# Parent Involvement in the Home, School, and Community

**George S. Morrison**
*Florida International University*

Charles E. Merrill Publishing Company
A Bell & Howell Company
Columbus    Toronto    London    Sydney

*To Betty Jane, who knew how
to help our children become
adults.*

Published by Charles E. Merrill Publishing Company
A Bell & Howell Company
Columbus, Ohio 43216

*This book was set in Times Roman and Helvetica.
The production editor was Jan Hall.
The cover was prepared by Larry Hamill.*

Cover photograph taken by William J. Stoll.

Photos on pages 51, 55, and 183 from the Bristol, Virginia Schools. All other photos by George S. Morrison.

Library of Congress Catalog Card Number: 77-91281
International Standard Book Number: 0-675-08393-1
2 3 4 5 6 7 8 9 10—85 84 83 82 81 80 79 78

*Printed in the United States of America*

# Foreword

Dr. Morrison makes a very significant contribution to the literature on the relatively new trend of building more meaningful ties between the home and the school. School leaders have missed an unusual opportunity to use the "teaching power" of parents to enhance their capacities to reach greater heights in teaching and learning. Dr. Morrison makes an eloquent case for parent participation in the education of their children as he traces the history and development of programs for parent involvement.

Over the past decade we have witnessed an unusual amount of social unrest. Traumatic changes have been shaking the structure of the institutions that provide the footing and foundation for our society. The home and the family have been victimized by these new forces that have demanded at least two bread winners in each family. Television, a permissive life-style, and a so-called new morality have generated the winds of change blowing through our institutional structure.

Education has been profoundly impacted by all of this. The teaching and learning process must have more appeal then it has ever had in the past. Parents are, indeed, the child's first teachers and the home is actually the first classroom. School officials must enhance the capacity of the parent to be a more effective and powerful influence upon the child. Dr. Morrison describes the problems and offers some persuasive prescriptions for active parent involvement in the entire education enterprise.

Every topic in this book discusses issues from the real world, matters of deep concern to educators and parents. The discussion is candid, spirited, and challenging. This timely text is a refreshing, insightful treatise written by an intelligent, practical-minded professional who has a rich background in the field of parenting. He has a great message and he says it well.

*T.H. Bell*
*Utah Commissioner of Higher Education,*
*former U.S. Commissioner of Education*

iii

# Preface

Current interest in parent involvement is essentially an effort to provide a wide range of opportunities for parents to have more control, authority, and direction in the development and education of their children and themselves. The rationale for this involvement is based on the belief that if parents are supported in developing knowledge, skills, and abilities relating to parenting and if families are involved in meaningful interactions with their children, then the long-range effect will be increased achievement of children in school settings, enhancement of their daily lives, and more involved and self-fulfilled parents. Presumably, as a result of the enhancement of the lives of children and families, soicety as a whole will benefit as a generation of children, reared by knowledgeable and interactive parents, in turn become "good" parents.

There are a great number of forces, including parent involvement programs, parenting seminars, and advocacy groups which would remold and alter the family as it existed, as we imagine it existed, or as it exists now. Herein is encountered a problem. Perhaps part of our infatuation and interest with parents comes from our desire to have or be a part of a romanticized family as we have remembered it in our imaginations and reveries. Quite often, this romanticized image of what a family was and is like consists of a 19th century victorian family where everyone was happy in the glow of a summer evening on a large front porch, secure in the patriarchal embrace of a traditional family unit. This type of family many people long for never really existed for very many people and probably never will exist in our future society. This condition, however, should not be viewed with alarm or forboding.

There are many forces which would radically alter the family as many people have actually experienced it. Artificial insemination, the growth of human life ex-utero, and the increase of single parent families promise to make parenting anonymous. Modern attempts at restructuring and redefining the family and child-rearing process such as the kibbutz and other forms of communal living may make the family unit as we have known it obsolete. How long society will be interested in promoting the active involvement of parents with their children remains to be seen and will depend on social forces we may only now dimly discern.

It seems appropriate, then, that in this time of crisis about the future of the family and the role it should play in educating and child rearing a book about parent involvement should be written. This book is designed to help anyone who wishes to become more involved in devising strategies and means for parents to become active in any educational endeavor. Hopefully, this will result in more self-directing and self-autonomous parents. The ultimate goal of this text is to promote parent involvement and development in order to create richer lives for families, parents, and children. As such, this text is intended for parents; paraprofessionals in day care, Head Start and preschool programs; preservice and inservice teachers; teacher aides in public schools; and graduate students. It combines both theory and practical methodology designed to help the reader become an active learner-participant rather than merely a reader about programs.

Chapter I, "Why Parent Involvement?" develops a historical rationale and contemporary social perspective for why we are currently interested in parents and parent involvement. It is my opinion that unless such a rationale is developed, the reader may lack the basis for synthesizing a comprehensive philosophy of parent involvement.

Chapter II, "What is Parent Involvement?" deals with a definition of *parent involvement.* Without this definition there is a very real danger that the subject of parent involvement may be viewed too narrowly. Consequently, this chapter defines parent involvement in a very broad sense and focuses on what parent involvement can do for the parent as well as what parents can do to help the programs they are involved in. It is this broad-based definition, with a focus on the development of parents, that makes Chapter II unique and consequently sets the tone for the rest of the chapters by embracing and developing the theme of parent involvement as that which benefits parents and children as well as programs.

Chapter III, "Parent Involvement Programs," takes a broad look at complimentary and contrasting programs of parent development. In this chapter, I have tried to be as representative as possible of some of the better-known programs for parent involvement, while at the same time providing the reader with information about some of the very good programs that are not necessarily reported in the literature. I think there is oftentimes a tendency to think of parent involvement programs as only those programs existing in the research journals or receiving national attention. It is my experience that there are many fine programs for parent involvement all across the United States. I have tried to provide the reader with this sense of involvement by describing some of these programs.

Chapter IV, "Parent Involvement in the Home," stresses the need for delivering a program of services to parents in their homes. A particular focus of this chapter is a description of home visitation by a home visitor. I hope this chapter will provide the reader some of the excitement and involvement that can occur from working with parents in the home setting.

Chapter V, "Parent Involvement in the Home: Some Considerations," examines some of the issues associated with any parent involvement program designed to deliver services to the home. In many instances, educators are much too casual about the kind of services they provide and the manner in which it is provided. Hopefully, therefore, Chapter V will cause the reader to examine some of the problems and issues encountered in a home visitation program.

Chapter VI, "Parent Involvement in Early Childhood Programs," discusses ways in which parents can become involved in early childhood settings other than the home. This chapter in some respects represents more of the traditional view of what parent involvement is thought to be. In this chapter, I have stressed the benefits that can accrue to parents by involvement in programs, as well as the benefits parents can provide to programs. In addition, this chapter stresses the necessity of training parents for involvement as a requisite for any successful program.

Chapter VII, "Parent Involvement with Handicapped Children," explores the problems and opportunities which confront parents of the handicapped. With the current emphasis on the handicapped, there will undoubtedly be more of an emphasis on involving parents of these children. It is only appropriate therefore that a chapter should be devoted to a discussion of ways to involve such parents.

Chapter VIII, "Programs for Parenting," takes a look at some of the currently available programs for providing individuals with information about child-rearing practices and child care. Some of the better known programs are discussed and examined.

Chapter IX, "Issues and Trends in Parent Involvement Programs," encourages the reader to establish an understanding of some of the real concerns associated with the field of parent involvement. It is my opinion that only by examining in a forthright manner some of the concerns, issues, and trends is it possible to work knowledgeably in a particular field. Too often we are so concerned with accomplishing a program that we fail to deal meaningfully with the problems that are apparent in the field and that may preclude our experiencing the success we should.

Chapter X, "New Careers in Education," encourages the reader to examine, on a personal, firsthand basis, some of the alternate possiblities that exist for employment in educational settings other than that of the traditional classroom teacher. Personally, I feel that too often people who are preparing for careers related to children overlook many of the varied and rich opportunities that exist for contributions to children and parents other than through classroom teaching. This chapter encourages the reader to participate in a self-exploratory examination of these alternative careers.

As a professor of early childhood education who daily teaches paraprofessionals and preservice and inservice teachers, it is my belief that students at all levels desire and deserve a text that is readable. By *readable,* I mean a book that students can understand while they are reading it and one in which they don't have to constantly refer to a dictionary. Some of my colleagues may interpret this as anti-intellectualism. I prefer to think of it as humanness and common sense. In a previous book written for Charles E. Merrill, *Early Childhood Education Today,* an overwhelming response from students who have used the text indicates that they appreciated a book that was readable, which did not contain a lot of statistics, and which did not provide an overwhelming number of research studies. Accordingly, in this text I have tried to include only that research which is appropriate to the topics being studied. I hope that students find this text a readable one also.

It is also my opinion that a textbook should not be bland and noncontroversial. Rather, it should present and deal with issues. As such, I have attempted to include as many issues as possible relating to a specific topic. Hopefully, these issues will provide a basis for classroom discussion, interpersonal student discussion, and a basis for the college professor or discussion leader to inject his own ideas as well as conflicting and supportive issues from the literature. This extablishes a framework for spirited, dynamic, questing learning.

In addition, I feel an author should present his personal points of view. This I have done. The reader will, I'm sure, be able to detect my biases and opinions throughout the text. There are those readers who will say that a text should be written as value free as possible. Quite the contrary. I feel a textbook should be written so that it includes as many different points of view as possible. By doing so, several processes can occur. First, a context of inquiry can be established which provides the means for the reader to challenge, reexamine, and compare values found in the text to those of his own. Second, a climate is created in which the instructor is afforded many opportunities to present alternate value systems, including his own, and this is as it should be.

As I have indicated, one of my personal and professional biases about texts is that they should be readable and interesting. The same criteria should also be true of books suggested for reading. I have read all of the books recommended for further reading and found them interesting and informative. This does not mean that there are not many other books that should be read. Some books I read were informative to me but were not suggested for further reading either because they were somewhat difficult to read or because of their technical and/or statistical nature. Also, the books selected are limited by my access to books. It is difficult to be aware of all books available or to have access to them when they are.

As with any creative endeavor, this text would not have been possible without the help and encouragement of many colleagues and friends: Ann O'Keefe, Florence Sequin, Evelyn Murray, Mary Kay Dishner, Berniece Andrews, Mary Beth Morrison, Irene Lubecki, George Farrow, Richard Wolf, Jane Thompson, Pamela McClane, Vicki Koster, Eileen Glotz, Phyllis Levenstein, The staffs of the St. Petersburg, Florida, and Schuylkill County, Pennsylvania, CFRP's and the Parkersburg, West Virginia, Home Start program. Jayne Turchich and Sherrie Mueller typed many drafts of the manuscript and assisted with the technical details associated with any writing endeavor. My wife, Betty Jane, provided the support and encouragement necessary for daily research and the process of sitting down and writing.

# Contents

# Why Parent Involvement?

## Teaching and Learning Goals

This chapter will provide the information, means, and opportunity to:

Examine and clarify issues and controversies surrounding programs designed to involve parents in the education of their children and in early childhood programs.

Develop a personal philosophy concerning parent involvement in early childhood programs.

Identify forces responsible for the current interest in parental involvement in early childhood programs.

Analyze a definition of *parent involvement* and compare and contrast it to one developed by the student himself.

Trace the historical development of programs for parent involvement and for delivering services to families in their homes.

Construct a rationale pro and con parent involvement and parent involvement programs.

Explore inter- and intrapersonal relations involved in the helping professions.

## Parent Involvement Is Not a New Idea

Why are the educational establishments, in general, and early childhood education programs, in particular, so interested in and infatuated with parent development?

1

Actually, the process of working with and providing services to families is not exactly a new one but has been around in one form or another for quite some time. It is only in the past decade that the dynamics of social, political, and educational forces have converged to promote the parent as a focal point around which many new programs and services can be developed as a means of enhancing the lives of all family members. The idea of working with parents and/or families in the home is not necessarily new either. What society is encountering is a renewed interest in parents. Because of all the accompanying publicity and new programs being developed for working with parents, we think that the process is new. While particular programs may be new, working with parents is not.

For example, one agency that has had a long and successful history of working with parents is the Visiting Nurses Association (VNA). This social service and public health agency, which exists in every state, delivers therapeutic bedside programs to anyone who is in need of care in the home. Examples of the kind of care that can be delivered are changing a catheter and giving a bath to a victim of a stroke. Other public health and social service agencies have also delivered services to families by providing parents and children with pre- and postnatal counseling and care.

Another program which has provided many services to individuals, youth, and family units is the Cooperative Extension Service. These agencies are administered through land grant colleges in all 50 states and are designed to assist in providing educational services in the following areas:

1. Youth (4-H). This is the head, heart, hands, and health organization in which many rural youth have been involved.

2. Family living and home economics. Examples of services in this area would be (1) providing educational resources and information to social service agencies, such as menu planning to Meals on Wheels, and (2) offering homemaking information and advice on a wide range of topics.

3. Agriculture. Services include such things as telling a farmer or home owner how much and what kind of fertilizer to use on his field or lawn and what kind of pesticides are environmentally safe.

4. Community development. Examples of services in this area would be (1) providing educational resources to help solve public problems, such as lending assistance to a taxpayers' organization so it can develop leadership skills necessary in effecting public change, and (2) providing leadership and expertise in developing a public playground.

## Emphasis on Child and Parent

Historically, therefore, there have been a number of agencies which have been concerned with children and families. What is "new," however, at least in the sense that new programs have been developed, is that the focus of new programs is toward the education of the parent and children for the primary benefit of the child, especially in the areas of school achievement and enhanced self-image.

Part of the efforts of many parent involvement programs is to make families aware of and help them utilize already existing services. It is not so much a case of programs not existing as it is a case of people not being aware of services. Consequently, many already existing services have been underutilized.

## Reasons for the Current Interest
## in Parent Involvement

If there have always been, to a greater or lesser extent, programs for parent and family education, the legitimate question can be asked, Why is the educational establishment suddenly interested in parents? The answers are diverse and come from many different, yet related, sources.

### *Research*

During the 1960s, there was a great deal of research dealing with how children learn and the conditions under which they learn best. Much of this research indicated that many of the traditional attitudes of home and school toward learning and the preschool child were not as beneficial for the child as was previously thought. During the forties, fifties, and early sixties, the predominant philosophy of pedagogy toward the preschool child advocated the following:

1. Not "forcing" or stimulating cognitive learning. This usually meant not teaching children to read or write before they were "ready," usually after entry into first grade.
2. Placing an emphasis on socialization. One of the primary purposes of preschool education was to provide a child time and opportunity to "learn how to get along with other children."
3. An emphasis on learning through play. This approach meant allowing the child to play pretty much as he wanted with little or no attempt on the part of parent or preschool teacher to encourage or promote learning through play.
4. A general understanding that "real" learning could be postponed and would not occur until the child entered public school, somewhere around the age of six.

*Important of Early Years.* Much of the research during the 1960s the wisdom of these traditional attitudes toward learning; the importance of the early years prior to entry into school; on the development of intelligence; and on future school achievement. Two researchers whose conclusions are frequently used to support this renewed interest in the young child's early learning experiences are Benjamin Bloom and J. McV. Hunt.

One of the conclusions reached by Bloom in his book *Stability and Change in Human Characteristics* was

> When a number of longitudinal studies are compared with each other and allowances are made for the reliability of the instruments and the variability of the samples, a single pattern clearly emerges . . . . Both the correlational data and the absolute scale of intelligence development make it clear that intelligence is a developing function and that the stability of measured intelligence increases with age. Both types of data suggest that in terms of intelligence measured at age 17, about 50% of the development takes place between conception and age 4, about 30% between ages 4 and 8, and about 20% between ages 8 and 17.[1]

---

[1]Benjamin S. Bloom, *Stability and Change in Human Characteristics* (New York: John Wiley and Sons, 1964), p. 88.

Bloom's findings support Hunt's contention that the quality and nature of early learning experiences have a lasting effect on the child's intellectual development. In his book *Intelligence and Experience,* Hunt concludes:

> In view of the conceptual developments and the evidence coming from animals learning to learn, from neuropsychology, from the programming of electronic computers to solve problems, and from the development of intelligence in children, it would appear that intelligence should be conceived as intellectual capacities based on central processes hierarchically arranged within the intrinsic portions of the cerebrum. These central processes are approximately analogous to the strategies for information processing and action with which electronic computers are programmed. With such a conception of intelligence, the assumptions that intelligence is fixed and that its development is predetermined by the genes are no longer tenable.
>
> In the light of these considerations, it appears that the counsel from experts on child-rearing during the third and much of the fourth decades of the twentieth century to let children be while they grow and to avoid excessive stimulation was highly unfortunate . . . .
>
> Further in the light of these theoretical considerations and the evidence concerning the effects of early experience on adult problem-solving in animals, it is no longer unreasonable to consider that it might be feasible to discover ways to govern the encounters that children have with their environments, especially during the early years of their development, to achieve a substantially faster rate of intellectual development and a substantially higher adult level of intellectual capacity.[2]

While many conclusions can be drawn from the above data, there are several which relate specifically to our topic of the importance of parents in the educative process.

First is the idea that the period of most rapid intellectual growth occurs from birth to age eight, or during the period the child spends most of his time in the home environment. What children are to become intellectually is measured on those devices which we call intelligence and school achievement tests and is determined long before they enter schools. There would seem to be three alternatives to this state of affairs:

1. Do nothing. This policy of doing nothing is basically what has been done previously. This approach is very popular with those who would pursue a *laissez-faire* approach to the young child.

2. Admit the child to a public or private preschool and/or some other educational program similar to good Head Start and day care programs.

3. Work with parents in providing an enriched home environment and experiences for the child. This rich home environment could ostensibly provide the child with the experiences necessary for optimum intellectual growth.

As will be discussed in following chapters, many educators are developing programs which involve a combination of the strategies suggested in points 2 and 3 above.

---

[2]J. McV. Hunt—*Intelligence and Experience.* Copyright© 1961, The Ronald Press Company, New York. Pp. 362-63.

A second conclusion which can be deducted from the above data is that it becomes increasingly evident that it is no longer a defensible position to view the child as being born into the world with a fixed intelligence. Instead, educators and parents must think in terms of developmental intelligence. This concept means that the child possesses, at birth, the capacity for intellectual development which encompasses a broad range. While heredity fixes or determines the range of intelligence, it is the environment (including experiences, culture, objects, relationships with others, etc.) which will determine the extent to which the intellectual potential of the child will or will not be developed.

If this interrelationship between heredity and environment is as crucial as many educators feel it is, then it would appear that there need to be more concerted efforts toward providing all children with the best environment possible. In order to make this kind of possibility a reality, many programs are being designed to help parents become aware of and provide for an optimal environmental setting.

A third implication the research has for educators and parents is that what happens to the young child early in life, prior to age eight, will have a life-long impact and influence upon his behavior and achievement. The simple fact is that early learnings and the effects of early experiences are extremely difficult to change, alter, or replace. What happens to the child early in life determines how he views the world and how be behaves intellectually, emotionally, and psychomotorically.

It seems obvious then that the time for an optimal learning environment is early in life. Since the environment that most children are reared in is the home, every home should be as good and as appropriate an environment as it is possible to provide.

For the above reasons, then, there has been an increased interest in working with parents to provide them with the support, information, and expertise to become the best educators of their children as it is possible for them to become.

*The interactions of parent and child during the early years play an important role in the development of the child.*

*Importance of the Family.*   Not only has there been a focus on the importance of the early years in the life of an individual, but there has also been an interest in the influence the family has on the life of children. Jencks and his colleagues, in examining factors related to inequality in the United States, arrived at the following conclusion:

> We found that family background had much more influence than IQ genotype on an individual's educational attainment. The family's influence depended partly on its socio-economic status and partly on cultural and psychological characteristics that were independent of socio-economic level. The effect of cognitive skill on educational attainment proved difficult to estimate, but it was clearly significant. We found no evidence that the role of family background was declining or that the role of cognitive skill was increasing. Qualitative differences between schools played a very minor role in determining how much schooling people eventually got.[3]

In commenting upon the inability of schools to eliminate inequality in our society, Jencks further comments, "There seem to be three reasons why school reform cannot make adults more equal. First, children seem to be far more influenced by what happens at home than by what happens in school."[4] The second reason given is that school reforms have little effect on those variables which affect a child's life, and a third reason is that the influence of the school does not persist into adult life.

Another study which supports the role and influence of the family in the educative process was conducted by Mayeske and his associates. In part, they concluded:

> This study has demonstrated that family background plays a profound role in the development of achievement, not only through the social and economic well-being of the family but through the values its members hold with regard to education, and the activities that parents and parental surrogates engage in with their children to make these values operational.[5]

In an effort to look at specific family environmental influences on the psychological development of the preschool child, White and his colleagues have studied the effects of various child-rearing practices. By observing how families do rear their children, White and his associates have been able to arrive at some tentative conclusions about the importance of the mother in the development of the child. In assessing the most important developmental growth period and parental impact upon it, White feels that the developmental time span of from ten to eighteen months is the most important in the child's life.

> Many people who study the development of children have made statements about the special importance of particular age ranges. In this regard, we are no different. Our study, even though incomplete at this writing, has convinced us of

[3]From *Inequality: A Reassessment of the Effect of Family and Schooling in America* by Christopher Jencks, et al.,© 1972 by Basic Books, Inc., Publishers, New York. P. 254.

[4]Jencks, p. 255.

[5]George W. Mayeske et al., *A Study of the Achievement of Our Nation's Students,* U.S. Department of Health, Education & Welfare, Office of Education, DHEW Publication No. (OE) 72-131 (Washington, D.C.: U.S. Government Printing Office, 1973).

the special importance of the 10- to 18-month age range for the development of general competence. At this time of life, for most children, several extremely important developments seem to coalesce and force a test of each family's capacity to rear children. The primary burden in most cases falls upon the mother.[6]

The important developments that White and Watts refer to are the capacity for receptive language, the emergence of locomotor ability, and the social development of the child with an individual identity. It is, in White and Watt's opinion, how the parent handles these three developmental processes which will ultimately and fundamentally affect the competence of the child.

> We will begin with the bold statement that the mother's direct and indirect actions with regard to her one- to three-year-old child, especially during the second year of life, are, in our opinion, the most powerful formative factors in the development of a preschool-age child.
>
> Further, we would guess that if a mother does a fine job in the preschool years, subsequent educators such as teachers will find their chances for effectiveness maximized. Finally, we would expect that much of the basic quality of the entire life of an individual is determined by the mother's actions during these two years. Obviously, we could be very wrong about these declarative statements. We make them as very strong hunches that we have become committed to, as a kind of net result of all our inquiries into early development.
>
> Let us quickly add that we believe most women are capable of doing a fine job with their one- to three-year-old children. Our study has convinced us that a mother need not necessarily have even a high school diploma, let alone a college education. Nor does she need to have very substantial economic assets. In addition, it is clear that a good job can be accomplished without a father in the home. In all these statements we see considerable hope for future generations.[7]

White further concludes:

> In our studies we were not only impressed by what some children could achieve during the first years, but also by the fact that the child's own family seemed so obviously central to the outcome. Indeed, we came to believe that the informal education that families provide for their children *makes more of an impact on a child's total educational development than the formal educational system.* If a family does its job well, the professional can then provide effective training. If not, there may be little the professional can do to save the child from mediocrity. This grim assessment is a direct conclusion from the findings of thousands of programs in remedial education, such as Head Start and Follow Through projects.[8]

White also maintains, *"To begin to look at a child's educational development when he is two years of age is already much too late,* particularly in the area of social skills and attitudes."[9]

---

[6]Burton L. White and Jean Carew Watts, *Experience and Environment: Major Influences on the Development of the Young Child,*Vol. I.© 1973, p. 234. Reprinted by permission of Prentice-Hall, Inc., Englewood Cliffs, New Jersey.

[7] White and Watts, p. 242.

[8]Burton L. White, *The First Three Years of Life,*© 1975, p. 4. Reprinted by permission of Prentice-Hall, Inc., Englewood Cliffs, New Jersey.

[9]White, p. 4.

*This mother is developing an interest in books by reading to her children. The role of the parent in the education process is an important one since school achievement begins in the home.*

White and his colleagues then have done much to focus the attention of society and educators on the role of the parents.

## Handicapped Children

The trend toward involving parents in the education of their children is particularly strong in the area of the handicapped. Indeed there is an effort on the part of educators to involve those parents of children with special needs, particularly when a specific educational program can be designed for dealing with these special needs. Quite often there seems to be a direct proportion between attempted parental involvement and severity of the problems which children possess.

A great deal of the interest in parents of handicapped children is because of state and federal laws. Court cases such as *PARC* v. *Pennsylvania* and federal laws such as Public Law 94-142, The Education for All Handicapped Children Act of 1975, have done much to increase public awareness and promote parent involvement. The PARC case, P.L. 94-142, and other factors influencing parental involvement with handicapped children will be discussed in more detail in chapter 7.

## Social and Cultural Changes

Changes that have occurred in our society constitute another reason for the renewed interest in providing parents help in the child-rearing and educating processes. During the last half-century, there have been a great many social and cultural changes in the world. One of these changes which has profoundly affected the parenting process is that it is no longer possible, in a great many cases, for parents to have role models for child rearing. Prior to World War II, when the mobility of the United States population was not as great as it is today, many new parents had their parents and, in many instances, their grandparents readily available for consultant purposes. Thus, there were experienced, trusted relatives close by to answer questions about child-rearing practices. With extended families, grandparents and parents may have lived in the same home. Or, it was not uncommon for newly married couples to establish housekeeping near one of the parents. In this way, the more experienced adults were near enough to provide instruction. However, the extended family is not as popular today as it once was. As a result, parents turned to Dr. Spock's book, *Baby and Child Care,* as a guide for information about common childhood diseases and about child rearing.[10] They found that they, for the most part, had no prior knowledge about how to be parents and lacked familiar resources to rely upon in deciding how and what to do.

## Parent Cooperative Schools

Parent cooperative schools are another reason for the interest in parent involvement. As the name implies, these schools are formed by parents. They are usually established out of parents' desires for good education for their children. Parents also view the cooperative process as one way in which they can participate in and influence policies through direct control and/or involvement in the decision-making process. A group of parents forms their own school, and through a parent board they set policies, establish curricula, and hire the teachers (who may be cooperative members), or provide the instruction themselves. Usually, when a teacher is hired on a fulltime basis, the parents provide help on a volunteer or paid basis. In some programs, the parents must meet the condition that they will spend time in the classroom either as a paid person or volunteer. Parent cooperatives exist primarily in large cities and/or in college and university towns. The point is, however, that once parents are used to operating their own school, they find it difficult to be satisfied with any less involvement. This tendency toward involvement carries over into the public school and other educational programs.

## Political Reasons

Some of the most pervasive reasons for the current interest in parent involvement can be attributed to political factors.

*Woman's Liberation/Feminist Movement.* Interest in parent education and involvement has increased because of the feminist movement. The role of women is changing, has changed, and will more than likely continue to change. Some of these changes are reflected in more equal opportunity, status, pay, and more emphasis on the right of women to lead life styles differing from those traditionally assigned to women. Traditionally, roles for women have been largely restricted to those associated with the home: homemaker (keeping the house clean, serving three balanced meals a day, etc.), lover (always available, always ready), and child rearer (seeing that the children are well fed, clothed, and earn straight A's in school).

However, as women have become unburdened from this role of homemaker and pursue more interests and specialized roles outside of the home, they will no longer have the time, energy, desire, or opportunity to assume some of these traditional roles. Undoubtedly, one of the roles that will be shed will be that of child rearer and

---

[10] Benjamin Spock, *Baby and Child Care* (New York: Pocket Books, 1957).

educator. Women will be more willing to relinquish this role and pay to have others do it for them.

As women pursue other roles, they are demanding and will demand more input into the educational process. The question of good child care, readily available and accessible during working hours will also become more of an issue, with increased efforts to have such facilities established. Advocacy groups for these services will become more strident in their efforts to make child care more of a national priority.

*Student Activism.*    The student political and social unrest of the 1960s and early 1970s, expressed through demonstrations, demands, and involvement led to a more active and militant student and a more frustrated and intimidated teacher. As a result of student unrest, students (a certain element at least) became more violent, disruptive, and less respectful (sometimes even expressing contempt) of schools, old-fashioned discipline codes, and traditional values. Suddenly, the old system didn't work to control students or to meet their demands. At the same time, in the face of this breakdown of previously used methods to control students, there was an accompanying lack of creative responses to the new enlightenment of students. As can be expected, teachers and other school personnel responded with more of the same old methods of repression, containment, and get tougher policies. At the other end of the spectrum, there was that other group of educators who responded with a passive indifference. This passivity was manifested by allowing students almost anything they wanted or demanded. This totally inadequate response, of course, resulted in chaos.

The result of both of the above responses to student activism has been inadequate. What has occurred is that, reluctantly, and after their own efforts have failed, teachers are beginning to turn to parents as a potential source for creative solutions to part of their problem.

There is also a growing realization on the part of the educational establishment that to wait until a student is in upper elementary, middle, or high school to begin to change the attitude of parent or child toward education and learning is much too late. By that time, the causes of the problems have already been in operation a long time, and the responses and attitudes have become rigid and, to a large extent, inflexible. The time to deal with attitudes is at the formative stage. Because attitudes and values are formed at an early age, there is an increased emphasis on working with parents of preschool and early elementary school children.

*The Civil Rights Movement.*    The civil rights movement has done a great deal to raise the consciousness and participation of people in programs. Not only have people become more aware of the rights they have under the U.S. Constitution and federal, state, and local laws, but they have also been encouraged to exercise and demand, where absent, the privileges provided. Particularly in the areas of educational practices has there been increased parent demand for involvement in control of and participation in the decision-making processes.

*Consumerism.*    The consumer movement of the last decade has encouraged parents to become involved more directly in economic and commercial factors affecting their lives. Parents are no longer passive about accepting those things which are not in the best interests of themselves or their children. Consequently, parents are expressing their objections to such things as flammable pajamas, unsafe toys, violent

*Parents are becoming more aware of their rights as consumers of products and services. This awareness encourages parent involvement. Parent involvement means in part, involvement of the parent in the community as a knowledgeable consumer.*

television programs, and junk foods. Parents feel that, unless they become involved in determining what are acceptable practices and products, the interest of the market place and profit margins will be served, not their own or those of their children.

## Federal and State Legislation

Many public school programs which have been developed to deal with problems and issues of young children's learning are financed and supported by federal monies. These programs have been established with monies obtained through the Elementary and Secondary Education Act (ESEA) of 1965—Public Law 89-10. The federal agency responsible for this act is the Office of Education, Department of Health, Education, and Welfare. There are many titles of the act which provide funding for many different programs, some of which provide for parent involvement. Some of the titles which fund programs discussed in this text include the following:

| *ESEA Title* | Purpose |
|---|---|
| Title I | To meet the educational needs of disadvantaged children. |
| Title I-B | To encourage greater state and local expenditures for education. |
| Title IV-C | To improve leadership resources of state and local education agencies, to support innovative and exemplary projects, nutrition and health services, and dropout prevention. |
| Title VII | To develop and operate programs for children 3-18 with limited English speaking ability. (bilingual education) |

Other public laws which have impact upon education agencies and provide support for programs encouraging parent involvement include these:

Community Service Act—Title V, (Public Law 93-644). The purpose of this act is to extend into primary grades educational gains made by deprived children in Head Start or similar preschool programs (commonly known as Follow Through).

Educational Amendments of 1974. National Reading Improvement Program. Title VII (Public Law 93-380 as amended by Public Law 94-194). Known as the Right to Read Program, this law encourages institutions, government agencies, and private organizations to improve and expand reading-related activities for children, youth, and adults.

Also, see chapter 7, "Parent Involvement with Handicapped Children," for information about The Education for All Handicapped Children Act of 1975 (Public Law 94-142).

In addition, there are state laws and programs which support and encourage parent involvement. For example, the state of California has an early childhood education program for children in kindergarten through grade three. One of the key features of this program is parent involvement in the planning, operation, and evaluation of school programs. This type of involvement is becoming more popular and necessary.

*Social Engineering and Governmental Programs.*  Parent involvement as we know it today is in a large measure a result of the "rediscovery of the poor" by the federal government in the early 1960s. Because of the adverse effects that poverty can have on parents and children, many of the New Frontier and Great Society programs of the Kennedy and Johnson administrations were initiated in order to counteract these adverse effects. One of the more significant pieces of legislation, at least as far as early childhood education and parent involvement is concerned, was the passage of the Economic Opportunity Act of 1964. This act created the Office of Economic Opportunity, and from this office, Project Head Start was developed and administered beginning in 1965. While it is possible to trace the pedagogical roots of parent involvement back to Pestalozzi, Comenius, and Froebel, the more modern and programmatic beginning is with Head Start.

Head Start has always been committed to the philosophy that if children are to be changed and improvements made in their lives, then corresponding changes have to be made in the lives of parents and teachers who are partners in the learning process. Head Start recognizes that it cannot hope to change the lives of children without involving parents. Therefore, one of the key Head Start component areas, in addition to health, education, and social service, is a parent involvement program. The following are objectives for this parent involvement component of Head Start:

1. Provide a planned program of experiences and activities which support and enhance the parental role as the principal influence in their child's education and development.

2. Provide a program that recognizes the parents as:
   A. Responsible guardians of their children's well being.

B. Prime educators of their children.

C. Contributors to the Head Start Program and to their communities.

3. Provide the following kinds of opportunities for parent participation:
   A. Direct involvement in decision making in program planning and operations.
   B. Participation in classroom and other program activities as paid employees, volunteers, or observers.
   C. Activities for parents which they have helped to develop.
   D. Working with their own children in cooperation with Head Start staff.[11]

These objectives reflect the idea that parents should be viewed as human beings who have needs and who have contributions to make to their children and the Head Start program. This is opposite to the viewpoint that sees a parent merely as someone who can provide a particular help and/or service. The main thrust of Head Start, however, still appears to be geared toward actualizing the parent to help the child as opposed to a comprehensive program of parent development.

## Parent-Citizen Involvement in Education Processes

Quite often, there is a tendency on the part of the educational establishment to think that parents and citizens in general do not want to be involved with schools and other educational agencies. This perception may be based upon previous experiences in which attempts to involve the public met with failure and/or limited success. However, oftentimes the problem is not that there is no parent interest, but it is the manner in which the parent involvement is solicited. Poor methods of solicitation are often confused with lack of parental interest and desire.

Also, lack of parental participation may be due in a great many instances to the fact that schools and educational personnel really don't want parent involvement. Educators frequently feel that the schools are there to operate and to do with as they, the professionals, see fit. This attitude and approach to parents has been labeled as arrogance by some critics of the public schools. Questions have been raised as to whether or not the public schools and other educational agencies can afford this arrogant attitude toward the public who ultimately pays the bills and salaries for the educational program.

### Parents Want Involvement

Based upon current information, the idea that parents are not interested or do not want to be involved in the educational process is not only a myth but also a gross error in judgment. Evidence to support the public's desire for involvement comes from the eighth annual Gallup poll of the public's attitudes toward the public schools, a project conducted by the Gallup poll and the Charles F. Kettering Foundation.[12]

---

[11]U.S. Department of Health, Education, and Welfare, Office of Child Development, *Head Start Program Performance Standards,* Head Start Policy Manual, OCD Notice N-30-364-1 (Washington, D.C.: U.S. Government Printing Office, January 1973), pp. 19-20.

[12]George H. Gallup, "Eighth Annual Gallup Poll of the Public's Attitudes Toward the Public Schools," *Phi Delta Kappan* 58, no. 2 (October 1976): 189-94.

When parents were asked how they felt the quality of the public schools could be improved, 51 percent of the parents polled felt that the public schools could be improved by devoting more attention to the teaching of basic skills (see table 1). Close behind that with 50 percent was to "enforce stricter discipline," and the third most frequent response was to "meet the individual needs of students," with 42 percent. For the purposes of this discussion, however, the most interesting response in fourth place with 41 percent was that there is a need to improve parent-school relations. This response is significant enough for educators to pay more attention to the parent involvement process than in the past.

When parents were asked if they thought it would be a good idea for the schools to offer courses to parents in order to help them help their children in school, the responses in Table 2 were given.

An analysis of table 2 will reveal that 77 percent of all of the parents polled felt that it was a good idea. This overwhelming affirmative response indicates that more schools should be interested in teaching these kinds of courses in order to help parents help their children. The significance of this response also has a great many implications for parent involvement.

One of the most often used methods of involving parents in an educational program is the citizen advisory committee. However, sometimes it is questionable how many parents get to serve on an advisory committee. Also, the effectiveness of advisory committees are often of limited value because of the way in which the committees are allowed to function. If a committee feels its recommendations are valued and will be followed within reason, then an advisory committee can be very beneficial.

Table 3 shows that not only would parents like to serve on an advisory committee but also 90 percent of the parents polled said that they would welcome an opportunity to serve. It is interesting that the second most sought after committee assignment would be that of dealing with student-teacher relations. This choice of student-teacher relations has implications for teacher-parent relations. One of the obvious ways to enhance student-teacher relations would be to improve parent involvement and support.

Interestingly, when citizens were asked to relate their reasons for the decline in national tests scores that has occurred over the last several years, 65 percent of all those polled said they felt that it was due to less parent attention, concern, and supervision of the child (see table 4). This response indicates that there is a need for more parent involvement with children. One of the ways that this parental concern which the public feels is lacking could be increased and enhanced is by schools developing programs for parent involvement.

There are then a great many reasons for the current rush to involve parents in some way and form in the educational process. This current interest began in the late sixties and early seventies. It is likely that the decade of the eighties will be identified as that time during which parents became a major focus in the educational process.

For the student who is interested in the historical antecedents of modern parent involvement programs, the field does have a rich and interesting history. A good

**TABLE 1** Which of these ways do you think would do most to improve the quality of public school education overall?

| | National Totals % | No Children in Schools % | Public School Parents % | Parochial School Parents % |
|---|---|---|---|---|
| Devote more attention to teaching of basic skills | 51 | 47 | 55 | 60 |
| Enforce stricter discipline | 50 | 47 | 52 | 64 |
| Meet individual needs of students | 42 | 39 | 47 | 44 |
| Improve parent/school relations | 41 | 43 | 36 | 47 |
| Emphasize moral development | 39 | 34 | 45 | 49 |
| Emphasize career education and development of salable skills | 38 | 39 | 36 | 37 |
| Provide opportunities for teachers to keep up-to-date regarding new methods | 29 | 27 | 32 | 29 |
| Raise academic standards | 27 | 28 | 23 | 38 |
| Raise teachers' salaries | 14 | 15 | 16 | 8 |
| Increase amount of homework | 14 | 12 | 17 | 21 |
| Build new buildings | 9 | 8 | 12 | 7 |
| Lower age for compulsory attendance | 5 | 4 | 6 | 1 |
| None | 1 | 1 | * | |
| Don't know/ no answer | 4 | 4 | 2 | 3 |

*Less than 1%
(Totals add to more than 100% because of multiple answers.)

**TABLE 2**  As a regular part of the public school educational system, it has been suggested that courses be offered at convenient times to parents in order to help them help their children in school. Do you think this is a good idea or a poor idea?

|  | National Totals % | No Children in Schools % | Public School Parents % | Parochial School Parents % |
|---|---|---|---|---|
| Good idea | 77 | 76 | 78 | 74 |
| Poor idea | 19 | 18 | 20 | 25 |
| Don't know/ no answer | 4 | 6 | 2 | 1 |

**TABLE 3**  Percentage of respondents selecting each committee on which they would like to serve.

| Advisory Committees | Percent Who Would Like To Serve on Such a Committee* |
|---|---|
| 1. Discipline and related problems | 47 |
| 2. Student/teacher relations | 31 |
| 3. Career education | 29 |
| 4. Student dropouts | 29 |
| 5. Teacher evaluation | 28 |
| 6. The handicapped student | 26 |
| 7. Educational costs/finances | 22 |
| 8. The curriculum | 21 |
| 9. Education for citizenship | 19 |
| 10. Work-study programs | 19 |
| 11. Home study and work habits | 19 |
| 12. Community use of school buildings | 16 |
| 13. Pupil assessment and test results | 15 |
| 14. School facilities | 14 |
| 15. Public relations of schools | 13 |
| 16. School transportation | 12 |
| 17. The athletic program | 12 |
| 18. Educational innovations | 12 |
| 19. Extracurricular activities | 11 |
| 20. Progress of recent graduates | 9 |
| None | 4 |
| Don't know/no answer | 6 |

*Totals more than 100% because of multiple answers.

**TABLE 4** Here are some reasons that have been given to explain the decline in national test scores. Look over these reasons and then tell which ones you think are most responsible for this decline.

|  | National Totals % | No Children in Schools % | Public School Parents % | Parochial School Parents % |
|---|---|---|---|---|
| Less parent attention, concern, and supervision of the child. | 65 | 64 | 65 | 72 |
| Students aren't as motivated to do well | 52 | 50 | 57 | 53 |
| Too much television viewing | 49 | 48 | 51 | 51 |
| Society is becoming too permissive | 49 | 47 | 49 | 61 |
| Teachers are giving less attention to students | 39 | 39 | 41 | 32 |
| It's easier to get into college now | 16 | 20 | 10 | 14 |
| Schools are expanding the number of courses offered | 10 | 12 | 8 | 4 |
| The tests are not reliable | 16 | 15 | 16 | 16 |
| Other and no opinion | 14 | 13 | 15 | 15 |

place to begin in an analysis of this historical foundation would be with Schlossman's account which starts with the child study movement of the 1880s and continues up until 1929. Particular emphasis in his account is placed on the evolution of the P.T.A.[13]

While there is, and probably will continue to be, a growing public fascination with parental involvement, the sad fact remains that schools and teachers have returned to or reconsidered parents reluctantly, for the wrong reasons, and much too late. Historically, the majority of teachers and schools have not welcomed and/or encouraged parent involvement. Some of the reasons for this state of affairs will be discussed in other chapters.

---

[13]Steven L. Schlossman, "Before Home Start: Notes Toward a History of Parent Education In America, 1897-1929," *Harvard Education Review* 46 (1976): 436-67.

# Bibliography

Bloom, Benjamin S. *Stability and Change in Human Characteristics*. New York: John Wiley and Sons, 1964.

Gallup, George H. "Eighth Annual Gallup Poll of the Public's Attitudes Toward the Public Schools." *Phi Delta Kappan* 58(2) (October 1976):189-94.

Hunt, J. McV. *Intelligence and Experience*. New York: The Ronald Press Co., 1961.

Jencks, Christopher et al. *Inequality: A Reassessment of the Effect of Family and Schooling in America*. New York: Harper & Row, 1973.

Mayeske, George W. et al. *A Study of the Achievement of Nation's Students*. Washington, D.C.: U.S. Government Printing Office, 1973.

Schlossman, Steven L. "Before Home Start: Notes Toward a History of Parent Education in America, 1897-1929," *Harvard Education Review* 46 (1976):436-67.

Spock, Benjamin. *Baby and Child Care*. New York: Pocket Books, 1957.

U.S. Department of Health, Education, and Welfare, Office of Child Development. *Head Start Program Performance Standards*. Washington, D.C.: U.S. Government Printing Office, 1973.

White, Burton L. *The First Three Years of Life*. Englewood Cliffs, N.J.: Prentice-Hall, 1975.

White, Burton L., and Watts, Jean Carew. *Experience and Environment: Major Influences on the Development of the Young Child*. Englewood Cliffs, N.J.: Prentice-Hall, 1973.

# Further Reading and Study

Badger, Earladeen D. *Mother's Guide to Early Learning*. Paoli, Pa: The Institute Corporation, McGraw-Hill Early Learning Company, 1973.

Contains many useful activities for parents to use in helping their young children develop and learn. It deals with such areas as visual attention, early eye-hand coordination, interest in objects, simple motor skills, socialization and imitation, matching, etc. Provides many activities to help develop these skills.

Kelly, Marguerite, and Parsons, Elia. *The Mothers' Almanac*. Garden City, N.Y.: Doubleday Company, 1975.

A good reference book for parents concerned with all aspects of child rearing, prenatal delivery, nutrition, discipline, toilet training, effects of moving, questions about sex, cooperative playgrounds, outings and creative play. Written by mothers for parents, the authors are in direct touch with the realities, experiences, influences, and expressions of parent-child relations.

White, Burton L. *The First Three Years of Life*. Englewood Cliffs, N.J.: Prentice-Hall, 1975.

A knowledgeable, easy-to-read developmental source of child-rearing ideas and advice which should be read by all parents, teachers, and anyone associated with children. The information is based on extensive research relating to actual child-rearing experiences. As the author states, "I tried over the years to accumulate dependable knowledge about what babies are like, what their interests are, and how to provide useful and beneficial experiences for them."

White, Burton L., and Watts, Jean Carew. *Experience and Environment: Major Influences on the Development of the Young Child*. Vol. 1, Englewood Cliffs, N.J.: Prentice-Hall, 1973.

A very interesting and informative account of the importance of mothering process and styles. Details the growth of competence in children as promoted by environments created by mothering styles. Of particular interest are chapters 4, 8, 9, 10, and 11. Should be beneficial for all who are teachers, parents, hope to be, or are involved in any way with parents.

Willis, Anne, and Ricciuti, Henry. *A Good Beginning for Babies, Guidelines for Group Care.* Washington, D.C.: National Association for the Education of Young Children, 1975.

Designed to assist in the development of infant day care centers, this book provides information on developmental learning, helping babies adjust, routine caregiving, health and safety of infants, and physical space and equipment. Since most of this information can also apply to the home, this book can be a useful guide to the new parent.

# *Activities*

1. If you were asked to give a talk to a group of parents about becoming involved in their children's program, what reasons would you give them for becoming involved?

2. Visit a Head Start program. Discuss with the director, teachers, and other staff members what their agency does to involve parents.

3. Interview parents who are involved in educational programs. Discuss with them what they enjoy most about being involved. Also, determine how they would improve their involvement process.

4. Visit public service agencies or invite program directors of these agencies to your classroom. What specific services do they provide for and to parents?

5. Isolation can and often does affect opportunities people and children can have. Isolation can occur on two levels, physical (distance) and intrapersonal (how people relate to each other).

 a. What specific effects could isolation that comes from distance (living many miles from a neighbor, town, store, etc.) have on parents? Children? On the interaction that occurs between parent and child?

 b. What specific effects could the isolation that occurs when people are afraid to leave their home/apartment have upon parents? Children? Parent/child interaction?

 c. Visit a children's ward of a hospital. (1) What evidence of isolation did you find? (2) Tell how you became involved with the children.

 d. Volunteer your services for several afternoons (or more) at a nursing home. How did you establish relationships with the residents? What kind of relationships did you establish? Was it difficult or easy for you to establish these relationships? Why? How is establishing relationships with adults different from or similar to establishing relationships with children? Why is it necessary for people who work with adults to be able to establish effective relationships?

6. Visit your local social service and/or welfare agency. Role play that you are in need of welfare benefits, food stamps, legal services, etc.

 a. How were you treated?

 b. What human relationships were most dominant? Which ones were lacking or ignored?

 c. What feelings did you have?

 d. What skills do you think are necessary to apply and receive social service benefits?

7. Conduct a poll (or use a questionnaire) of the parents in your neighborhood. Determine:

 a. If parents would like to become more involved in their children's education.

 b. If parents feel they are wanted by the local school, Head Start, preschool, etc.

 c. What kinds of school/education related activites parents would like to become involved with.

8. What evidence can you cite which supports the idea that the environment of the young child has a profound influence on him.

9. Begin to keep a journal or log relating your observations of and interactions with children, parents, and teachers. Be sure to include your feelings, impressions, ideas, concerns, etc. Periodically share your journal with some of your classmates and friends. Discuss with them your insights and learnings.

# What Is Parent Involvement?

# 2

---

## Teaching and Learning Goals

This chapter will provide the information, means, and opportunity to:

Re-examine traditional concepts of parental roles and functions.

Examine the social and cultural forces which have changed and are changing the traditional family.

Consider alternate definitions of parent and family.

Analyze cultural, social, and political issues involved in any attempt to provide services to children, parents, and families.

Compare a definition of parent involvement to one developed by a student, to one presented in the text, and to one developed by others.

---

## A Narrow Definition

In the past, there has been a tendency to have too narrow a definition of *parent involvement*. Such a definition, has usually emphasized getting parents involved in the education of their children in public schools and private preschool programs as well as limiting parents in programs and viewing them as people who provide help and/or augment the educational program. According to this definition, a parent is viewed as a custodian, teacher aide, or helper in delivering services to children in the classroom or center. Consequently, this view of parent involvement places the emphasis on what the parent can do for the program, rather than on what the program can do for the parent. Unfortunately, this view of the parent as a provider of services is increasing in popularity particularly in public schools where the alternative to hiring additional teachers or teacher aides is the recruitment of parent volunteers. Thus, parents are not only pictured as a source of services, but the services they render are also viewed as free or considerably less expensive than union negotiated salaries of classroom teachers.

Another problem with a narrow definition of parent involvement is that it may emphasize providing services for parents rather than *with* parents. This process of doing *for* rather than *with* should not be encouraged for it does not view the parents as a partner and, therefore, tends to demean parents and their role.

Sometimes, too, there is a tendency for educators to view their relationship with parents as similar to traveling on a one-way street. In this instance, the question they often ask is, "How can the parent help us?" In the parent involvement process, the interaction between parent and educational program should be viewed as a reciprocal one of two-way interaction. The central question then becomes, "How can the parents help us and how can we help the parent?"

## A Comprehensive Definition

What is needed is a concept of parent involvement which is comprehensive and which conceives of parents as having talents and skills which can be utilized for their own welfare and well-being as well as the welfare of their children, school, or educational agency. At the same time, the definition should recognize that parents have many needs including mental, physical, emotional, and social, which can be met through parent involvement. Any less of a concept of parents and parent involvement is demeaning both to parents and to those who seek their involvement for whatever reason.

Consequently, *parent involvement* is a process of actualizing the potential of parents; of helping parents discover their strengths, potentialities, and talents; and of using them for the benefit of themselves and the family. The essential shift in emphasis in this definition is from child and educational agency to parent. The parent becomes the focus of development. Without this comprehensive definition, parent involvement runs the risk of being a sham and a self-serving endeavor.

## Different Meanings of Terms

Throughout this text three terms which will be used frequently are *parent involvement, parent development,* and *parent education.* These three terms are used interchangeably because for me they are essentially synonymous terms. When *parent involvement* is used as defined above, it has all of the elements that we would expect in terms of education and development. The ultimate expression of education and development, then, is involvement. We cannot educate and develop simply to achieve these ends. Formal education has pursued this course of action for too long so that education becomes an end in itself. This should not be so. When we educate for a particular end, we miss the essence of the process. We become so concerned with the ends that we are indifferent toward or insensitive to how we achieve these ends. It is difficult to find a more appropriate approach than learning by doing. As Dewey expressed in his famous *My Pedagogical Creed,* "education, therefore, is a process of living and not a preparation for future living."[1] This process can best be achieved through involvement.

You should be aware, however, that some educators use the terms differently than defined here. One way that the term *parent involvement* is frequently used is to mean the inclusion of parents in classroom and early childhood center activities. *Parent education,* on the other hand, for some means the teaching of parents through group sessions, seminars, etc. However, both of these definitions used in this way are too narrow. Consequently, the term *parent involvement* is comprehensive and more accurately describes what it is we hope to accomplish for families, children, and parents.

## Parenting

*Parenting* is another term that is being used with increasing frequency. Parenting means the process of developing and utilizing the knowledge and skills appropriate to planning for, creating, giving birth to, rearing, and/or providing care for offspring. There has been a rapid growth in the past decade of programs and processes designed specifically to help individuals parent. Some of these programs and issues involved in parenting will be discussed in chapter 8.

*The definition of parent and family has and will continue to change. Many children are being reared by grandparents and other parent surrogates.*

## The Family: A Changing Institution

What constitutes a family and/or a parent has undergone a radical change in the past ten years. A family no longer consists of a white mother and father with an income of $20,000, a dog, two cars, a four-bedroom home, and 2.3 children (the national

---

[1]Reginald D. Archambault, ed., *John Dewey on Education—Selected Writings* (New York: Random House, 1964), p. 430.

average). Indeed, if this is your concept of a family it probably is quite different from the family which most children come from. There is a tendency for all of us to think very casually about what a family is. However, if we are going to work and become involved with families, we must be sensitive to what they are like.

## Nuclear Family

One way of thinking about families is in terms of definitions. This is an approach that is often used in textbooks and in formal discussions about the family. In the United States we think that most people live in a *nuclear family*. The nuclear family, as usually thought of, consists of a wife, husband, and children. This nuclear family, at least as it exists in the United States and Canada, is also *neolocal,* meaning the family as a unit lives apart from parents and grandparents. The nuclear family also represents a distinct and separate social unit. While our definition of a nuclear family is very precise, the reality is that it is becoming more difficult to say exactly what it is that constitutes a family.

Death, divorce, remarriage, nonmarriage, etc., play a role in confusing our traditional concept of a family. As these forces restructure the family unit, it makes it more difficult to define what a family is as many sociologists and anthropologists have discovered.

## Changing Family Roles

What a nuclear family does for its members is also changing as society and culture change. We typically think of the role of the family as including the functions of socialization, education, and physical care of its members. However, the role of the political state in industrialized Western society is, with increasing frequency, assuming more of these traditional family roles, particularly in the area of education. This assumption of roles is evidenced by political units which are providing the services directly or furnishing funds for their implementation, for example, day care, Head Start, and other programs discussed throughout this text.

*Advantages of the Nuclear Family.*   There may be a tendency to think that the nuclear family is outmoded for the latter decades of the twentieth century. Perhaps it is. What form of family unit, if any, will emerge to take the place of the nuclear family? Several advantages of the nuclear family are worthy of mentioning:

1. It is small enough to respond to the mobility of society.
2. It permits a couple to be free from the control of their parents.
3. It provides an opportunity for shared (if not always equal) responsibility between partners.

*Functions of the Nuclear Family.*   Regardless of what forms of child-rearing institutions emerge in the future, there are several basic functions which they will have to fulfill:

1. Basic physical care of the child.
2. Emotional support and attachment. Studies with primates and institutionalized children attest to the consequences that occur from emotional deprivation.

3. Basic educational processes resulting in socialization, for example, being able to live in (hopefully productively) society.

## Household

Rather than use the definition of a nuclear family as our guideline throughout this text, it would be more appropriate to use the term *household*. A *household* is a group of individuals living together, unified by such bonds as kinship, sex, friendship, economic dependence, compatibility, dependence, legal obligations, etc. Used in this way, the term *household* more realistically describes many of the characteristics of arrangements of living together that are currently present in our society.

## Parents and Family: Changing Relationships

We also need to determine what we mean by *parents,* for just as our concept of family may not (probably does not) agree with reality, so too with our concept of parent. Examples of the kinds of households with their resultant parent/ child interaction patterns are as follows:

1. Single family parent due to death of the spouse, illegitimacy, or divorce. This single parent family also may be a conscious decision on the part of a parent who desires to rear a child or children as a single parent. If the family is a single parent family because of divorce, custody of the children may be vested in one parent or the other.

2. Single parent family with a lover or casual adult present. This other adult in the home may, for good or bad, influence the child in many different ways. The presence of this adult cannot be overlooked or ignored but must be included, if possible, in any effort toward parent involvement.

3. Two parent families. This family pattern is becoming more common in American society as the divorce rates continue to spiral. As remarriages occur some of the resulting family patterns are:

    a. The children of only the one parent are present in the family. This situation may mean that the parent without children may or may not take an interest in and be involved with the children. This attitude of the parent also has implications in efforts at parent involvement.

    b. Both parents are involved in the child-rearing and educating process even though only one parent has children in the family.

    c. Both parents have children in the family, and both parents are concerned and involved.

    d. What often happens in remarriages is that parents bring their own children to a new marriage and children are also born to the two parents. Consequently, the children represent three different unions or marriages.

4. Grandmother and/or grandfather as basic caregiver. This pattern may exist for a number of reasons, some of which are (1) the natural parent has abandoned the children, (2) the child is illegitimate and the parent has turned over responsibility for child rearing to the grandparent, and (3) the parent may not be physically able or mentally competent to provide adequate care for the child. In cases where the grandparents are rearing the child of their children, they may or may not have

custody over the children. This question of custody may affect, to some degree, how the grandparent is involved in any parent involvement program.

5. Foster parent as the caregiver. The foster parent may have permanent custody or temporary custody. Sometimes a foster parent will have permanent assignment of the child but without rights of adoption because the natural parents would or will not grant permission for adoption. Foster family care is a social service providing substitute family care for a planned period of time for children who have to be separated from their natural and legal parents. The purpose of foster family care is to provide children with adequate environments and family development, essential to growth and development.

6. Adoptive parents. In the situation where a child is adopted, the parents have full legal responsibility for the child. This adoptive child or children may be part of a family which also includes natural children of the parents. Some parents have found that a sure way of having natural children of their own is to adopt a child.

7. Surrogate parents. In a family situation where there is a household of adults living together, the natural parent may not be present or may be unknown to the child. In place of the parent, the household group as a whole assumes responsibility for child rearing. This latter type of child rearing is common in communal living patterns. Also, it is not uncommon for aunts, uncles, and cousins to live with natural parents and assume child-rearing responsibilities for nieces, nephews, cousins, etc. In addition, there are many instances in which, due to the death of natural parents, guardians become surrogate parents. The guardian, often appointed by a social or legal agency, may or may not be familiar to the child.

## Reduction of Family Functions

As a particular society grows in sophistication, the functions and roles that a family exercises tend to become fewer. This reduction of functions seems to be most prevalent in societies or parts of societies that are economically and scientifically advanced. In these technological societies, roles of individuals tend to become highly specialized, and less time and talent are needed for the direct satisfaction of personal needs through farming, hunting, fishing, etc. Consequently, there is less need for a family or family members to assume specialized role functions such as growing food, producing goods, and educating offspring. Learning survival skills such as home-making, taught best at the knee of the mother, is not as important today as it was in the 1700s and 1800s. Other skills are more important.

This phenomena of the interrelatedness between specialized personal skills and reduced family functions can be seen rather clearly in the United States. The role of the family in providing direct services to its members is not as great today as it was 50 years ago.

This same process can be observed in the socioeconomic pattern of our society. As a family's socioeconomic status increases there is more of a tendency to have other people, especially those who have specialized roles, perform services for the family. This includes educating the children. Having others educate children can be a status symbol and, in some instances, it is fashionable not to rear or educate one's children. Those who can afford it hire nannies and send their children to preschools. Those who cannot afford it because of socioeconomic status are more involved in educating their own children.

## *Breakup of the Family*

Many people decry the breakup of the American family. Those who do so cite as evidence of this breakup the family's reluctance to assume responsibility for traditional roles. Some social scientists feel that schools should not assume responsibility for traditional family functions such as health care because it tends to further weaken family roles and functions. However, this loss of roles is a natural evolutionary process of the family structure and organization. As discussed previously, it is a result of the increase in specialized individual roles due to economic and technological factors. You cannot have an advanced technological society and expect the nuclear family to fulfill the roles and functions it might have one hundred years ago. A nineteenth century family could not meet the needs of technological man. Modern society demands institutions appropriate to its needs. A new family structure and appropriate roles will undoubtedly evolve as society changes, for it is society which determines the kind of individual institutions which will serve its needs. In this respect, families and parent roles change to meet the needs of society, not the other way around.

It is interesting, then, to consider the idea that current efforts to reinforce and improve parent's roles as educators of their children in the home may represent a conservative process, tending to preserve the status quo! Many people feel that home-based and other parent involvement programs represent a somewhat radical innovation. In reality, the truly radical approach to the family may well be to further specialize the educative process and remove it entirely from the home. However, if this does occur, it will be a gradual process extending over a period of time and will

*Much of the current interest in parenting is directed toward improving skills as educators and care givers of children. This parent provides her child with love and affection necessary for normal development.*

be subject to attack by conservatives who will surely charge it with the breakup of the home.

## What Is a Parent?

Just as the definition of what a family is has to be consistent with what exists in the real world, so too does the concept of what a parent is have to be attuned to the twentieth century.

Throughout this text, the term *parent* means any individual who provides the child with basic care, direction, support, protection, and guidance. This definition means that a parent can be a natural parent, foster parent, surrogate parent, aunt, uncle, or any adult related to the child. Being a parent has no relationship to age. This definition of *parent* does not fit the usual conception of what most people mean when they think of or use the word *parent*.

A parent is no longer necessarily married, female, and an unemployed homemaker, free the majority of the time to respond to the needs of children. Consequently, we have parents who are

1. Employed full- or parttime. It is not unusual for both parents to work. Quite often parents may work shifts differing from each other. One parent may work the first shift; and the other, the second or third. Frequently, the times parents work are different from the hours in which the school or preschool is in session. Perhaps a parent has a job as a custodian from 6 a.m. to 2 p.m. This means that the parent is not home to get the child off to school. The child either has to do it himself or have a surrogate assume the responsibility.

2. Single woman. Being a single woman parent increases the likelihood that the parent has to work. It is estimated that 15 percent of the heads of households are women. The number of single-parent families is likely to increase in the decades ahead.

3. Single male. There is also a growing number of heads of households who are single males. It is surprising how often we think that the single parent should be female. Also, we quite often assume that in involvement with parents we will work with the mother. So much of our attitude and way of thinking toward the parent is oriented toward the female image. This image and mind set will have to be altered to include the male.

4. Unmarried. Many of our concepts of what the parent is like is also oriented toward assuming that all parents are, were, or should be married. Indeed many people are choosing not to be married while living together and are choosing parenthood without marriage as an appropriate and fulfilling life style. In addition, the number of illegitimate births is on the increase in the United States. Nationwide, for the year 1975, 14.2 percent of all births were illegitimate, and according to projections, this number is likely to increase. The geographical area where one is living and teaching may have a greater or lower rate of illegitimate births. For example, for 1975, in Washington, D.C., over one-half of the births were illegitimate.[2]

---

[2] "Illegitimacy Rate," *Newsweek,* November 22, 1976, p. 36.

5. Unemployed. Just as we assume that one parent is staying home and caring for the family's children, we also assume the other parent works. This can be a terribly erroneous assumption. It may well be that both parents and/or the parent is unemployed either because they choose to be, because no work is available, or because they are underskilled or overskilled. (There are many Ph.D.s who cannot find employment in their area of specialization.)

6. Uninterested in their children. Again we assume quite erroneously that a parent or parents are interested in their children's education and are capable of doing something about providing significant experiences for their children. We also assume that because people have procreated children they have their best interests at heart and they know what to do for their children. We also make the classic assumption that because a person has children they are a good parent.

The parent with five or six children may not have the time and/or energy to do what he or she would like to do for the children. On the other hand, the parent who was a single child may not have any experience with children and/or child rearing; so it is simply a case of not knowing what to do.

Many teachers also think that parents who are home with their children are involving them in learning activities. However, besides not knowing what to do, parents may have so many problems and other obligations that they cannot deal with teaching their children.

You are encouraged to add to the list of the kinds of parents with whom educators must work. In this way, you will become more aware of and sensitive to the different kinds of parents. In addition, you will begin to understand that the word *parent*, which we often use so casually, has a wide range of meanings, most of which don't fit our previously stereotyped images.

## Parents: Changing Roles

Just as our concept of what a parent is has to be changed, so also must we alter and expand our concept of what a parent does. Table 5 lists some of the roles that parents assume in our society. Hardly ever is any one particular role isolated from the other, but many intertwine, overlap, and are complementary to others. The roles as listed were not meant to be exhaustive, nor are any meant to be demeaning, sexist, or limiting. Rather they are meant to convey the incredibly far-ranging and difficult task that being a parent has become. It is hard work, requires a great deal of energy, and is very time-consuming. Being a twentieth century parent demands a wide range of skills and knowledge. Whether we like or agree with the list, a parent in any typical day is expected by society, institutions, and other parent/partners to fulfill all or most of these roles! No wonder being a parent is considered the most difficult job in the world. It is also the job for which we provide the least amount of training prior to being a parent and the least amount of help once one becomes a parent.

## Parents Need Help

A child is the responsibility (as well as the heir) of her parents. This responsibility is determined both by social force and custom as well as by legal determinations.

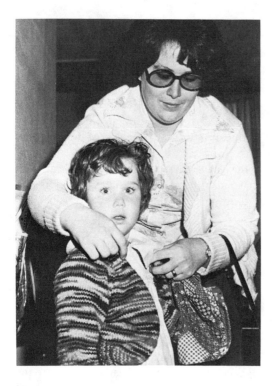

*Being a parent has been called the most difficult job in the world. Parenting is also a job for which society provides very little training.*

## TABLE 5

1. Arbitrator
2. Babysitter
3. Breadwinner
4. Caregiver
5. Chauffeur
6. Community Worker
7. Companion
8. Consoler
9. Counselor
10. Dietician
11. Disciplinarian
12. Economist
    (Shopper, Budget Maker)
13. Entertainer
14. Father
15. Financier
    (Budget, Bank Account, etc.)
16. Friend
17. Groundskeeper
    (Landscaper, Gardener, etc.)
18. Guardian

19. Handy man
    (Plumber, Electrician, etc.)
20. Healer (Doctor/Nurse)
21. Homemaker (Cook, Maid, etc.)
22. Housewife
23. Income Provider
24. Janitor
25. Lawmaker/Judge
26. Learner
27. Listener
28. Lover
29. Mother
30. Nurse
31. Peacemaker
32. Playmate
33. Psychologist
34. Seamstress
35. Security Provider (Guard)
36. Teacher
37. Volunteer

Consequently, a child derives her social position (as a member of the family), legal rights (protection, inheritance, etc.), and achievement orientation from her family. This position and these rights that a child lays claim to as a result of birth are without question the most pervasive factors that will influence her life. Indeed there are sociologists and educators (including the author) who would agree that these forces are more influential and deterministic than the ability of the educative process to ameliorate, alter, or counteract their influence.

It would not make sense then to stand by and idly decry the breakup of the family. To point the finger of accusation at parents for not doing their job is not the answer. It is unjustifiable also for educational agencies to refuse to provide help to families or for them to give back to families certain functions, for example, health examinations, school lunches, etc. What is needed is help, not indifference. There are those who would argue that the public schools should not become involved in the education of the child for sexual awareness and parenthood. This argument is often based on the idea that it is the responsibility of the home and/or church to provide this information. However, it would appear to me that because of the increase in illegitimate births and lack of effective parent training programs, schools would realize that they can do no less than provide a comprehensive program in these areas.

Regardless of individual preferences or biases of educators, program agencies, teachers, etc., programs for working with parents will have to be developed at all levels.

## Bibliography

Archambault, Reginald D. *John Dewey on Education—Selected Writings.* New York: Random House, 1964.

"Illegitimacy Rate." *Newsweek,* November 22, 1976, p. 36.

## Further Reading and Study

Becker, Wesley C. *Parents Are Teachers (A Child Management Program).* Champaign, Ill.: Research Press Company, 1971.

This book describes a systematic approach to positive reinforcement. Parents can use this approach to become more effective teachers of their children. The program is designed so the parents can work in a group or individually. This is an easy-to-read book which will assist the parents in teaching and helping their child in positive ways.

LeMasters, E. E. *Parents in Modern America.* Homewood, Ill.: The Dorsey Press, 1974.

This is a well-written and informative account of the many important issues and problems that face American parents today. LeMasters covers the topics of parents in modern American society, folklore and myths about parenthood, social classes, minority group parents, single parents, mass media and its effects, social change, and the counseling of parents.

Levine, James A. *Who Will Raise the Children? New Options for Fathers (and Mothers).* New York: J. B. Lippincott Co., 1976.

This book is about men and the care of their children. It explores the growing phenomenon of "househusbands" and how this change in tradition affects child, father, and mother. This timely book is important for all parents to read because it provides insights into the complexities of child care, as well as the difficulties involved in being a single parent or househusband.

Recruitment Leadership and Training Institute. *The Role of Parents as Teachers.* Philadelphia, Pa.: Temple University, June 1975.

This booklet, designed especially for parents, contains activities and games in the areas of language, math, and creative activities. A section on the growing child presents suggestions for working with children and outlines characteristics of the three, four, and five year old. A final section deals with practical information for preparing the child and parent for school.

Smart, Mollie Stevens, and Smart, Laura S. *Families, Developing Relationships.* New York: The MacMillan Co., 1976.

This book provides extensive coverage of all areas of family relationships between parent/child, husband/wife, brother/sister, etc. Topics investigated include the areas of love, communication in the family, sexual relationships, partnerhood, parenthood, learning and living with children, domestic skills, family planning, health care, budgeting, and crisis in the family. An excellent textbook on the all-important job of living in and raising a family.

Stein, Sara Bonnett. *New Parent's Guide to Early Learning.* New York: A Plume Book, New American Library, 1976.

This excellent account of parenting provides the reader with an understanding of what it is to be a parent. The author does not give rules or procedures but encourages the opening of minds, eyes, ears, and feelings to the child. It helps parents realize they are the experts when it comes to their children.

## Activities

1. Interview someone who is living on what is considered a poverty income. Determine for what their money is spent. Compare these figures and data to a family whose income is higher and who is considered middle class.
   a. What conclusions can you draw?
   b. What suggestions would you make for both families?

2. Interview personnel from Head Start, day care, welfare, and other social service agencies to determine their income-level requirements for participation in their various programs. Do you think there should be a minimum or maximum income requirement for participation in federal programs? Why? Why not?

3. Visit and gather information from a family planning clinic. Simulate with your classmates a visit with a parent about family planning.

4. Cite particular ways in which the family has changed in the last 50 years. Do you personally approve/agree with these changes? Why? Why not?

5. List the roles that you remember your parents assumed. As a group, compare the lists of roles of your parents. How are they similar and different? Why do certain parents assume roles which differ from other parents and from what we consider traditional roles for parents?

6. Historically, families have assigned traditional roles to family members; i.e., the father earns money, the mother stays home and cooks. How is the current emphasis on the equality of the sexes and the feminist movement changing traditional roles? What problems/opportunities does this change create? What effect will these changing roles have on our concept of the traditional family?

7. How will the role of children in the family change? What new roles may be assigned to children?

8. Compare family characteristics such as size, composition, socioeconomic status, etc., of your family with those of your classmates. How are they similar and different? What implications do these similarities and differences have for parent involvement programs?

9. Do you think the traditional family as you have known it is disappearing? Why? Why not?

10. Do you think it is necessary to rear children in a nuclear family? Why? Why not?

# Parent Involvement Programs

# 3

---

## Teaching and Learning Goals

This chapter will provide the information, means, and opportunity to:

Become knowledgeable about parent involvement programs.

Compare and contrast philosophies, activities, and features of programs dealing with parent involvement.

Develop an attitude toward parent involvement programs and provide supporting evidence for these attitudes.

Examine rationale for parent involvement programs.

---

## Introduction

In trying to describe programs for parent involvement, it is difficult to classify them according to any one particular criteria because there is a great deal of commonality among programs. The majority of programs that have been or are being developed have originated because of the presence and availability of federal monies and research grants or because of federal or state mandates which make parent involvement a condition for the receipt of programmatic monies. In addition, most programs involve parents of preschool and early childhood youngsters. For these reasons, this chapter will discuss selected programs that are designed to involve parents in the education of children without regard to the funding source or sponsoring agency.

The three most frequently given reasons for parent involvement programs are:

1. To promote the comprehensive development of children.
2. To enhance the role of the parent as the primary educator and caregiver of the child.
3. To help parents develop and use knowledge and skills which will enhance the lives of families.

Other reasons for parent involvement that are frequently given include these:

1. Federal and/or state programs (such as Head Start) mandate parent involvement as a condition of funding.
2. It is more economically advantageous to use parents as aides or volunteers than to pay professionals.
3. To make parents a part of the solution to the problem of discipline, control, and underachievement found in some educational settings.

Whenever you encounter a parent involvement program, you should inquire about the purposes of its activities and the reasons for its existence. The goals and objectives of a program will determine to whom, how, and the extent to which services are provided.

## Home Start

Although it was by no means the first or one of the first ventures in parent involvement, the Home Start Demonstration Program was both an innovative and, in many ways, a pioneer effort in the implementation of a child development program utilizing parents as the primary focus in the delivery of services. Home Start's primary function was to deliver comprehensive services to the home using the parent as the primary educator of the child.

Part of the underlying rationale for the inauguration of the Home Start program included the following:

1. By providing services through the home, the potential existed for reaching more people with more services. In this way parents, children, and other adults could be included in the program.
2. The role of parent as educator and primary care provider for the family could be supported and enhanced.
3. Research from other parent-based programs indicated that both children and parents could benefit from home-based and parent involvement efforts.

The Home Start Demonstration Program was inaugurated in 1972 as a three-year demonstration project by the Office of Child Development (Office of Human Development, Department of Health, Education & Welfare) as a part of the Head Start program. Whereas Head Start efforts are directed toward center-based programs, with teachers' aides and volunteers, Home Start sought to use the home, the parent, and home visitors as a means of providing child and family development programs and services. Head Start enrolls children, Home Start enrolled families. In this sense, Home Start was designed to determine the feasibility, procedures, and problems involved in delivering Head Start type services to preschool children in the home. It was anticipated that existing Head Start programs across the nation could then adapt to their own local situations the procedures developed by the Home Start program. In order to implement Home Start at the national level and to provide services to as wide a cultural and ethnic background as possible, sixteen demonstration centers were funded in fifteen states throughout the United States. These demonstration centers were located at Huntsville, Alabama; Fairbanks, Alaska; Dardanelle, Arkansas; Fort Definace, Arizona; San Diego, California; Wichita, Kansas; Gloucester, Massachusetts; Reno, Nevada; Binghamton, New York; Franklin, North Carolina; Cleveland, Ohio; Harrogate, Tennessee; Houston and Laredo, Texas; Logan, Utah; and Parkersburg, West Virginia. Each of these centers was funded with approximately $100,000 a year and served approximately eighty families each.

As a Head Start demonstration program, the Home Start program delivered a comprehensive program of services in the areas of education (physical and intellectual), nutrition and health, social services, and psychological services. These programs of services were delivered through the parent as the focal person and, as such, sought to enhance, encourage, and support the parent's role. Every effort was made not to have program personnel do for, or substitute for, the parent. Because of this operational method, it was Home Start which popularized and in many ways refined the role of the home visitor as a professional who interacted with the family as a direct supporter and helper.

Each home visitor in the initial demonstration project had a case load of ten families. While the home visitor worked with and through the parent to provide services to children, the strengths and needs of all family members were accounted for. This was achieved either by delivering services to meet unique family problems, for example, providing transportation to a doctor's office, or by expediting and coordinating the delivery of already existing community services, for example, using the legal aid society to help secure help in getting a landlord to fix faulty plumbing.

The Home Start Demonstration Program ended in June of 1975. Some of the findings related to the program were

> 1. Home Start parents were more involved with their children through verbal interaction; allowed their children to engage more in household tasks; provided more books and read more to their children; and engaged in more thought provoking questions with their children than did a control group.
>
> 2. Home Start children were more ready for school; were more task oriented and received better medical and dental care than a control group.
>
> 3. Home Start was as effective as Head Start in providing comprehensive services to children.
>
> 4. The cost of operating a Home Start Program was about equal to that of operating a Head Start Program.
>
> 5. Paraprofessionals can be trained as home visitors to provide effective services to families in their homes.[1]

---

[1]John M. Love et al., *National Home Start Evaluation: Final Report, Findings and Implications* (Ypsilanti, Mich.: High/Scope Educational Research Foundation; Cambridge, Mass.: Abt Associates, March 1976).

In order to provide training to Head Start and other programs which were interested in providing home-based programs as an option to the center-based programs, the Office of Child Development in 1975 funded six training centers throughout the United States. Five of these six were original Home Start training centers. These Home Start Training Centers (HSTC) are located at Parkersburg, West Virginia; Tazewell, Tennessee; Portage, Wisconsin; Russellville, Arkansas; Millville, Utah; and Reno, Nevada. More direct information about both Home Start and the Home Start Training Centers may be obtained by writing: Home Start, Office of Child Development, Department of Health, Education & Welfare, P.O. Box 1182, Washington, D.C. 22213.

## West Central West Virginia Community Action Program

This program is located in a rural Appalachian area of West Virginia around Parkersburg and covers a ten county area of 3,200 square miles with a population of 51 people per square mile. Services are provided to children and their families in the four areas of health/nutrition, education, parent involvement, and social services. These four programmatic areas are integral components of the national Head Start program. In the Parkersburg program, these services are delivered through a home-based option as well as center-based programs. There are 180 children in center-based programs and 160 children in the home-based program. Children who can be transported to a Head Start center within a reasonable amount of time (a child may be on a bus 30 minutes) and distance are provided the opportunity to participate in the center format. This transportation consideration, however, is a logistical one and is not necessarily the most important criteria for enrollment in the home-based program. The primary considerations for determining if a family should be enrolled in the home-based program are family needs. The following are some of these family needs:

*Reasons for Enrolling Families in the Program:*

1. If a family does not work or is unemployed. (There has to be some adult in the home to whom to deliver the services.)
2. If the parents want a home-based option.
3. If parents' needs are such that they would benefit most from the home-based program.
4. The geographic consideration is such that transportation to or access to a center program is not easy. (In this sense, a low density population area may be one of the reasons for consideration of a home-based program.)

### Rationale for a Home-based Option

The following are reasons for enrolling parents in a home-based option. These are not peculiar to the Parkersburg program but include reasons that many home-based programs throughout the nation give as reasons for their programs. Of course, there will be local needs and circumstances which will necessitate different rationale.

Rationale for the Program:

1. To support and enhance the parent's role as the primary educator of the child. Staff personnel are committed to the process of having parents help set goals for their children in all the component areas.

2. To enhance the skills of children and parents. Efforts are made to actualize the lives of parents so they can be self-determining.

3. To provide whole family help and services. In this manner, the needs of the entire family can be assessed and met. The Parkersburg program feels it cannot hope to deal with the needs of children without meeting the needs of families. Staff personnel feel that since the child lives in a family, he needs a stable, functioning family in which to live.

4. Resources can be brought to parents which might not be available to them otherwise. For example, health services and learning materials can be brought to parents.

5. Geographic factors such as population density and distance from centers and schools make a home-based option an attractive alternative.

*Home Start Training Center.* In addition to operating a home-based option, the Parkersburg program also functions as one of the six national home-based training centers funded by the Office of Child Development. As a national training center, the program provides home visitor training services to Head Start, Child and Family Resource Programs (CFRP) throughout the United States. Programs desiring to have staff members trained enroll them in the training session which is held on a quarterly basis.

The Home Start training center operates on the premise that in order to help children, parents have to be helped to deal with environmental problems (food, clothing, shelter) that often act as obstacles to the solution of educational problems. Parents who are unhealthy, undernourished, and lack adequate shelter can hardly be expected to devote their full attention to developing in their children attitudes and abilities which will result in school competence. A priority of the training center is to train professionals who will help parents deal with the roles usually expected of parents.

In developing skills and programs to help parents, parent involvement specialists are taught to do the following:

1. Assess the strengths and needs of each family they work with.

2. Help parents understand child development.

3. Help parents apply appropriate educational and social strategies to promote the full development of their children both educationally and emotionally.

4. Make each parent aware of the environmental resources that can be employed in the solution of family problems and in living fulfilling lives.

5. Provide parents with the necessary skills which will enable them to function autonomously, in the absence of the home visitor.

6. Help parents interact effectively with their children.

7. Encourage and promote the parents' involvement in group processes and in the community.

In conducting a training program to help home visitors become competent in helping parents in the above-named ways, the training focuses on these things:

1. Evolving home-based programs.
2. Developing skills necessary for working with parents.
3. Establishing roles and responsibilities of home visitors.
4. Planning and record keeping.
5. Conducting a home visit.
6. Evaluating strategies relating to:
   a. Home visits
   b. Home visitor effectiveness
   c. Programmatic effectiveness
7. Understanding resources which can be used in developing an effective parent support system and home visitation program.

The primary method for training home visitors is participation in actual home visits. In this process, an experienced home visitor who has been trained to be a trainer of home visitors helps a trainee prepare for, participate in, and evaluate home visits. This visitation, under the expert tutelage of a peer, provides a realistic and meaningful learning experience.

Unique features of the training program include the following:

1. Participation in actual home visits. This onsite training also includes an analysis and critique of the visit by the home visitor trainer and the trainee.

2. A humanistic base for the structuring of the program format and materials. All staff members are concerned for the needs and feelings of parents and home visitor trainees as persons. As such, the program has a humanistic approach based upon a genuine concern for people.

## The Child and Family Resource Program (CFRP)

While there are almost as many models for working with parents as there are programs, there do exist several national programs funded by the federal government for working with parents, children, and families. One of these is the Child and Family Resource Program.

> The Child and Family Resource Program (CFRP) is a national Head Start demonstration program. It was funded in June, 1973 by the Office of Child Development (OCD), in the Office of Human Development of the U.S. Department of Health, Education, and Welfare and is part of the Head Start Improvement and Innovation effort. The program is a child-centered family service program, designed to provide family support services that are crucial for, and directly related to, the sustained healthy growth and development of children from the prenatal period through age 8.
>
> Normally, Head Start programs enroll 3-5-year-old children of low-income families and provide them with education, parent involvement, health services, and social services. However, a Head Start which is part of the CFRP enrolls families.

It then tries to promote child development and meet children's needs by working through the family as a unit. The CFRP provides the same services as Head Start and additional services tailored to the needs of each family.[2]

The CFRP then is a component of the already existing Head Start program and, as such, builds upon the services and programs currently offered by the national Head Start program and local Head Start programs. This approach to providing increased and more comprehensive services to all family members makes sense in that, by utilizing already existing programs, duplication of time, talent, and money is avoided and the services of current staff is maximized.

Since the CFRP is concerned with children from birth to age eight, services are provided in the following ways:

0-Age 3    Home Start (or through a home visitor)
4-5    Head Start
6-8    Public school liaison and home visitor

There are eleven nationally funded CFRP's located at New Haven, Connecticut; Poughkeepsie, New York; Pottsville, Pennsylvania; St. Petersburg, Florida; Jackson, Michigan; Oklahoma City, Oklahoma; Gering, Nebraska; Bismark, North Dakota; Las Vegas, Nevada; Salem, Oregon; and Modesto, California.

National objectives for all these CFRP's are as follows:

1. To individualize and tailor programs and services to children and their families.

2. To link resources in the community so that families may choose from a variety of programs and services while relating primarily to a single resource center for all young children in the same family.

3. To provide continuity of resources available to parents, enabling each family to guide the development of its children from the prenatal period through their early school years.

4. To enhance and build upon the strengths of the individual family as a child-rearing system, with distinct values, culture, and aspirations. The CFRP will attempt to reinforce these strengths, treating each individual as a whole and the family as a unit.[3]

While Head Start programs emphasize the delivery of services to children between three and five in center-based programs, the CFRP seeks to provide services to families. The family is viewed as the crucial institution through which services to children from birth to eight years, parents, other family members, and expectant mothers of all ages can be provided.

Since the delivery of services is focused on the family, it is essential that a very careful and thorough analysis of the family needs, strengths, weaknesses, values, aspirations, etc., be accomplished prior to working with the family. This prior

---

[2] *The Child and Family Resource Program: An Overview,* DHEW Publication No. (OHD) 76-31087 (Washington, D.C.: U.S. Government Printing Office, 1975, p. 1).

[3] *The Child and Family Resource Program . . . ,* pp. 3 and 4.

ass˄ssment is the key to successful family involvement since it permits several things to occur:

1. It focuses attention on family needs and goals prior to the development of a program. While this process of prior assessment may appear somewhat obvious, this is not always the case. It is surprising the number of programs which try to operate on preconceived needs of clients. Where programs are built on preconceived needs, quite often clients are delivered services whether they want them or not and, in some instances, whether they need them or not. It is the old case of someone (usually a bureaucrat far removed from the situation) deciding what is good for someone else. Frequently, no one ever thinks to inquire of the people for whom the services are intended what they feel their needs and priorities are.

2. The prior family assessment process permits and encourages the individualization of services. While there are certain generic needs that are basic to all families, the specificity, complexity, and intensity of these needs vary tremendously from individual to individual and from family to family. Also, there are needs that may be peculiar to an individual family or family member that can be ascertained and met only through a process of individual assessment.

This assessment process is viewed by the CFRP staff as an ongoing and continuous procedure. Consequently, efforts are made to constantly monitor progress and change service delivery modes and content in response to the continuous monitoring process.

Also, one of the basic premises of the CFRP is that it is the family to whom and through whom services can and should be delivered. This assumption recognizes the

*The child grows and develops within a family or household. The practices of this childrearing unit determine many of the characteristics and attitudes of the child. For this reason, there is a growing interest in providing parenting information and guidance.*

family as a necessary and vital social institution. To deliver services outside of, in opposition to, or in spite of the family would only tend to weaken it and defeat the purpose of the program. The delivery of services through the family supports the family as a basic social institution and recognizes and reinforces its role as a primary educator, socializer, and supporter of its members.

## The St. Petersburg, Florida, CFRP

The St. Petersburg, Florida, CFRP provides services in an urban setting to 137 families and 249 children. Six of these families are white and 131 are black. Most of the families are one-parent families with only twenty-six family units consisting of married parents. For purposes of recruitment of families into the program, the head of a household is considered to be the person who is responsible for holding the family unit together. In addition, everyone who lives in the same family dwelling is considered part of the same family unit and, consequently, is provided services. The majority of the enrolled families are receiving welfare benefits and are considered low-income families (for example, a nonfarm family of four with an income of less than $5,500.00 is considered below income and eligible for CFRP services). The program headquarters is located in a former hospital in the middle of a square-mile area where most of the target families reside in housing developments subsidized by municipal, state, and federal funds.

### Services of the St. Petersburg CFRP

The majority of the CFRP services of the St. Petersburg program are provided through the following:

1. Home visitors.
2. Contract services provided by other agencies.
3. Parent/child centers.
4. Dissemination of information through the media and local program printed material.

The basis for the programmatic services is the family recruitment and assessment process and the subsequent delivery of services designed for the family based on this analysis. Without this analysis there would be no real understanding of the family and the services they need.

Table 6 shows the total process for providing services in the St. Petersburg CFRP. (See page 44.)

### Family Recruitment and Analysis Process

*Eligibility Criteria.* In order to qualify and be eligible for the St. Petersburg CFRP, a family must meet these criteria:

1. Have one or more children currently enrolled in Head Start.
2. Have an income at or below the federal poverty guidelines, for example, $5,500 for a nonfarm family of four.

3. Express a desire and commitment to participate in the services of the program.
4. Twenty-five percent of the families may come from referrals from other agencies; however, they must meet the income requirements.

The 137 families currently enrolled in the program represent the maximum that can be adequately serviced with current financial support and staff. Ultimately, two fundamental questions have to be asked in relation to the fiscal and personnel resources of a program. First, Who needs the service most? and second, How many families, out of those who need the services the most, can we provide meaningful services to? A program that overextends itself by trying to service too many clients really does more of a disservice to its clients than it provides benefits.

**TABLE 6**   Family recruitment, intake, and analysis process in the St. Petersburg, Florida, CFRP.

1. Identification of eligible families
2. Orientation to the program, goals, objectives, and procedures
3. Invitation to families to enroll
4. Follow-up orientation in the home
5. Agreement of family to participate
6. Intake process
   a. Identification of head of household
   b. Social history of family compiled
   c. Case study of the family written by the home visitor
7. Assessment team reviews family case study and plans strategies
   a. Identifies strengths and weaknesses for individuals in family and for family as a unit
   b. Devises and recommends plan of activities
8. Implementation of plan through home visitors, contracted services, parent/child centers, and supporting information
   a. Monitoring of family activities and achievements
   b. Support of family through specific activities
   c. Counseling
9. Reassessment process at six-month intervals.

## Orientation to the Program

Once eligibility is established, an orientation session is held for the families in which they are told about the CFRP, its goals, objectives, benefits, and expectations. Following this orientation program, families are invited to enroll. Not all families who are eligible to enroll do so, nor is any pressure exerted by the agency to insist that they do. The rationale for this process is that families should be willing to give a commitment to the program. This level of commitment need not he the same for everyone, but it should be present in some degree depending on the family situation.

A follow-up orientation is held by a home visitor in the homes of all families who enroll. In this follow-up session, programmatic features and services are explained in detail. Also, expectations of the program for the family are explained. Some of these expectations are keeping appointments, attending parent meetings when possible, becoming involved in educational activities with their children, showing a willingness to try and participate in program activities, and providing information about the family necessary for the operation of the program. As a pledge of their commitment, the family signs an informal agreement to the effect that they will be involved. This informal agreement is the last step in the enrollment process and is followed by the intake process.

## Intake Process

It is at the initial part of the intake process that the head of the household is identified. This process is important primarily because, without this identification of the head of the household, the program as it is implemented in the home would lack leadership and direction.

## Social History

Following the identification of the family head, the home visitor compiles a social history of the family. Some of the data in this history include demographic data relating to names of people belonging to the family, such as their ages and sexes and health backgrounds, and housing information, etc. This social data is then compiled into a case history by the home visitor. The case history also includes the family's own goals and expectations from the program, family and individual strengths and weaknesses, activities which will help achieve family goals, and specific recommendations of activities by the home visitor.

## Assessment Team

The family case history, when completed, is forwarded to an assessment team for further analysis and recommendations. This assessment team consists of the following:

1. Director of CFRP.
2. Coordinator for family counseling.
3. Supervisor of social and economic services.
4. Public school liaison person.
5. Director of special projects for a child and family center (a private agency).
6. A representative from the public health department.
7. A representative from the county social service agency.
8. A representative from Vocational Rehabilitation (a state organization).

*Example of the Assessment Process.* During the assessment team's deliberations, for example, a specific strength of a particular parent might be identified as: "Desires to hold the family together under adverse circumstances." The circumstances consist of: five children between the ages of two and nine, an alcoholic husband, a tendency on the part of the parent toward child abuse, feelings of rejection by society, and a poor self-image.

Some of the possible solutions that might be suggested by the assessment team could be these:

1. Family planning counseling.
2. Family marriage counseling.
3. Head Start for two of the children.
4. Physical health screening for the entire family.
5. Encouragement and support for the husband to join Alcoholics Anonymous.

A weakness of a parent as identified by the team might be: has poor self-concept and image; lacks self-confidence; would like to find a job but feels there is nothing she is capable of doing. A proposal to help overcome these weaknesses might include such things as these:

1. Provide encouragement in locating a job.
2. Provide transportation to job interview if necessary.
3. Help parent clarify what she would like to do.(This could include aptitude testing.)
4. Provide assistance in resume writing.
5. Take the parent to lunch (to enhance self-image).
6. Increase the number of home visits from one to two a week in order to provide more counseling.

## Family Accomplishments

The accomplishments of the family are constantly monitored by the home visitor. Specific accomplishments might be recorded as follows:

1. Parent is taking birth control pills.
2. Parent is continuing to be encouraged to participate in family counseling (attempts so far have been unsuccessful).
3. Children were taken to dentist to have their teeth cleaned, repaired, and receive fluoridation treatments.
4. Emergency funds ($25) were given to buy food for the family when mother's purse was stolen.
5. Transportation was provided to a job interview.
6. Children have been enrolled in summer Head Start program.

## Reassessment

Every six months, the assessment team reassesses the goals and accomplishments of the family. Following this reassessment, new priorities for the family and individual family members are established. It is hoped that through the process described above, families will come to be more independent and self-autonomous so they can deal effectively as a family with their family needs.

## Home Visitor Roles

The role of the home visitor in the St. Petersburg CFRP basically consists of two roles:

1. A modeler of behavior, expressed through specific activities for showing the parents how to involve and become involved in their children's learning.
2. A counselor and helper. In this role, the home visitor attempts to support the parents in their efforts to become self-actualizing. The four home visitors in the program generally have a case load of twenty-eight families with an average home visit lasting approximately one hour.

## Parent/Child Centers

In the parent/child centers operated by the program, parents are encouraged to become involved in a wide range of activities designed to help them in their everyday lives. Some of these activities and services are cooking and sewing classes, seminars dealing with child development, small group sessions designed to show parents how to teach their children in the home, a library of pamphlets and materials, and transportation to the center when necessary.

## Unique Features

A particularly strong feature of the program and one which also contributes to its success is that its efforts are concentrated in a specific, limited geographic area. Rather than spread its resources over a wide area and serve only a few families from all of the possible target areas, program personnel decided to concentrate their efforts in one specific area. Consequently, time, effort, and personnel are marshalled to deal with family problems, and wasted efforts are avoided or minimized. It would be appropriate, indeed, if all families who were in need could be helped and supported according to their needs. However, until society sets priorities, other than those it now has, and provides the necessary financial support to make such services readily available, priorities for available services will have to be established and only a few select families will receive aid. As such, the CFRP is a demonstration project and is designed to provide services to a limited number of families. This helps explain why it makes sense for the St. Petersburg CFRP to concentrate its services in a specific, well-defined, geographic area.

The offices of the CFRP are also housed with many other social service agencies in the former hospital complex. Because of this intimate proximity to other programs, the program is able to establish a working rapport with and have almost immediate access to other program personnel. The problems of distance, decentralization, and the accompanying problems of anonymity and disinterest are thus avoided. Being able to accompany a parent down a hall to the office of a support agency is much more effective than having to communicate via telephone or letter and deal with the problems of transportation which are involved in going somewhere else. A portion of the success of being able to have many of their family's problems referred to and handled by other support agencies can be attributed to the rapport, trust, and close working relationship the program has been able to establish with these other agencies throughout its four-year existence.

The CFRP also employs a public school liaison person who is primarily responsible for acquainting public school personnel of the Head Start and CFRP services previously rendered to child and family and of services which the CFRP can continue to provide. This process of informing the public schools about the availability of Head Start type services for children through age eight (grades one to three) represents one of the more pressing problems facing many preschool programs.

## Schuylkill County Child Development Program

This program is located in central, rural Pennsylvania in what was once a booming anthracite coal region. The decline of the mining industry over the last several decades has left many miners and others in coal-related industries unemployed. As is common in much of central Pennsylvania, small textile industries devoted specifically to the manufacturing of clothing have been established. Most of these light textile industries employ women. Consequently, the Schuylkill County Child Development Program has developed a program of services to meet the needs of many of its clients who work. It should be understood that simply because an individual is employed, this does not mean that he or she earns enough income to be above the federal poverty level of $5,500 for a nonfarm family of four. It may well be that even though a person works, he or she is eligible for federal and state low-income program benefits and services.

The Schuylkill County Child Development Program includes a Head Start program, Title XX day care, a County Fee Pay program, and a Child and Family Resource program. Services provided through the CFRP include a full-day/full-year, center-based program for infants and toddlers from birth to age three, and an infant home-based program for children from birth to age three.

The CFRP, operating under the umbrella of the Schuylkill County Child Development Program, provides comprehensive developmental services to children and their families on an individual basis. To meet this goal, the program has initiated a CFRP advisory board composed of the directors of the human service agencies within Schuylkill County. This agency helps establish a community resource link which enables the families enrolled in the CFRP to choose from a variety of programs and services while enrolled. An assessment committee works with the CFRP staff and the individual families in identifying needs and developing action plans directed toward the satisfaction of these needs.

Services provided to the families served include the following:

1. Child care.
2. Preschool education.
3. Parenting education.
4. Parent involvement.
5. Family social services.
6. Physical and mental health services.

7. Nutrition.

8. Preschool linkages creating (or attempting to create) a link between the home and school, for example, explaining the program of the school to the home, assessing preschool children's needs, etc.

The rationale for implementing a home-based option within the Schuylkill County Child Development Program was based on several conditions. First of all, some parents do not live near enough to a center-based program to have their children conveniently transported. There is a practical limit beyond which young children can and should be transported. What that limit is depends on many factors, including distance to be traveled, time needed to travel, age of the child, physical condition and needs of the child, and money allocated to local programs for transportation. Second, some families prefer a home-based program to a center-based program. Even though center-based programs may be available, not all parents feel it is desirable for their children to attend a center-based preschool program.

The rationale for a center-based program also is premised on several factors. First, many parents work. Consequently, they are not at home to receive the services of a home-based program. Second, the life style and cultural attitudes of some families is not conducive to a home-based program. A center-based program provides more opportunities to deliver services to children and parents in order to help them develop to their fullest potential. Third, some children have special needs, including handicapping conditions. These needs can more readily receive the attention of specialists in a center-based program. Fourth, there are instances of child abuse. Some children, because of parental attitudes, are the recipients of abusive treatment. These children need the services, care, and protection that a center can provide. (The reader should also be aware that the number of cases of child abuse in the United States is on the increase. Part of this increase, of course, is due to the better detection of such cases. Part is due to the increased pressures of child rearing. Also, case studies seem to indicate that a child who is the victim of abuse is likely to become a parent who in turn abuses his children.)

## The Home-based Option

The home-based option of the Schuylkill County Child Development Program employs five home visitors, who are responsible for providing supportive information and services to sixty-four families. These families are visited at least twice a month (more often, if necessary) to insure delivery of program services. The length of an average home visit is approximately one hour with the home visitor's schedules designed to provide for longer or shorter visits when necessary.

The emphasis during the home visitation is on parenting. In order to develop skills and knowledge, each family in cooperation with their home visitor designs an individual family action plan which establishes their goals. These goals will be achieved with community resources. A typical home visit includes the following processes:

1. Involving the parent(s) in a review of their child's progress in the activities developed during the previous visit. When necessary and appropriate, the home

visitor will help the parent design alternative approaches. There may be reasons why a suggested or planned activity didn't work.

2. Providing equipment and activities for children during the home visit. All activities are developed to be developmentally stimulating and to support children's individual needs.

3. Involving the parents in the individual family action plan through activities designed to achieve long-range as well as short-term goals. These activities can include such things as providing and insuring parents' understanding of pamphlets or other printed materials or setting up an appointment with a community agency and, where necessary, transporting the family to their meeting with that agency.

4. Informing the parents of specific programs and community activities. This process can also include an explanation of how they can benefit from these services.

5. Encouraging parents to become involved in community affairs, Head Start activities, and other programs. This process is designed to help parents become self-actualizing, self-fulfilled persons and contributing members of the community.

6. Supporting and encouraging parents in their endeavors to become the prime educators of their children.

Parenting education, an integral part of CFRP, is provided in five parenting centers located throughout the county. All parents and their children are encouraged to participate. The parenting centers are places where parents become involved in and knowledgeable about their children's total development. The center atmosphere provides for socialization, interaction, and group experiences which support parents in becoming caring, competent, and involved individuals.

Parenting workshops are conducted monthly and are designed on the basis of an interest survey completed by the parents. Workshop sessions include these topics:

1. Discipline. Whose Responsibility?
2. My Child and His/Her Body.
3. Masturbation. What's A Parent to Do?
4. Let's Get Ready to Read. What Parents Can Do to Help!

## Unique Features

Unique feature of the Schuylkill County CFRP include the following:

1. All of the services provided by the Schuylkill County Child Development Program are under the auspices of a single agency. This enables the program to combine resources, maximize the use of personnel, and avoid duplication of effort.

2. The needs of families and children are met individually in many different ways. There are a number of options available to parents which permit a wide range of alternative solutions to family problems and needs. Families are not restricted to one program nor must they go without an alternative because of a lack of programs.

3. Parents who are employed have child care services available to them on a sliding fee scale basis. This means that those parents who are employed and who are not eligible for Head Start and day care services also have services available to them,

based upon their ability to pay. This is significant because quite often parents who are not eligible for federally supported programs are left with no alternative other than the uncertainty of finding a babysitter.

*In the Bristol Virginia Schools, emphasis is placed on parent involvement. By providing materials and support to parents, children's chances for success in school are increased.*

## Bristol, Virginia, Public School Program

A noteworthy program for the involvement of parents in the education of children is conducted by the Bristol, Virginia, school system. This program is supported by funding through the Virginia Department of Education under Title IV-C of the Elementary-Secondary Education Act (ESEA) of 1965 and local school board monies. Title IV-C provides, among other things, monies for public school districts to provide services to disadvantaged elementary and secondary school children.

### Goals

There are five goals of the Bristol, Virginia, program:

1. To provide inservice training to the Title III-IV C staff members, special education teachers, teachers of preschool children, and parent groups.
2. To develop materials which enable parents to teach their children at home.
3. To develop a toy lending library for parent groups.
4. To encourage community agencies in supporting and assisting in parent-child-teacher involvement.
5. To develop the perceptual-psychomotor skills of young children.

While the main emphasis of the program is to enhance young children's functioning in the psychomotor and cognitive domains, the program uses the process of parent involvement to achieve increased child functioning in these areas. By recognizing that the chief influence on the child is the parent, the program seeks to maximize this influence and promote its development to help children learn better in home and school. Consequently, while the program seeks to increase the learning potential of children, the main focus of its efforts is toward the parent.

The program is designed to provide services to children between the ages of two and seven. This range of before school and school-age children necessitates two complementary yet separate programs, one for the parents of preschool children and the other for parents of children already attending school. The program provides services to approximately 300 parents and 375 children.

## Eligibility Criteria

An extensive program of recruitment is conducted in order to assure that all parents and children who are eligible have an opportunity to participate. Priorities for admission of families into the program are:

1. Families with siblings of children who have experienced previous problems and/or failure in school.
2. Results of preschool screening tests indicate that children may have difficulty adapting to the school program.
3. Teacher observations of preschool children specify those who could benefit from extra and/or special programs.
4. Vacancies, if any, after the above priorities have been met are filled by children whose parents want them in the program.

## Preschool Program—Mobile Van

The program for delivering services to parents of children ages two to four is centered around a mobile home van converted to serve as a classroom on wheels for children and their parents. This mobile van also acts as a demonstration program for parents. The classroom van travels once a week to nine different locations in the district for a two-hour stop at each location. At each stop, approximately eight parents and eight to ten children are welcomed onto the classroom van by the teacher. The classroom van teacher (officially known as a home-school coordinator,) and an aide are the teaching team responsible for delivering the program of services. While the teacher aide begins the "classroom" portion of the program, the classroom van teacher greets and consults with the parent or caregiver, either in a group session or on an individual basis as the need may be.

*Parent Van Program.*   During the consultation time between the parent and teacher the focus is toward three things:

1. Instructing each parent in the content and use of a weekly learning activity packet.
2. Discussing problems relating to the previous week's learning activities or learning problems of individual children.
3. Making announcements about finalizing arrangements for and encouraging responsibilities associated with small and large group parent meetings.

*Children's Program.*   The children participate in the educational program on the classroom van for a two-hour teaching session which reinforces, extends, and anticipates activities in the weekly learning packets provided to each parent. During the time the children are attending "classes" on the classroom van, the parents are free to stay and become involved or go shopping, keep doctor's appointments, or engage in whatever other activities they wish. A parent volunteer schedule is arranged so that one parent volunteer is always present on the classroom van. In this way, parents are helped to appreciate and learn about the classroom setting and are instructed in how to accomplish specific teaching tasks.

Not all children are brought to the van by their parents. Some are brought by their care providers. The program personnel believe that simply because parents work is no reason why they should be denied services in the program. Also, by providing services to a caregiver, there is usually an important spin-off effect in that this caregiver will not only teach the parent, but will also use the knowledge learned with his or her own children.

## Learning Packets

The weekly learning packets provided to the parents include the following:

1. Objectives for the weeks activities.
2. A list of the activities and what is necessary to complete them such as directions for cutting and pasting.
3. A detailed set of directions which explain the methods and procedures for conducting the activities.
4. Materials necessary for conducting the activities. Quite often, enough materials to complete an activity are furnished in the packet. The parent is encouraged to provide other or similar materials to extend or repeat the activity; for example, strips of colored paper are provided to make a basic chain. Paste has been supplied previously. Parents are told what other materials they can use to make more paper chains, for example, strips cut or torn from newspapers, grocery bags, etc.
5. A locally designed and produced workbook containing activities to teach or reinforce particular cognitive concept, for example, likenesses and differences of shapes.
6. A "contract" for each parent. This contract has space for each parent to list the activities he participated in with his children during the week and the amount of time parent and child spent in the teaching process. Approximately 90 percent of the parents return these contracts. The completed contract also helps form a basis for teacher-parent interaction during the weekly classroom van visits.

The community is involved in creating these learning packets. Each parent packet is produced by senior citizens in two local nursing homes, and the public high school graphic arts department helps print many of the materials used in the program.

## Kindergarten and First Grade Programs

Once a child enters the public school, a program is provided for the parents by the kindergarten and first grade teachers. Each of these programs provided by the individual teachers is complementary to the others. However, the teachers are encouraged to be creative in providing unique programs for the parents. The commonality of each program is that each teacher gives parents a monthly learning packet which contains materials to reinforce, extend, and supplement classroom learning activities. Directions for conducting the activities, along with all necessary materials for completing the activities, are also provided.

*Individual Classroom Programs.*    Here are some of the alternative kinds of programs developed by the teachers for involving parents:

1. Parents "inservicing" parents. In this unique kind of program, a kindergarten teacher teaches a group of parents who in turn go into the community and teach other parents. The group sessions conducted by the parent revolve around school learning activities and how to conduct and extend them in the home.

2. Teaching parents basic skills. A first grade teacher teaches parents the skills which their children are learning in school. If a parent does not know how to write in manuscript or cursive writing or how to help the child write at home, then the teacher shows the parents how to do this. Parents come to the classroom before and after school and in the evenings to learn these skills. (Teachers often assume quite erroneously that parents know how to do the basic skills of reading, writing, and arithmetic which they are teaching to their children.)

3. Teaching parents "at home" skills. A first grade teacher teaches parents how to read to their children at home. This process of teaching may also include teaching the parents how to "read" when they, the parents, cannot read.

4. Parents' reading club. This program emphasizes the role of the mother as reader. The theory is that if children see the parent reading, they will also value reading. Conducted by a first grade teacher, this program brings the community and school libraries to the parents by providing them with library cards. Sessions are also held in which parents are shown how to use the library. Children also join the reading club and are given points for extra reading they do. These reading points are then used to earn prizes donated by local businesses. For example, fifty reading points may earn a hamburger at a fast food outlet or an ice cream cone from a local dairy bar.

## Parent Group Meetings

The Bristol, Virginia, system also focuses many of its activities around a comprehensive series of parent group meetings. For all parents in the program, a series of monthly meetings are held. These deal with topics selected by the parents themselves and include such things as these:

1. A panel composed of parents in which they discuss how they teach their children at home.

2. A discussion of the learning problems of children, conducted by a staff member from a local medical college.

In addition to the monthly meetings, all teachers hold a series of from two to six small group meetings a month for parents to attend as they desire. The mobile classroom van is also taken into the community for group meetings of the parents of the two to four-year-old children.

*Toy Lending Library.* The mobile classroom van also acts as a toy lending library. As such, parents can check out for use in the home commercial toys and games. In addition, there are locally produced learning materials, such as learning packets, which the parent can check our for use.

## Curriculum Goals

The activities of the program, especially the activities relating to children, are based upon a curriculum developed by the local program which emphasizes perceptual-psychomotor skills. It is these two learning skill areas which receive the majority of the focus in the developing and designing of activities for classroom and home use. In addition, the program can be described as diagnostic and prescriptive since all children's achievement and skill levels are diagnosed when they enter the program and learning activities are prescribed according to achievement level and learning needs.

The Bristol program is currently operated by a staff of eleven professionals consisting of a program director, four classroom teachers, and six learning aides. These professionals are provided with an intensive program of inservice training in order to acquire the attitudes and skills necessary to operate such a comprehensive program of parent-child-school involvement.

## Discussion

The Bristol, Virginia, program is an excellent example of what can be accomplished by a small group of dedicated professionals operating on what would be considered a

*These children can benefit from a preschool experience inside a mobile van classroom operated by the Bristol, Virginia Schools.*

small budget. This program seems to be doing a great deal with a limited financial base. Part of the reason it is able to accomplish so much (and perhaps one of the reasons why it doesn't need a great deal of money) is because of its efforts to combine parent involvement with community support. Consequently, it is using already existing community resources to help support the program, and this is how it should be.

In the delivery of services to parents, each teacher is encouraged to become a manager of his own environment and programs. There is every indication that this approach is succeeding and is one of the reasons why the program is so successful. The teachers are free from many external constraints and have the support of the administration, thus operating in a setting in which self-actualization can occur.

## Brookline Early Education Project (Beep)

One of the more widely publicized and nationally recognized programs involving children and parents is the Brookline Early Education Project at Brookline, Massachusetts. This pilot project is operated by the Brookline Public Schools through grants from Carnegie Corporation of New York and The Robert Wood Johnson Foundation of Princeton, New Jersey. These grants enable the Brookline school system to conduct educational programs and secure the assistance of Children's Hospital Medical Center in conducting a diagnostic medical program.

### Goals

The primary programmatic goal of the project, which was initiated in February 1973, is to help parents provide a home environment which will enhance and support the comprehensive development of preschool children and promote school competence. This approach is based on the recognition that, developmentally, the preschool years are the most important for children.

### Clientele

Between February 1973 and fall 1974, 285 families were enrolled in the project. Any family who was expecting a child during this time span was eligible to enroll. Thus, children were enrolled during the last trimester of pregnancy or at birth. There are currently 210 children and families in the project representing a wide range of socioeconomic, educational, and ethnic backgrounds.

BEEP does not attempt to "train" parents for a particular style or method of parenting or child rearing but rather seeks to provide educational information and diagnostic medical services which will assist parents in providing an environment to promote the maximum development of the child. Since all children, families, and their environments are unique, BEEP staff feel that to create a program of services which is "best" for all children and families would be counterproductive to the individual needs of families and children.

### Services

In order to promote the major program goal of "developing school competence for each child," BEEP provides the following basic services:

1. A diagnostic program consisting of early and periodic detection, screening and follow-up for each child including physical and developmental assessments beginning shortly after birth and continuing up through entry into school,
2. Support for parents in the rearing of their children by providing knowledge and human resources,
3. Direct educational programs for children beginning at 24 months of age with a playgroup experience and later on with a preschool program.[4]

As a pilot project, BEEP is involved in trying to determine what particular early education strategies and delivery systems school districts could choose for implementation depending upon their particular needs, staffing patterns, and budgets. Thus, BEEP provides three different levels of programmatic services which are individualized to the needs and preferences of each family. Within each level to which they are assigned, each family may choose what services they desire and whether they will attend particular meetings, seminars, etc.

## Educational Services

When families enter the project, they are randomly assigned to one of the three levels of educational services. This randomness of assignment is done primarily to help determine the cost of the three levels of services. With knowledge about what it costs to deliver the services, communities desiring to select one of these levels for implementation can do so based on the resources they have available to them.

There are three educational levels of services to families:

*0-12 months*

Level A. This level represents the highest frequency of contact initiated by BEEP staff. Specific services include:
1. Home visits, one every three or four weeks depending on family need and desire.
2. Child care services, three times a month, with sessions of two hours in length.
Level B.
1. Home visits every six weeks.
2. Child care services at the BEEP center two times a month.
Level C. A center-based program.
1. Individual parents initiate contact with center for information about child development and rearing.
2. No child care services are available.

*12-24 months:* Continuation of previous educational services for all families.

Level A. Small group educational sessions are held once a month. These focus on a discussion of children's developmental stages.

Level B. Small group meetings are held every six weeks.

Level C. Initiative for specific help and information continues to depend on parents.

---

[4]"A Brief Description of the Brookline Early Education Project: Overview," mimeographed (Brookline, Mass. :BEEP Project, August 11, 1976).

*24-36 months:* The emphasis of the educational program shifts from parent to the child with the enrollment of children in playgroups. The participation of children in these playgroups is for all children regardless of the levels of family assignment. Playgroup sessions are held once a week for two hours. Parents meet individually with the playgroup teacher to discuss parent observations of children's learning styles and skill development. Parents also meet in groups to discuss child development topics.

Teachers meet with A-level families once a month; B-level families, every six weeks; and C-level families, twice a semester.

There are children's services which are available to all families. These include parent lounges, play areas for babies and toddlers, lending libraries of books and toys, and workshops and seminars. Transportation is provided to families when it is necessary for participation in the program.

The curriculum of the educational program of BEEP depends upon the abilities and interests of children and the needs and desires of all families involved. Specific content areas include focus on child development and environmental conditions which affect the development of skills and abilities. In addition, management techniques and decisions related to how the parent will manage and interact with the child are emphasized.

## Prekindergarten

In this phase of the project, the emphasis is on a prekindergarten program rather than contact through home visits, with parents choosing between three or five half-day sessions. Other services provided include: parent-cooperative extended day services, home visits and center visits occurring on an as-needed and desired basis, and parent group programs structured around the needs and interests of the parents. Home visits are sharply reduced and are no longer a major emphasis in the program. If a mother works and cannot come to a center, a home visit is made.

The educational program for each child becomes more prescriptive during this phase of the program. Based on the recommendations of a diagnostic teacher and data gathered by the medical and developmental team, a teaching prescription is developed for each child.

It is at this time that parents are asked to share in the expense of the program. Tuition is paid according to a sliding fee scale based upon family need. Full tuition of $650 a year (ten months) is less than what is charged by private nursery schools in the area.

## Medical Services

All families, regardless of their assigned level of educational involvement, have identical diagnostic medical services. These medical services include the following:

*0-12 months:* Gathering of medical data and history of parent and child and assessment of the child's health by a diagnostic medical health team composed of a pediatrician, nurse, and psychologist. Developmental evaluation of fine and gross motor and perceptual skills begins. Examinations are conducted at 2 weeks, 3½ months, and 6½ months, and an 11½ month examination is provided if BEEP staff and parents feel it is necessary. The *Bayley Scales of Infant Development* and the *Denver Developmental Screening Test* are administered at ages 3½ months, 6½ months, and 14½ months. Orthopedic examinations are also begun.

*12-24 months:* At 14½ months, physical, neurological and sensory screening; developmental evaluations continue with the administration of the *Bayley Scales of Infant Development* at 24 months. Evaluations of social and language development are also made. Lead and anemia screening are conducted, and at 18 months, dental screening.

*24-36 months:* At 24 months, evaluation of developmental abilities continues: *Bayley Scales* are administered. At 30 months a Stanford-Binet (an individual intelligence test) and the *Denver Developmental Screening Test* are given along with language and abstract abilities testing. At 30 months, dental screening reoccurs, and physical, neurological and sensory exams are administered.

*42 months;* The administration of *McCarthy's Scale of Children's Abilities* and the *Denver Developmental Screening Test;* direct observation of the child in the preschool setting occurs. Updating of medical and life events history; physical and dental screening; and neurological developmental examinations.

*54 months;* Individualized examinations for children with special needs; all medical and developmental data are reviewed jointly by staff and parents. At this time, parents and BEEP staff decide what information, if any, is provided to the public schools in helping them develop an educational plan for the child. The final decision concerning the release of information is made by the parents.

During all of the diagnostic processes and evaluations, the family is present as a source of information. In addition, each time evaluations of any kind are conducted, there is a minimum of a half-hour feedback session with each family about the results of the examination. BEEP is not in the position of health care, and the results of all examinations can be provided to the family doctor. BEEP also provides consultation with medical specialists as the need arises. In addition, social service workers help families develop linkages with community agencies that can assist in meeting family needs.

## Unique Features of Beep

There are several features of BEEP which makes it distinctive from other parent involvement projects:

1. The project recognizes that parents play the major role in the education of their children. Therefore, efforts are made to help parents understand child development and how to use the home environment as a means of enhancing growth and development.

2. The project involves the efforts of a public school system to become involved in and provide services to families *prior* to children's entrance into kindergarten or first grade. As such, the Brookline Public Schools have gone on record as recognizing that the preschool years are as important as the elementary and secondary years.

3. It provides a coordinated program of diagnostic medical and educational services to children and families during the first five years of life.

4. In so far as possible, programmatic services are provided on an individualized basis to families.

5. Diagnostic and prescriptive educational services are individualized for each child based on the results of diagnostic medical examinations and developmental diagnosis and screening.

6. The program does not attempt to develop one model for the delivery of services to be duplicated in or by other school districts. Rather, BEEP seeks to develop a format within which a range of services can be implemented in many different school districts according to local needs and constraints.

## The Mother-Child Home Program (MCHP)

One of the earliest efforts to provide home-based service to parents utilizing a home visitor is the Mother-Child Home Program directed by Phyllis Levenstein.[5] Initiated in 1965, the Mother-Child Home Program was developed by and continues to be researched by the Verbal Interaction Project, with Dr. Levenstein as principal investigator. The Verbal Interaction Project which includes the Mother-Child Home Program, is located in Freeport, New York, and is sponsored by the Family Service Association of Nassau County, New York, and the State University of New York at Stony Brook.

### Prevention of Educational Disadvantage

The general goal of the program is to prevent educational disadvantage in young children. As such, the program seeks to prepare children both intellectually and socially for school experiences, while enhancing the quality of family life. The main method for achieving this goal is to encourage verbal and social interaction between child and parent and between family and child. The theoretical base of the program is the concept that cognitive growth can be enhanced and encouraged by stimulating the children's language development. For verbal development, a child is mainly dependent upon the interaction that occurs between himself and his primary caregiver, who is usually the mother. Since the period of rapid language development in children is between the ages of two and four, the MCHP concentrates on enhancing and increasing the language development and ability of children between these ages. Designed for low-income families, this program provides the opportunity and means for increased and enriched verbal interaction between parent and child.

### Verbal Interaction Stimulus Materials (VISM)

The basis for verbal interaction between parent and child is the Verbal Interaction Stimulus Materials (VISM). The VISM are commercially available toys and books selected according to a list of criteria developed by the project. An example of a commercial toy used as a VISM is a hammer and wooden peg bench, and one book used is Ezra Jack Keat's the *Snowy Day*. VISM used in the project will change from year to year depending upon feedback received from parents, toy demonstrators, and the availability of the material on the commercial market.

[5]Phyllis Levenstein, "The Mother-Child Home Program in *The Preschool In Action* 2d ed., eds. M. C. Day and R. K. Parker (Boston: Allyn and Bacon, 1977), pp. 28-49.

## Toy Demonstrators

The program of services is delivered to the homes of families by "Toy Demonstrators." These Toy Demonstrators who are individuals sincerely interested in working with children, consist of two groups. One group is paid to serve as Toy Demonstrators because they are usually parents with a high school education or less and are eligible for low-income classification. The other group consists of volunteer Toy Demonstrators who are usually college graduates and do not qualify for the low-income classification. All Toy Demonstrators are provided with intensive training prior to an initial home visitation and with continuing inservice education during the home visitation processes.

The case load for a home visitor is anywhere between one and ten families. Each family is visited twice weekly, with each session lasting approximately one-half hour. During the first of two weekly visits to the home, the Toy Demonstrator introduces a toy and/or book to the parent and the child. The second weekly home visit consists of a review, follow-up, and reinforcement session in relation to the learning materials and their use.

Each Toy Demonstrator follows a guide sheet prepared by the program. This guide sheet, actually an abbreviated curriculum, outlines methods, procedures, and suggestions for using the material and is left with the family following the visit. During the home visit, the Toy Demonstrator models verbal interaction and encourages the parent to become involved with the child, using the VISM as a means of promoting verbal stimulation. The Toy Demonstrator does not "teach" the mother and/or the child but encourages the mother from the initial home visit, to become involved with the child through the VISM and other materials. Therefore, the Toy Demonstrator becomes more of a guide, director, and catalyst rather than "teacher." The emphasis in the home visit is on an interactive process rather than upon a didactic process, with the focus of attention on the parent and the promoting of verbal and social interaction.

The process which provides the basis for interaction between mother and child is the child's play encouraged by the VISM. The Toy Demonstrator encourages the mother to participate in the play activity of the child with the VISM. In this manner, the mother learns, by doing, the methods and skills of encouraging, soliciting, and extending the child's conversation. This verbal interaction also supports social interaction between the mother and child. Whenever necessary the Toy Demonstrator models this interaction.

The VISM that are used in the project are permanently assigned to each family. These materials are introduced into the home on alternate weeks, i.e., one week a toy is introduced and the next week a book is introduced. In this way at the end of a year's participation in the program, the child and family have permanently assigned to them eleven toys and twelve books.

The Toy Demonstrator is not considered a counselor in terms of family problems. This is primarily because counseling is not the intent of the program, and, in addition, Toy Demonstrators have not been trained for the counseling role. Should family members need help, guidance, and/or counseling, the Toy Demonstrator will refer this request to one of the staff members of the Mother-Child Home Program who is trained to handle such problems.

## Research Results

Results of the effectiveness of the Mother-Child Home Program are encouraging. According to research data from the program:

> The long-term results have thus far been encouraging, and, insofar as IQ scores may be taken as an index of level of cognitive functioning, the children who received two full years of the MCHP do not appear to be laboring under the cognitive disadvantage usually associated with the demographic attributes which determined their acceptance into the program.[6]

## Unique Features

There are several unique features of the Mother-Child Home Program which make it different from other kinds of programs that deliver services to the homes of families:

1. The emphasis in the MCHP is placed on the parent by providing the skills necessary for verbal stimulation and interaction with the child. While the child is not ignored by any means, the purpose of the program is to prevent educational disadvantage via verbal interaction. The main emphasis, then, is to get the parent to function in a verbal and social relationship with the child. Quite often in other parent involvement programs, the emphasis is on the child and providing specific kinds of services for the child. In the MCHP, while the parent and child are treated as a dyad, the emphasis is still on the parent.

2. The purpose of the program is specific: to encourage verbal interaction between parent and child. Very often in parent involvement programs, there is a tendency to have a large number of goals encompassing the areas of health, nutrition, education, and social services. In such cases, it is very easy to try to provide too many services and or provide services which lack depth. Since the goal of the MCHP is addressed to the one specific area of verbal stimulation, there is no risk of spreading the services of the Toy Demonstrators too thin.

3. The use of commercially available toys and books demonstrates that it is not always necessary or desirable to have homemade or project-designed materials.

4. The emphasis on involving the parent by doing is a refreshing and often-ignored process. Many programs are too anxious to do things for or to people, and as a result, little learning and involvement occur.

5. Through role modeling and immediate involvement in the process, parents are provided skills which can be used repeatedly with the child in the home. Thus the parent operates independently of the Toy Demonstrator.

6. The books and toys which serve as curriculum material are permanently assigned and are left with the child for continuing reinforcement. This procedure, of course, differs from those in which the materials are merely loaned for the duration of the program.

---

[6]John Madden, Phyllis Levenstein, and Sidney Levenstein, "Longitudinal IQ Outcomes of the Mother-Child Home Program," *Child Development* 47, no. 4 (December 1976), p. 1024.

# Mobile Van Library

The Penncrest School District, located in northwestern Pennsylvania, covers 410 square miles. In this large, sparsely populated rural area, access to the few preschool programs that do exist is limited by distance and lack of public transportation. In addition, families living in a rural setting are isolated from meaningful interaction with other families. Many mothers find the problem of isolation compounded by having no private transportation available to them during the day, since the family automobile (when there is one) is used by the husband as transportation to work. This isolation, resulting in reduced interaction with people, places, and things, can have a deleterious affect on the development of the preschool child.

In order to provide parents of preschool children with help and support in the education of their children, the Penncrest School District operates an Early Childhood Outreach (ECHO) Program. This program is supported in part with ESEA Title III and IV monies.

The services to parents and children are delivered through:

1. A home visitation program
2. Parent group meetings
3. A mobile van library

The mobile van library is a van-type truck that has been converted into a library on wheels and is carpeted and climate controlled. Especially designed shelves and storage areas provide space for children's books, toys, audio-visual materials, and parent books. These materials are loaned on a bi-weekly basis. In addition, materials such as crayons, paper, pencils, scissors, etc., are "loaned" on a permanent basis. The driver of the van has received special training in order to help facilitate parent and child selection and use of the materials. There are over 1,200 book titles in the current collection available from the van library.

The mobile van libary makes approximately forty stops a week at various locations throughout the district. These stops are located at churches, grocery stores, centrally located parent homes and other places wherever it is convenient for parents and children to congregate, such as existing day care centers. A stop may last anywhere from twenty minutes to one hour depending on the number of families serviced.

Materials are selected for inclusion in the van libary so there is available a broad range of learning activities related to school readiness. Some of these materials are:

1. *Puppets.* These can help children in the development of language skills and provide parent and child many opportunities to role play various situations.
2. *Puzzles.* A wide range of different puzzles can assist in developing eye-hand coordination, visual memory and recall and can help increase attention span.
3. *Blocks.* A selection of many shapes, sizes, types, and textures (e.g. parquetry; house shapes, round, square, hard and soft wood, etc.) help promote cause and effect relationships, eye-hand coordination, and motor skills.

4. *Pegboards.* These materials help facilitate visual perception and fine motor development.
5. *Sequential Story Boards.* Designed to involve children in telling stories about what comes first, second, third, etc., these materials promote language development and reasoning ability.

All these materials are loaned with the idea that parents will use them in "educating" and interacting with their children. The home visitor, during a weekly home visit, instructs parents in material use and helps guide the selection of new materials at the next mobile library visit.

Parents, for their own development, have a wide range of books to choose from. Their selection of books include standard references such as *Baby and Child Care*[7] and *I Saw a Purple Cow*[8] which contain activities designed to promote parent/child interaction.

## Summary

There are a great many parent involvement programs designed to encourage and promote family, parent, and child development. While improving the lives of people may be a common goal for the majority of the programs, there is no universal agreement about how this should be accomplished. The methodologies are diverse and divergent. This diversity permits the application of many differing methodologies to all types of situations. In this way, it can be determined which programs work best in certain geographic, social, political, educational, and cultural circumstances. Table 7 outlines the differing types of parent involvement programs.

The programs for parent involvement that have been presented in this chapter represent only a few of the many operational programs. They are representative of the good programs being conducted in many different locations. You should make every effort to become familiar with programs in your area through visitation and interaction with program personnel.

[7]Benjamin Spock, *Baby and Child Care* (New York: Simon and Schuster, 1968.)
[8]Ann Cole, Carolyn Haas, Faith Bushnell, and Betty Weinberger, *I Saw a Purple Cow* (Boston: Little, Brown and Company, 1972.)

**TABLE 7** A classification of parent involvement programs.

A. Sources of Funding and Support
  1. Federal Government
     a. HEW/OCD, e.g., Home Start/Child and Family Resource Programs (CFRP), and Head Start
     b. Elementary and Secondary Education Act (ESEA), Title I & IV, e.g., Bristol, Virginia Public Schools
  2. State monies, e.g., Department of Welfare, social service agencies, etc.
  3. Local school district or private agency (usually nonprofit)
  4. College or university
  5. Any combination of the above
B. Person or Group for Whom the Service Is Designed (Sometimes Called Foca! Person or Group)
  1. By specific person(s) or group
     a. All family members
     b. Parents
     c. Children
        (1) Birth to age 3
        (2) Ages 4 to 5
        (3) School aged, e.g., Follow Through (a continuation of Head Start type services in grades 1-3)
        (4) Combinations of the above
  2. By income. This eligibility requirement usually follows federal or state poverty guidelines. The majority of parent involvement programs designed to date are for low-income groups. The income eligibility requirement for a nonfarm family of four is $5,500.
  3. By minority groups, e.g., American Indians, Mexican Americans, black Americans, Spanish Americans.
  4. By exceptionality. *Exceptionality* is usually defined as deviating from the "average" in physical, mental, social, and emotional characteristics. Many parent involvement programs have been designed in order to assist parents in learning how to help their exceptional children.
  5. By geographic area
     a. Urban
     b. Rural
C. Intent or Purpose of the Program
  1. Enhance the role of the parent as the primary educator of the child
  2. Strengthen and support the family
     a. Alleviate and rectify family problems
     b. Increase ability of family to function as a unit
  3. Enhance the development of the child
  4. Prepare children for school
  5. Prevent school failure
  6. Increase parental interest in the school

7. Utilize abilities and talents of parents
8. Extend services of social service agencies to children
9. Utilize a narrow focus, e.g., educate the child
10. Utilize a comprehensive focus, e.g., a full range of health, social, nutritional, and educational services to children and families
11. Break intergenerational cycles of poverty (the original intent of Head Start)
12. Satisfy or meet federal and/or state guidelines in order to receive programmatic monies
13. Provide employment to parents who are low income, unemployed, etc.

D. How the Programmatic Services Are Delivered

1. Home visitor
   a. Different roles and functions of home visitors
      (1) Teacher of child and/or family members
         (a) Works directly with child and bypasses parents
         (b) Works directly with parents who, in turn, work with child
         (c) Works directly with parent. Child-home visitor role models appropriate behavior and the parent mirrors this modeling behavior
         (d) Tells the parent without showing
         (e) Leaves or provides printed material
      (2) Counselor, works from problems as told by parents or as discovered while visiting
         (a) Encourages parents to be self-supportive and autonomous
         (b) Provides advice on family and personal problems
      (3) Resource person
         (a) Brings materials and supplies, e.g., vitamins, learning materials, recipes
         (b) Makes schedules, appointments
      (4) Provider of information
      (5) Facilitator, makes things happen
         (a) Tells parents how to accomplish things, where to go, etc.
2. Parents as teachers, parents "inservice" parents
   a. Parents are taught by an "expert," and they in turn teach or inservice other parents
3. Parent groups, organized and used to disseminate information and solve problems
   a. PTA
   b. Discussion groups
      (1) Group consultation model
         (a) Personal growth groups
         (b) Therapeutic groups
      (2) Groups convened for specific purposes
   c. Parent book clubs and reading groups
   d. Specific projects
      (1) Fund raising
      (2) Book fairs
      (3) School-wide projects, e.g., field trips
4. Communication media
   a. Newspapers for parents written by:
      (1) Parents for parents

        (2) Administrators for parents

        (3) Teachers for parents

        (4) Children for parents

    b. Telephone

        (1) Parents call parents

        (2) Automatic answering service equipment

           (a) Special events are announced

           (b) School menus

           (c) School closings

    c. Radio/TV used for announcements and solicitations

  5. Mobile classroom

    a. Take services and materials to:

        (1) Parents

        (2) Children

        (3) Community

  6. Classroom teacher

    a. Reporter of information

        (1) Parent conference

        (2) Letters to parents, etc.

    b. Teacher of parents, e.g., as in Bristol, Virginia program

  7. Parent/child centers

    a. Parent group meetings

        (1) Seminars

        (2) Training sessions

    b. Places for parents to gather

        (1) Parents interact with other parents

        (2) Parents relax, read, discuss, etc.

        (3) Parents attend meetings, seminars, classes

  8. Interdisciplinary team

    a. Education specialist

    b. Social service worker

    c. Health services coordinator

    d. Psychologist

    e. Counselor

  9. Television, films, and multi-media programs

    a. "Sesame Street"

    b. "Mister Rogers Neighborhood"

    c. "Captain Kangaroo"

    d. Specially designed TV, film, and media programs for parent involvement

10. Referral to agencies and contracting for services

    a. "Contracting" of services for parents from public service and or private agencies

    b. Referral of parents to already existing agencies rather than duplicate services

E. How Parents Are Involved

  1. Policy advisory and/or policy-making body

2. Direct services
    a. In home
    b. In classroom
3. Discussion groups
4. Formal classes and seminars
5. Aides, volunteers, etc.
6. Training sessions, e.g., teaching parents specific skills
7. Paid assistants, teachers, etc.

# Bibliography

"A Brief Description of the Brookline Early Education Project: Overview." Mimeographed. Brookline, Mass.: BEEP Project, August 11, 1976.

Levenstein, Phyllis. "The Mother-Child Home Program." In *The Preschool in Action,* 2d. ed., edited by M. C. Day and R. K. Parker. Boston: Allyn and Bacon, 1977.

Love, John M. et al. *National Home Start Evaluation: Final Report, Findings and Implications.* Ypsilanti, Mich.: High/Scope Educational Research Foundation and Cambridge, Mass.: Abt Associates, March 1976.

Madden, John, Levenstein, Phyllis, and Levenstein, Sidney. "Longitudinal IQ Outcomes of the Mother-Child Home Program," *Child Development* 47, no. 4 (December 1976): 1024.

*The Child and Family Resource Program: An Overview.* DHEW Publication No. (OHD) 76-31087. Washington, D.C.: U.S. Government Printing Office, 1975.

# Further Reading and Study

Bell, T. H. *Your Child's Intellect: A Guide to Home-Based Preschool Education.* Salt Lake City, Utah: Olympus Publishing Co., 1972.

A how-to-do-it approach for educating children in the home. Outlines and describes activities for children from birth to five years of age. Illustrated with photographs that depict the activities being used in the home.

Bronfenbrenner, Urie. *A Report on Longitudinal Evaluation of Preschool Programs, Vol II, Is Early Intervention Effective?* Washington, D.C.: U.S. Department of Health, Education, and Welfare, Office of Child Development, 1974.

In attempting to answer the question posed in the title, the author undertook an analysis of seven programs designed to aid in the development of preschool children. This report provides interesting and informative information about the projects and their effectiveness as well as some insightful conclusions and recommendations about early intervention programs. The content will appeal most to researchers, graduate students, and program developers.

Gordon, Ira J., and Breivogel, William T. *Building Effective Home-School Relationships.* Boston, Mass.: Allyn and Bacon, 1976.

Discusses the selection, recruitment, and training of home visitors. The roles of teachers, parents, and administrators are outlined and explained. Evaluative strategies for home-school programs are also presented.

U.S. Department of Health, Education, and Welfare, Office of Human Development, Office of Child Development, Home Start. *A Guide for Planning and Operating Home-Based Child Development Programs.* DHEW Publication No. (OHD) 75-1080. Washington, D.C.: U.S. Government Printing Office, June 1974.

A rather comprehensive document which provides many practical ideas for parent involvement in the home. While many of the ideas relate to Head Start and Home Start, the suggestions could be readily adapted to other programs.

## *Activities*

1. Among your classmates, make a survey of the different kinds of family patterns present.

2. How would the different types of family patterns discussed in this chapter affect how you, as a teacher or home visitor, would communicate with the home?

3. If you could create an "ideal" family unit, what would it be like?

4. What functions do you feel the family should exercise but does not? What family functions could be accomplished better by other agencies?

    a. Do you think education about sex role and function is better accomplished in the home or by an external educational agency?

    b. What functions do you feel the family you came from should have performed but did not? What functions did they perform that you do not agree with?

5. Analyze the strengths and weaknesses of your family.

    a. Explain why you chose the strengths and/or weaknesses you did.

    b. What do you consider the greatest strength of your family? Why? The greatest weakness? Why?

    c. Develop a plan and activities for correcting or alleviating the weakness.

    d. Develop a plan to support and maximize the strength.

6. Critique the objectives of the CFRP. What goals would you delete or change? What different ones would you add? Explain your reasons for all additions and changes.

7. Develop a questionnaire you could give to parents to find out their needs and ideas about home-based and center-based early childhood programs.

8. Collect journal and magazine articles about working with parents. Save only those which give you specific ideas and tips.

9. Develop a set of criteria you could use in deciding which families would be eligible for a home-based education program.

10. What are your opinions and feelings about parent involvement in early childhood programs? Discuss these with your classmates.

11. Conduct a poll of parents to find out

    a. How they think early childhood programs and schools can help them in educating their children.

    b. How they think they can be involved in early childhood programs.

    c. What specific help they feel they need in child rearing/educating.

    d. What activities they would like in a home visitation program.

# Parent Involvement through Home Visitation

**4**

---

## Teaching and Learning Goals

This chapter will provide the information, means, and opportunity to:

Examine in detail specific strategies for parent involvement in the home.

Clarify personal values and attitudes toward parent-home involvement programs.

Develop personalized and localized strategies for parent-home involvement.

Assess particular strategies of parent involvement to determine if they are sufficient, comprehensive, and practical.

Compare parent involvement programs discussed in the text to other programs for parent involvement.

Experience vicariously a home visit.

Examine factors and conditions necessary in planning and executing a home visit.

Critique suggested competencies for home visitors.

---

## Many Kinds of Programs

There are a great many parent involvement programs designed to be used with the parent in the home. There are also combinations of programs in which part of the services are provided through the home and part through a center. All in all, there are almost too many types and kinds of programs to know about or be aware of.

In addition, while a program may be designed as a home visitation or parent involvement program, its goals, objectives, and methods may be quite different from another program which is also billed as a home visitation or parent involvement program.

The programs that are discussed in this text are only examples and representatives of the many different kinds of programs that could be discussed. You should make every effort to become aware of other programs and compare and contrast them to the ones in this text.

Not only are parent involvement programs becoming very popular and numerous, but nationally there is a great deal of emphasis on programs that involve a home visitation component. It seems as though a parent involvement program isn't worthy of the name unless it provides for visitation in the home! Unfortunately, there may exist instances in which such a component is included just to be educationally fashionable!

A parent involvement program is no different from any other good educational program. To be effective and meaningful, it must be planned for. This means that staff and program developers must address the problems, issues, local needs, and constraints of any such program.

## Rationale and Objectives Needed

In order to develop an effective program of parent involvement, it is necessary to base this development on meaningful rationale and objectives. Such questions as the following must be asked by all program staff:

1. Is a home visitation program necessary for the success of our overall program?
2. What do we hope to accomplish by a home visitation program?
3. What can we achieve in a home visitation program that it would not be possible to achieve otherwise?
4. What will the home visitation program cost?
5. Can we afford the cost of the program?
6. Will it be necessary to secure sources of outside funding?
7. Are federal and state monies available for what we want to do?
8. What kind and amount of training will be necessary?
9. Is the program good for families, parents, and children?

Of course, these questions are merely representative of the kind that can and should be asked.

## Reasons for Home-based Programs

Usually the reasons given by most programs for initiating a home visitation program include the following:

1. To provide children with educational and developmental services during their formative and critical years of development.

2. To help children succeed in school.

3. To reduce failure in kindergarten and the primary grades.

4. To involve and encourage parents in the development and education of their children.

While the above are the primary reasons usually given for a parent involvement program, here are some additional reasons:

1. To support parents in their role as primary caregivers and educators of their children.

2. To provide services to all members of a family.

3. To provide services to children and families it might not ordinarily be possible to serve because of distance from the program.

4. To comply with federal, state, or local guidelines specifying parent involvement.

5. To be eligible to receive supplemental monies (e.g., $200 additional for each child whose home is visited, parent involved, etc.) for the conduct of a parent involvement program.

6. To enlist parental cooperation in solving school- and/or center-related problems, for example, discipline.

7. To utilize parents as a source of help and assistance, for example, as paid or unpaid aides in the classroom.

A particular program may have any or all of these objectives for parent involvement depending upon local desires, needs, and sources of funding. As a general rule, those programs which are federally and/or state funded are usually more comprehensive and broader in scope than those programs which do not have such support. Also, federally funded programs usually serve lower socioeconomic families in rural and urban areas.

## Home Visitors/Parent Involvement Specialist

There is a tendency in education to use words and terms casually. One of these terms is *home visitor*. A home visitor is a person who provides some kind of service to parents. Usually the home visitor provides the services in the home. However, since a home visitor also provides information and services to parents at their places of employment, in a hospital, at a neighborhood center, in a church, etc., it is not always accurate to use the term *home visitor.*

In instances where the services are not always or regularly provided in the home, a term that is sometimes used to describe the person doing the servicing is *parent involvement specialist* (coordinator). This term more accurately describes the role and intent of personnel who are involved in promoting parent involvement.

### Selection of Parent Involvement Specialists

Once the objectives of the home visitation program have been stated and a source of funding secured, a next logical step would be the selection of people to work in the program as parent involvement specialists. This selection is no easy task. Usually several problems are encountered in the process:

1. There may already be staff in the program who are in need of employment and, therefore, will have to be employed. I don't mean to imply that providing employment for staff is bad or wrong. However, oftentimes, circumstances or regulations prohibit programs from hiring personnel who are *best* suited for the position being filled.

2. There may not be a readily available labor pool for the job under consideration. This unavailability of personnel is sometimes due to a lack of real knowledge about and understanding of the role of parent involvement by the general public. This circumstance means that in order to increase the labor pool supply, a recruitment and orientation program will have to be conducted.

*A home visitor should be a person who has the ability to work well with both children and adults. This home visitor has developed a good working relationship with this family.*

## Recruitment of Parent Involvement Specialists

The recruitment process for parent involvement specialists should be all-inclusive and comprehensive. It should involve the components outlined below and in figure 1:

1. A wide dissemination of information about the job. Everyone who is eligible must have an opportunity to know that the job is available. This does not mean merely advertising in a newspaper, for many families don't subscribe to the paper. Here are methods that should be used for the dissemination of information:

    a. Newspaper notices and advertisements.

    b. Telephone canvasses.

    c. Public announcements.

    d. Notices in centers, schools, churches, hospitals, etc.

e. Distribution of circulars by boy scouts, girl scouts, etc.

f. Door-to-door convassing or recruitment.

g. Notices sent home with school children.

The point is that there should be a wide-ranging effort to reach all who potentially can and want to become involved.

2. An honest description and explanation of the role of a parent involvement specialist. Quite often in searching for jobs, people are given the wrong impression about what the job involves. This job description should also include sample duties as well as the salary or hourly rate being paid.

3. A screening process to find the most capable people. This screening process should focus on those qualities which a parent involvement specialist should possess. The following are among the most often reported necessary qualities:

a. Ability to communicate with people.

b. Experience with the child-rearing process either by extended experience such as having been a day care mother or teacher or by being a parent.

c. Ability to establish rapport with the socioeconomic and ethnic group being visited.

The sophistication and comprehensiveness of the parent involvement specialist selection process will depend, to a large extent, on the goals and purposes of the program. Regardless of what type of person the program wants to select, there is still a need for a selection process of some type.

## Training Program

Following the recruitment and selection of the parent involvement specialists, a training program will have to be formulated and conducted. The importance of this training session cannot be minimized. One of the keys to the success of the entire parent involvement process will depend upon how well the program personnel are trained for what they are to accomplish.

This training session is necessary because people who are being helped respond better to visitors who are competent and know what they are doing. In cases where there is a lack of confidence, credibility is lost between the specialist and parent.

Training also is necessary for the self-image of the specialist. Nothing promotes success quite so much as a feeling of ability and competence. By knowing that you are competent in what you are doing, your likelihood of success increases.

### *Training Components*

The training process should include the components listed below and shown graphically in figure 2:

1. Orientation to the role of a parent involvement specialist. This orientation should include the following:

a. A discussion of the goals and objectives of the program. Ideally, the personnel being trained should be involved in the goal-setting process.

**FIGURE 1** Recruitment and Selection Process for Parent Involvement Specialist

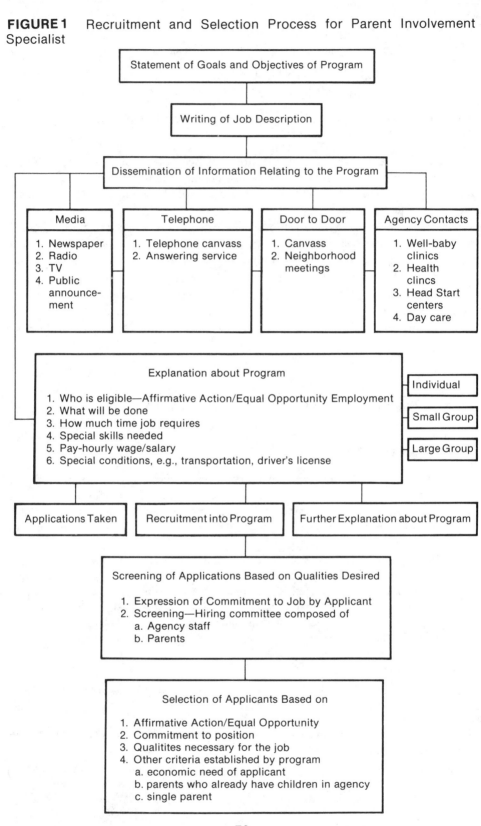

**FIGURE 2** Training Process for Parent Involvement Specialists

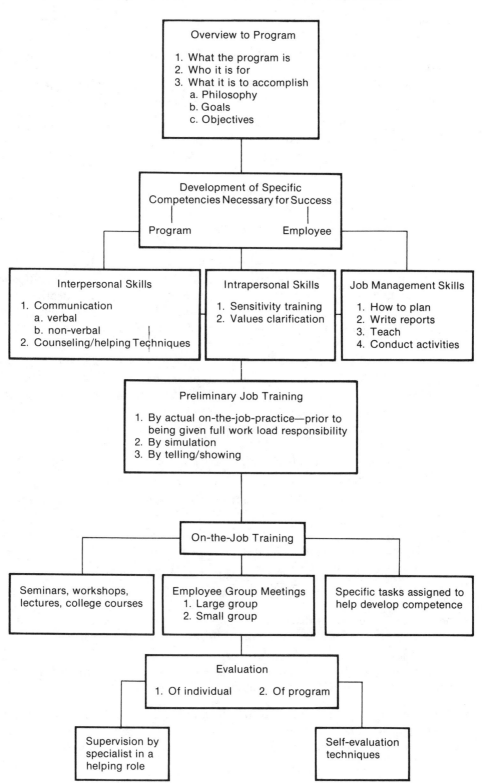

Overview to Program

1. What the program is
2. Who it is for
3. What it is to accomplish
   a. Philosophy
   b. Goals
   c. Objectives

Development of Specific
Competencies Necessary for Success
| Program | Employee |

Interpersonal Skills

1. Communication
   a. verbal
   b. non-verbal
2. Counseling/helping Techniques

Intrapersonal Skills

1. Sensitivity training
2. Values clarification

Job Management Skills

1. How to plan
2. Write reports
3. Teach
4. Conduct activities

Preliminary Job Training

1. By actual on-the-job-practice—prior to being given full work load responsibility
2. By simulation
3. By telling/showing

On-the-Job Training

Seminars, workshops, lectures, college courses

Employee Group Meetings
1. Large group
2. Small group

Specific tasks assigned to help develop competence

Evaluation

1. Of individual    2. Of program

Supervision by specialist in a helping role

Self-evaluation techniques

b. A discussion (explanation) of the rationale for the program. The "why" of the program needs to be explained.

c. An explanation of whom the program is for and who will be visited, provided services, etc.

2. Specific training related to attitudes toward home visiting. Ideally, this training should include activities and processes which encourage and facilitate the following:

a. Sensitivity to the needs and feelings of others.

b. Clarification of one's value system in relation to

(1) The job that will be performed (Do you believe in and like what you will be doing?).

(2) The socioeconomic-ethnic-educational background and life styles of the population which will be visited.

c. Communication with people. Communication skills are extremely important, and training should deal with these topics:

(1) How to facilitate communication among adults and children.

(2) The different kinds and levels of communication necessary in different situations. For example, communicating with a school superintendent requires particular skills and interactions. Communicating with a distraught parent about her child's poor adjustment to the first grade may require different (yet complementary) communication skills.

(3) Nonverbal communication. Emphasis should be placed upon the role that nonverbal behavior plays in interpersonal communication. Emphasis should be placed on such areas as: attending to the person being communicated with through eye contact and postural positions.

3. Specific training related to knowledge and skills needed on the job. This training can include these topics:

a. Being aware of the local agencies that can be called upon for assistance.

b. Knowing what materials are necessary to take on a home visit.

c. Knowing how to fill out mileage forms, work plans, family information forms, etc.

d. What to specifically do and *not* to do on a home visit.

e. Acceptable manners in the home of a parent.

f. Ethics—confidentiality of what is seen, heard, and confided.

4. Visitation under supervision. Prior to conducting a home visit alone, the new parent involvement specialist should spend time with an experienced specialist in conducting a home visit. If this is not possible, then a simulated home visit where the parent involvement specialist visits other trainees could be provided for.

5. On-the-job training. It is essential to a smooth-functioning program that continuous training, based upon the needs of the program and the parents, should be conducted. Without this built-in system of training, the program will not long exist.

The question of the time period for which the initial training session should be designed depends on local needs and constraints such as time, money, and availability of personnel to train. The session can be as short as one day or as long as two weeks. However, depending on the particular role of the parent involvement specialist, a satisfactory and effective training program can be conducted in two to three days.

There may be a tendency on the part of program planners to short-circuit or minimize training. When and if this occurs, it is unfortunate since training of personnel is a key to the success of any program.

## Role Definition

Regardless of how well a training program is structured, it will not succeed unless it is structured around a role definition of the parent involvement specialist. Quite often, training programs are developed without clearly addressing in understandable terms what it is people who are being trained are expected to be able to do as a result of the training program. Competencies must be written to support this role definition. Consequently, the issue of competencies has to be examined.

### What Is a Competency?

There has been a great deal written about competencies and how to write them. Much controversy surrounds the competency-based education movement. It is not the intent here to rekindle or augment this debate but to provide a basis for rational discussion.

A *competency* is something which an individual is able to do. Consequently, a competency is the performance of a task by an individual. A *competency statement* is a written expression which declares what task or skill a person should be able to do. If a competency statement does not represent something which an individual is capable of doing, then it is not a competency or cannot be considered a good competency statement. The following is a competency statement:

The parent involvement specialist writes weekly lesson plans for each parent in the program.

This statement represents a competency statement because what the statement calls for, i.e., the writing of a lesson plan, is an act which the parent involvement specialist can do or perform.

By inference then, a competency should be capable of measurement by observation (seeing the person write the plan) or by observable data (the plan itself or a statement from a responsible person such as a teacher or supervisor saying she saw the plan being written or that the individual is competent in writing lesson plans). The individual must be seen performing, or there must be evidence that performance has occurred in order for there to be a competency.

Oftentimes, people will confuse the knowledge base necessary to complete or perform a competency with the competency itself. For example, note the following:

A parent involvement specialist should know the five main points of a lesson plan.

This is not a competency but a knowledge base or *enabler* which provides the doer with the necessary knowledge to achieve the competency of writing a lesson plan. Obviously, someone cannot write a lesson plan unless she knows how. A knowledge base is needed to do so. Likewise, simply because someone knows how does not mean she can do it. The proof of knowledge is performance!

## Writing Competencies

How are competencies written? Ideally, they should flow from and reflect the *role* that we have described or prescribed. The definition of the role of the parent involvement specialist is as follows:

> A parent involvement specialist provides parents with the support, means, abilities, and skills necessary for dealing with life problems and for effective involvement with children, families, and other adults in the home, school, and community.

This role definition is used as a guideline in writing competencies. Without the role definition, it would be impossible to write competencies with the clarity and specificity with which they need to be written. The role definition is a process which must occur *prior* to writing competencies. However, it is a procedure which is often overlooked, ignored, or not considered. If a role definition is not written, how would we know if we are writing competencies for a parent involvement specialist or a day care center teacher?

In writing competencies, many people confuse what a person is able to do (a competency) with what a person should be like (a quality). A quality is not a competency and vice-versa.

A statement such as, "a parent involvement specialist should be a caring person," merely describes the nature of the individual, not what she is able to do. Table 8 shows a list of competencies for parent involvement specialists. Table 9 provides a list of qualities. Compare the two tables to see the difference between a competency and a quality.

## Performance Level

Another point about competencies that is worth mentioning is that nowhere is anything mentioned about the quality of the performance. The competency merely states that a lesson plan for parents will be written, not how well it will be written. There are several ways that this issue of performance level can be dealt with:

1. Have a minimum level of performance specified for everyone.

2. Write several competencies, one reflecting a minimum level of performance expected of everyone and another competency (or two) reflecting higher levels of performance or competence. This method is also one way it is possible to deal with the grading issue. A minimum level competency performance earns a C grade and higher level competencies earn a B and/or A. However, it is not always easy or even possible to write higher level competencies. For example, if a competency states, "A parent involvement specialist is always on time for the scheduled visit," one cannot do better than always being on time!

3. Write a different competency statement to fit the ability level of each parent involvement specialist being trained.

4. Ignore the issue of levels and expect different performance levels for different people. This procedure often leads to trouble, however, for some people often object if they have to do more than is expected of everyone else.

## Competencies for a Parent Involvement Specialist

The competencies listed in table 8 are neither all sufficient or all-inclusive. They should by no means be adopted without critical examination and revision. They may or may not be appropriate for a specific program. Remember that specific competencies used in any program have to be developed from the role definition of what a parent involvement specialist does and from the objectives of the local program. Many of the competencies listed here apply specifically to a parent involvement specialist who is involved in a comprehensive parent involvement program. The same caution also applies to the role definition.

The following competencies are based upon experience with parent involvement specialists, visitation to programs, and consultation with experts in the field. Although they are by no means exhaustive or comprehensive, they represent kinds of competencies which should be written.

**TABLE 8** A role definition and list of competencies for parent involvement specialists.

*Role Definition.* The role of a parent involvement specialist is to help parents develop the support, means, abilities, and skills necessary for dealing with life problems and for effective involvement with children, families, and other adults in the home, school, and community.

*The parent involvement specialist is able to:*

1. Help parents select and plan learning activities appropriate to the age, development, and interests of the children.

2. Involve parents in activities with their children.

3. Explain to parents the purposes of specific learning activities.

4. Provide information about resources and activities to parents.

5. Help parents decide if activities conducted in the home and/or school helped the children learn.

6. Use parent ideas in developing a program of activities for children, the parents, and other family members.

7. Show respect for the value system of parents by not interfering with the values of the parent and the value system which exists among parent, children, and family members.

8. Provide parents opportunities to express their feelings and opinions about their children's learning as it relates to activities and the involvement program.

9. Evaluate the parent involvement program by suggesting areas for improvement.

10. Explain the program of parent involvement (goals and procedures) to parents and others not familiar with the program.

11. Use observation as a basis for planning for parent and child activities.

12. Show parents how to use the home environment (materials, articles, space, and outside area) as a basis for children's learning.

13. Discuss with parents developmental skills and competencies normally expected of children at ages six months, one years, two years, three years, four years, and five years.

14. Encourage parents to examine many viewpoints in arriving at a decision about a child.

15. Counsel with parents about family and life problems.

16. Plan for each parent involvement session or program.

17. Notify parents by a phone call or through a colleague when he/she will be absent.

18. Demonstrate punctuality by being at the meeting/appointment at the indicated time.

19. Keep accurate and up-to-date records relating to the home visits, family progress, etc.

20. Analyze family/child background, needs, strengths, weaknesses, etc.

21. Establish goals and objectives for family/child development.

22. Develop a plan of action for family/child improvement and involvement based upon the strengths, weaknesses, and needs of parents and children.

23. Utilize in the parent involvement process, materials (worksheets, papers, art work, etc.) made by the child at home, the center, or school.

*A home visitor can provide children with many learning opportunities. Where possible, the use of household items as learning tools can be encouraged.*

## Qualities for a Parent Involvement Specialist

In addition to doing a great many different kinds of things and demonstrating a number of skills, there are also certain qualities which parent involvement specialists should possess. These qualities are ones which many people who have worked with parents say are necessary for being effective. Table 9 lists qualities often associated with being a good parent involvement specialist.

Hardly anyone would suggest that these qualities are unworthy ones or are ones which anyone who is working with people in human service programs should not possess. However, the problem with specifying qualities which people should possess are several:

1. We would *expect* anyone working with children and families to possess these qualities.

2. These qualities are difficult to teach to an adult who does not possess them.

3. They are difficult to measure objectively.

4. Specific qualities can mean different things to different people. Friendliness to one person may not mean friendliness to someone else, especially when different kinds of parents are involved.

There seems to be a consensus of opinion by those professionals who train parent involvement specialists that if an individual does not possess the qualities mentioned in table 9, that person will not make a good parent involvement specialist. Apparently you are either a good parent involvement specialist or you are not. No amount of training or experience (because you might not last long on the job) will develop these qualities which seem to be developed much earlier in life than when one begins to work in the area of parent involvement. Admittedly, this assessment of the development of qualities may seem rather pessimistic to many readers. While individuals may be changed and/or provided with qualities which they didn't possess prior to being hired, the process of changing people without these qualities is an expensive and lengthy one.

**TABLE 9** A list of qualities for parent involvement specialists.

*The parent involvement specialist should be:*

| | |
|---|---|
| understanding | tactful |
| honest | resilient |
| trusting | kind |
| compassionate | empathetic |
| caring | cheerful |
| helpful | dedicated |
| sensitive | enthusiastic |
| friendly | warm |
| supportive | courteous |
| loving | motivated |
| patient | persistent |

## Knowledge Base and Conditions for Being a Parent Involvement Specialist

In addition to the competencies and qualities thought necessary for a parent involvement specialist, there is also a knowledge information base which some professionals feel is necessary for parent involvement. This information base includes knowledge of the following:

1. Child growth and development.

2. Child-rearing practices.

3. Effective parenting practices.

4. Instructional processes (especially as they relate to individualizing instruction).

There are several other conditions or attributes which some professionals feel are necessary for success as a parent involvement specialist. Here are two of the more important of these:

1. Similar cultural, socioeconomic, and ethnic background to the families visited or involved.
2. Success as a parent.

The question is often raised concerning the qualifications of those who work with parents. Should anyone be hired to work with parents in the homes and schools? A similar question would be: Should anybody be trained to become a teacher of children? The answer in both cases is no. There should be screening of personnel into the teaching profession and into parent involvement programs, both similar in terms of importance.

Too often the assumption is made that just anyone can teach or anyone can work with parents. Many people are not emotionally equipped or culturally sensitized to participate in home visits. Some home visitors experience cultural shock by going into homes where values of cleanliness, order, and education are different from their own. In a training program I was operating for home visitors one trainee refused to continue going to a home because she feared that one of the adults in the home had a contagious skin disease. Obviously the trainee did not long remain in the program; as a result of counseling she voluntarily withdrew. In this sense, training programs act as a screening mechanism. Selection and training should be based on the previously discussed competencies and qualifications.

## The Home Visitation Process

One very pervasive impression has been communicated to me when talking with parent involvement specialists and accompanying them on their home visits. It is that their role and duties are underestimated by the general public and the educational profession. To be a competent and meaningful home visitor requires hard work, long hours, and dedication. This, of course, is exactly the same set of conditions that is necessary for successful teaching at all levels. As can be determined by a thorough examination of figures 3-7, the home visitation process is a very involved one. In addition, it requires a great deal of preparation and planning.[1]

### Planning and Preparation

The planning process prior to a home visit is extremely important. A weekly plan sheet should be used. Figure 4 shows a completed weekly plan. This form, or one similar to it, helps set goals and establish priorities for both the family and the visitor. Objectives for any program must reflect the goals of a particular program. The objectives in a Head Start home-based program will quite naturally reflect the four component areas of health/nutrition, education, social services, and parent involvement since these are national components. The weekly plan illustrated uses these four

[1] The author is grateful to Bernice Andrews, Director of the Parkersburg Home Start Training Program and her staff for providing the information on which this section is based.

**FIGURE 3**  The Home Visitation Process

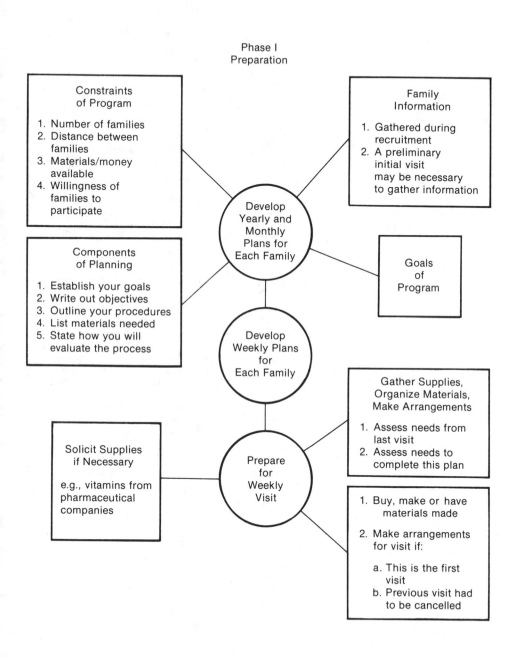

Phase I
Preparation

Constraints
of Program

1. Number of families
2. Distance between
   families
3. Materials/money
   available
4. Willingness of
   families to
   participate

Family
Information

1. Gathered during
   recruitment
2. A preliminary
   initial visit
   may be necessary
   to gather information

Develop
Yearly and
Monthly
Plans for
Each Family

Components
of Planning

1. Establish your goals
2. Write out objectives
3. Outline your procedures
4. List materials needed
5. State how you will
   evaluate the process

Goals
of
Program

Develop
Weekly Plans
for
Each Family

Gather Supplies,
Organize Materials,
Make Arrangements

1. Assess needs from
   last visit
2. Assess needs to
   complete this plan

Solicit Supplies
if Necessary

e.g., vitamins from
pharmaceutical
companies

Prepare
for
Weekly
Visit

1. Buy, make or have
   materials made

2. Make arrangements
   for visit if:

   a. This is the first
      visit
   b. Previous visit had
      to be cancelled

Continued on pg. 86 & 87

**FIGURE 3, continued**

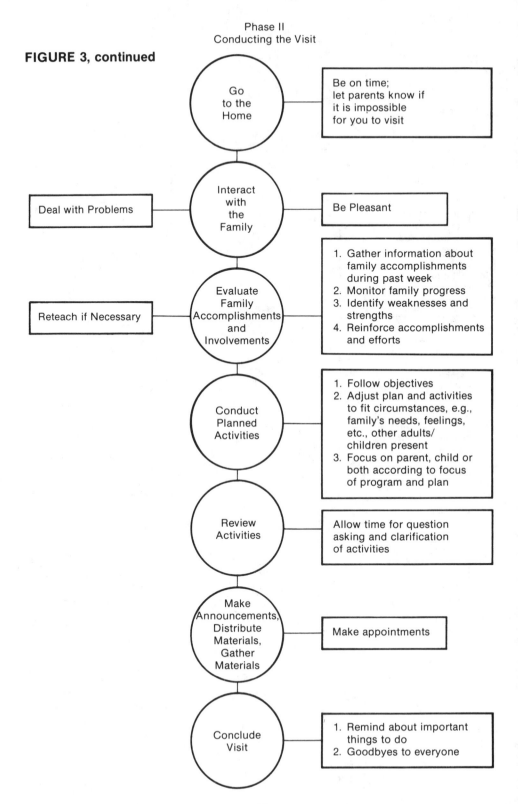

**FIGURE 3, continued**

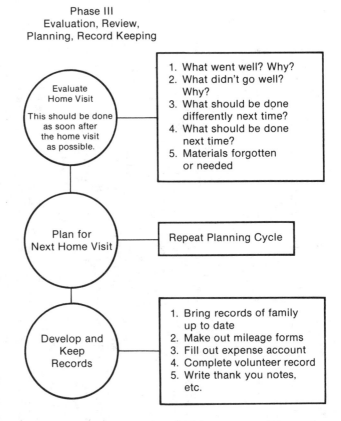

Phase III
Evaluation, Review,
Planning, Record Keeping

Evaluate
Home Visit

This should be done
as soon after
the home visit
as possible.

1. What went well? Why?
2. What didn't go well?
   Why?
3. What should be done
   differently next time?
4. What should be done
   next time?
5. Materials forgotten
   or needed

Plan for
Next Home Visit

Repeat Planning Cycle

Develop and
Keep
Records

1. Bring records of family
   up to date
2. Make out mileage forms
3. Fill out expense account
4. Complete volunteer record
5. Write thank you notes,
   etc.

areas as a basis for planning. Of course, programmatic priorities may be different for different programs, depending on the particular emphasis of that program.

The objectives that are set for a particular family should reflect data gathered in the recruitment process and in the initial preliminary visit. Objectives should be compatible to family needs and desires and should be developed in consultation with the family.

## Family Recruitment

Family recruitment for any type of parent involvement is basically a process of referral by the following:

1. Word of mouth.
2. Social service agencies, such as crippled children's agencies and schools.
3. Inquiring at post offices.
4. Placing ads in newspapers.
5. Announcements in churches.
6. Contacting former clients.
7. Knocking on doors.

**FIGURE 4** Home Visit Plan

Parent Involvement Specialist: Susie Jones    Family:  Applered Family
January 3-7, 1977

| Objectives | Objectives Focused toward Parent/Children | Activities | Materials | Visitor Assessment of Visit | Suggestions for Next Visit |
|---|---|---|---|---|---|
| To discuss with family use of vitamins, teeth brushing, and flossing. | Family Focus | Informal questions about brushing and vitamin usage. | Monthly calendar of vitamin usage and brushing. | This process occurs following the visit. Such questions as the following should be asked: Did I accomplish what I said I was going to? Were there problems? How did I deal with them? | 1. Take more dental floss. 2. Continue checking the brushing chart. |
| To assess the general health condition of the family. | Family Focus | Observation of health status, informal questioning. | Thermometer | Child feverish/took temperature/parent hesitant to take child to doctor/suggested tepid bath. | Will check later in the week on condition of child, will arrange doctor's appointment if necessary and desired. |
| To provide alternate ways to use fruit as a snack. | Family Focus | Preparing a fruit salad, e.g., washing, cutting, etc. Emphasize fruit names, taste, color, texture, etc. | Apples, grapes, pears, oranges. | Parent and two children were involved in preparation, eating, and cleanup of the snack. More emphases should be placed on names for fruits. This activity took more time than I thought it would. I will have to plan better for *how* to complete this. | Design a future activity dealing with same fruits. Be sure to ask parent if they had a fruit snack and if children were involved. |

| Objective | Who | Activity | Materials | Observations | Notes |
|---|---|---|---|---|---|
| Promote, increase, and extend vocabulary. Enhance parent/child interaction. Provide a time for parent-directed learning. | Parent/Child | Story telling with puppets made during the previous home visit. (The parent is responsible for this activity.) | Sock puppets, cardboard props. | The parent spent a great deal of time in preparing for this activity. | Probably did not praise *parent* enough. Must make more of an effort to use praise when needed. Also reinforce purpose of activity. |
| Further explore family attitude toward applying for food stamps. | Parent | Informal discussion about benefits and cost of food stamps. | Literature from U.S. Department of Agriculture | Parent not receptive to renewed discussion Said to me, "I don't want charity." | Talk about increased prices of food as means of reintroducing topic of food stamps. |
| Provide the opportunity for the parent to help plan a field trip for home-based families to the Children's Museum. | Parent | Informal discussion about need for field trip. Suggest ways parent can help. | Brochures from museum, plans from another field trip. Suggest ways parent can help. | Parents were hesitant about own ability to do. Said they had never done anything like this before. Parents may be afraid to travel and commit themselves to a group task. | Tell parents of other parents who are helping. Have other parents call to encourage participation. |

This recruitment process must be energetic and comprehensive. It is no good to operate a program if you are not going to provide services to the intended clientele.

## Family Information Gathering

The family information-gathering process, when used, is usually not attempted until a rapport has been established with the families. When this occurs, the home visitor fills out the form with the parent(s).

This information gathering process is necessary and beneficial for the following reasons:

1. It helps set goals for the family and the agency providing the services.
2. It provides an opportunity for parents to tell their problems.
3. It involves the family in the process of setting and establishing goals.

However such information gathering, while necessary, can do the following:

1. Make the parents self-conscious about their status, background, etc.
2. Cause some families to feel the home visitor is prying into their business.

The form depicted in figure 5 will provide the reader with an example of the kind of information that can be collected during an enrollment process or during the parent involvement/home visitation process. The specific content of the form can be changed and/or adapted to fit the particular circumstances and goals of the parent involvement program. For example, such data as family income, language used in the home, ethnic background, health status and conditions of family members, etc., could also be included.

## The Home Visit

The following narrative of a home visit reflects the culture, life style, morals, etc., of an Appalachian rural family. A one-way trip to the family is thirty-five miles, a distance which is quite common in a rural area.

The home visitor drives to the Applered's home. Three children are eagerly waiting for her, for this is a highpoint of their week. The children are ages two, three, and four. The mother, age twenty-four, opens the door and greets the home visitor. She is dressed in a light cotton dress. Her feet are bare. It is cold outside, and the home visitor hurries up on the porch and into the house so that the mother won't get cold.

The children quickly surround the home visitor. She hugs them all and picks up the youngest. The father, age thirty-eight, comes into the house from outside where he has been cutting wood. He is currently unemployed. His third-grade education and lack of a specific skill make employment particularly difficult for him. When his automobile is in running condition, which isn't too often, he works in a local marble factory. The lack of reliable transportation is a problem for the family. If the father can't keep the car in running condition, then he cannot get to work. The father is included in the home visit, and he too looks forward to the home visitor. He urges the home visitor to take her coat off and be seated.

The home visitor inquires how things have been going with the family during the past week. Past experience has shown the visitor that there are usually problems with

**FIGURE 5**  Family Information Form

Name of Family _____

Address _____

Directions for Going to Family Home _____

_____

Phone Number _____

Individual Family Members

Father _____ Age _____

Educational Background _____

Place of Employment _____

Mother _____ Age _____

Educational Background _____

Place of Employment _____

| Children | Age | Sex | Grade in School |
|---|---|---|---|
| _____ | _____ | _____ | _____ |
| _____ | _____ | _____ | _____ |
| _____ | _____ | _____ | _____ |

Special Problems of Family

Father _____

Mother _____

Children _____

_____

Reasons for Enrollment of Family into Program

_____

_____

_____

What Family Hopes to Achieve Through Program

_____

_____

_____

91

the children, for example, the oldest daughter, six years old, has been experiencing seizures. The home visitor has helped the parents go to the Crippled Children's Society to get free medical services in order to have the seizures diagnosed. This process has taken approximately one month. The daughter is now on medication and goes to the doctor for a diagnostic examination and maintenance therapy once a week. The home visitor has helped provide transportation for these examinations. In addition, the home visitor has arranged for a senior citizen volunteer to provide transportation service. The volunteer is given fifteen cents a mile to transport the child and mother to the medical appointment.

In order to reinforce dental and health practices of the family, the home visitor inquires of the parents, "Are the children taking their vitamins and brushing their teeth everyday?" "Are Mom and Dad doing it too?" The family has put hooks on the wall by the sink which are used to hang up the toothbrushes. Each family member's name is put by a hook along with a record chart for each person to check when they have brushed.

The home visitor also provides vitamins, toothpaste, dental floss, etc., to the family. These supplies may be bought with programmatic funds or drug companies may provide toothbrushes and toothpaste. County medical programs may provide vitamins. If the family does not have fluoridated water, fluoride tablets may also be furnished. In addition, vitamins with iron are given if the hemoglobin content of the children is found to be low. Through medical screening, a blood analysis of all family members has been conducted. This blood analysis will yield a complete blood content (CBC) which will determine, among other things, if the hemoglobin content is low. The usual ways for increasing the hemoglobin count is through intake of iron and protein.

Through conversation, the home visitor will inquire about the children's breakfast. "What did you have for breakfast?" "Pancakes?" This can lead to a conversation about how the pancakes tasted, what the children put on them, etc. Sometimes the children may say they didn't have anything to eat. When children respond that they have had nothing to eat, the home visitor will determine if this is a persistent and chronic occurrence. If it is because of a lack of food, money, parent initiative, family problems, etc., this will more than likely be an area in which the home visitor will spend time developing activities and reinforcing concepts with the parents concerning the importance of good nutrition. In addition, the family will be helped to deal with these problems. At Christmas time, the home visitor may take baskets of groceries and from time to time, will get an emergency food order from the Community Action Agency or Department of Welfare so that the family may have food. It could also be the case that this family isn't aware of the federal food stamp program. If so, this will also be an area in which the home visitor will provide help. (The amount of money a family spends for food stamps, if any, depends on family income, bills, and other family responsibilities.)

The family is next asked to get their monthly plan so it can be reviewed by the family and the home visitor. This monthly plan is discussed with the parent each month and is developed with their help. Parents are always asked if they have any ideas for conducting activities, solving problems, etc. Quite often the parents do suggest different ideas, for example, using coffee cans and buttons for conducting a classification activity.

During the visit, the children will also show the home visitor what they have done the past week. The mother tells what she did with the children. For example, the mother throughout the week has been having the children find things in the house that are red and has had the children help with sorting the clothes prior to washing them. They have also played together the game, I Spy.

The father is very involved in teaching the children and although he cannot read, will teach the children the names for the tools in his tool box. The father also "reads" to the children by naming pictures in picture books left by the home visitor. The home visitor makes it a practice to leave several books every week. Magazines also are left for the parents. In this case, magazines are more effective than books since the parents do not read. (While magazines are very good teaching devices, culturally they are very middle class. Many of the homes, fashion, etc., are beyond the means and ability of many families to achieve. In addition, many of the advertisements can cause frustration because of the inability to achieve what they advocate.)

In this particular home, learning is a reciprocal process since the home visitor also learns a greal deal. The father shows the home visitor and children how to cut wood, how to start a fire in a woodburning stove, and how to fix the automobile. The home visitor encourages these kinds of learning activities.

The next activity which the home visitor helps the family with is a craft activity of stuffing a necktie. Everyone is shown how to make a "snake" stuffed animal toy. There is a discussion about what the animal is, its color, shape, length, etc. (Stuffed animals such as these can also be made by parents and sold at the Parent Committee Sales.) In addition, activities such as these are good to use in introducing the children to sewing and stitching. Of course, they are also excellent as props for encouraging language development.

For the younger children, as a follow-up activity, a piece of cardboard can be punched with holes to form shapes, initials of names, designs, etc. These pieces of cardboard can then be "sewn" with string. The home visitor brings the cardboard, and the parent provides the needle, string, etc. This is an important process since the home visitor doesn't want to do everything for the family.

At this particular home, the home visitor inquires if the parent is continuing to receive a social security supplement for a handicapped child. This is a follow-up discussion since over the previous six months, the home visitor has helped the family receive this benefit.

The home visitor checks on the family supply of learning materials. "Do you have plenty of paste, scissors, and paper?" These supplies are furnished by the agency. The home visitor makes sure that these supplies will be used by the children throughout the week by leaving activities to color, cut, paste, etc. It is surprising how inexpensive these materials are. Consult a school supply catalogue to determine how little paper and pencils do cost.

Prior to the conclusion of the visit, the home visitor shows the mother activities she wants her to do with the children the coming week. In this particular case, they are a review of the concepts of color, shape, size, classification, and weight. These concepts had been introduced before. The home visitor also reminds parents of the forthcoming parent meeting. Arrangements are made to have a neighbor provide the mother with a ride. The father has volunteered to baby-sit so the mother can attend the meeting.

The home visit is concluded by the home visitor's wishing everyone a good week and giving the children a hug. The children don't want the home visitor to leave since the visit has been an enjoyable time for them.

The home visit usually takes two hours but can be lengthened or shortened depending on the family and the particular schedule of the home visitor.

## Assessment of the Home Visit Plan (Based on Figure 4)

1. A great deal of "education" and "cognitive" content occurs in all of the activities even though not all the objectives are formal, educational ones.

2. It may be impossible to achieve all of the goals or objectives one has planned for in one visit.

3. The home visitor's assessment of the visit and suggestions for the next visit should be completed as soon after the home visit as possible.

4. It is very important that the goals and objectives of the weekly visit be based on the following:

   a. The needs, interests, and desires of each family member should be considered.

   b. While the lesson plan may not reflect it, effort and plans should be made to individualize activities for each family and for each person within each family. For example, one activity may not be suitable, sufficient, or appropriate for all the children in a family. Therefore, several activities may be necessary.

   c. It is very easy to plan a home visit on the basis of thinking up activities that would be "nice" or "good" for families to do. However, this approach to teaching and involvement at any level is educationally unsound as well as procedurally wrong. All planning should begin with goals. Unfortunately, this process of setting goals and objectives is one which most human service professionals (especially teachers) don't want to do.

5. A home visit (any other activity for that matter) is only as good as the planning which occurs prior to the visit.

6. The plan provides primarily for family and parent focus activities and, consequently, includes all members of the family. There is a strong tendency in a home visit process to focus only on the child. Quite often this focus can occur to the point of excluding other family members. The focus of the visit will depend upon the goals of the program.

7. In planning, there is a tendency to focus on cognitive goals, for example, teaching people how to do things, providing information, etc., to the exclusion of affective goals such as enhancing self-image, helping parents clarify their own values, promoting communication among family members, etc. Consequently, affective goals should be established and provided for in the program of activities. These, of course, should be based on the needs of the family.

## Home Visitor's Schedule

Figures 6 and 7 depict the schedules of two different home visitors. These schedules are different from each other for a number of reasons. Here are some of the factors which cause them to be different:

1. The personality and visiting modality of the home visitor. *Visiting modality* refers to the way in which the visitor delivers the services to a family.

2. The goals and objectives of the home visitation program.

3. The number of families in the program.

4. The budget of the program. Some programs may purchase more materials than other programs.

5. The geographic and demographic nature of an area. One home visitor may have to travel a great distance to particular families; whereas, another home visitor may not have to travel at all.

6. The problems, needs, desires, and strengths of each family, which determine how the visit is conducted.

Not only should we expect home visitor schedules to vary from program to program, but we would also expect them to vary within programs. Indeed, it is desirable that they should. We don't expect teachers to teach identically to each other; we should not expect home visitors to function identically to each other.

## Home Visitation Materials

In making home visits, a parent involvement specialist has to take to the homes materials needed to support and complete the planned for activities. What specific materials are taken depends upon what has been planned for each family. Table 10 lists some materials which are representative of the kind that might be included in a home visit.

**TABLE 10**  A list of materials needed for a home visit.

Health/Nutrition

Vitamins
Thermometer
Pamphlets relating to health
Newspaper articles relating to
  measles and vaccinations
"Mr. Yuk" stickers (Poison Prevention and Control Center)
Chart of poisons and antedotes

Education

| | | |
|---|---|---|
| Scissors | Books | 3 X 5 Cards |
| Paper | Toys | Construction paper |
| Crayons | Games | |
| Pencils | Learning Materials | |
| Rulers | 1. Teacher made | |
| Paste | 2. Purchased | |

Social Services

Pamphlet describing food stamps

Parent Involvement

Printed announcements of parent meetings at center

**FIGURE 6**  Home Visitor Schedule

| | 8 A.M. | 9 A.M. | 10 A.M. | 11 A.M. | 12 noon | 1 P.M. | 2 P.M. | 3 P.M. | 4 P.M. |
|---|---|---|---|---|---|---|---|---|---|
| MONDAY | Office Prep time and a staff meeting | Office | | HOME VISITS | | Sack Lunch | | HOME VISITS | |
| TUESDAY | Take family to Dr.'s office and Crippled Children's Society | | | HOME VISITS | | Sack Lunch | | HOME VISITS | |
| WEDNESDAY | Trips to legal services, health department, grocery stores, thrift shops, picking up and delivering (food, furniture) | | | HOME VISITS | | Sack Lunch | | HOME VISITS | |
| THURSDAY | HOME VISITS | | | HOME VISITS | | Sack Lunch | | HOME VISITS | |
| FRIDAY | Planning all day. Write out lesson plans (weekly). Help write and assemble monthly plans. Create activities. Plan and attend one parent meeting a month, held on Friday. Schedule appointments with social service agencies. Complete paper work for coming month, such as mileage forms, inkind contributions forms (*inkind* means providing services for which one is not paid), etc. Prepare supplies and materials for the coming week. | | | | | | | | |

96

**FIGURE 7** Home Visitor Schedule

| | A.M. | P.M. |
|---|---|---|
| MONDAY | Staff meeting and/or planning time. | Two home visits scheduled. Made first visit but had to cancel the second because it was necessary to take one family to the doctor because the family car broke down. Also, made arrangements with a neighbor to drive the family to the doctor on subsequent visits. Went to welfare department for information about a new program. |
| TUESDAY | Two home visits. | Planning and family analysis. |
| WEDNESDAY | Two home contacts (a contact is a brief follow-up of a visit. It can last anywhere from 15 minutes to a half hour.) | One home visit. Transported family to the county hospital. |
| THURSDAY | Two home visits. | One home visit. Took the public health nurse along in order to assess a child for a potential physical handicap. |
| FRIDAY | Two home visits. | One home visit. Remainder of day spent on paper work. |
| SUNDAY | Get materials at home together for following week. Plan in detail for week's activities. | |

In addition to the activities presented, the following monthly activities will have to be attended: parent meetings, parent socials, fund-raising affairs, field trips, staff meetings (many of which occur in the evening).

97

## Typical Functions of Home Visitors

When an analysis is made of what a home visitor does, some of the roles or tasks which emerge are those listed in Table 11.

**TABLE 11**   Percent of home visitor's time spent in each role category (based on 40-60 hour week).

| | |
|---|---|
| Teacher | 10% |
| Expeditor | 20% |
| Coordinator | 20% |
| Counselor | 20% |
| Transporter | 10% |
| Record Keeper | 10% |
| Planner | 10% |

The time spent in the roles of expeditor and coordinator seems to overshadow the time spent as a teacher. Of course, how much time is spent on a particular function depends on the focus of the program and the strengths of a home visitor. However, a home visitation program should exercise a monitoring function of the visitor's activities to assure that the amount of time spent in a particular role does not inordinately exceed the amount of time that should be spent on a particular function. Some home visitors may find it easier, more convenient, or more in keeping with their particular style of visiting to spend more time on a particular function. This overemphasis in a particular area can lead to weaknesses in the program.

*Opportunities exist for working with parents in many different ways. Here a parent involvement specialist teaches parents how to help their children. A follow-up visit to the home will reinforce and extend what was taught.*

## Case Load of a Home Visitor

There seems to be a great deal of variation and difference of opinion concerning the family case load that a home visitor should carry. In some programs, a case load of eight to ten families is considered average, while in other programs a case load of twenty-five to thirty families is considered normal. The case load that an individual home visitor carries seems to be dependent upon the following kind of factors:

1. Goals and objectives of the particular program. Where the goals and objectives of a particular program dictate that a rather broad and comprehensive program of services will be delivered to the family and home, then it is going to take a much longer time for the home visitor to do this. The home visitor will, of necessity, be much more involved with the family than if these services were not so comprehensive. For example, if the home visitor is delivering a full range of health, nutrition, and educational services with supplemental services in the areas of housing, counseling, family living problems, etc., then to plan for, make arrangements for, deliver, and follow up on these services is going to take a much longer time than it would if a visitor were delivering a narrow range of services. If the function of the home visitor is to go into the home and teach the parents a specific educational activity, which could be used with their child in the absences of the home visitor, then this activity will not take as long as a comprehensive program. In a comprehensive program, a home visitor may take anywhere from an hour to a half day or more. In a less comprehensive program, the home visit may last anywhere from a half hour to forty-five minutes.

2. The distance which a home visitor has to travel in order to visit homes will have an effect on the case load that the visitor can carry. In rural settings, where homes are located on isolated back roads difficult to traverse even in good weather and where distances between homes may be ten miles or more, it will take the home visitor much longer to see individual families. Because of this transportation factor, fewer homes can be visited. On the other hand, in an urban setting where the home visitor can walk from one home to another, the number of home visits can be greater. If home visitors are delivering services in a housing development, they need considerably less time between visits.

3. The style of home visitation that an individual develops also affects her case load. Some home visitors use a visiting modality which incorporates a counseling function and a format which encourages interaction. Consequently, visits are freer, more relaxed, and promote an empathy with parents. Where this type of visit occurs, there will be a tendency and a need to stay longer in the home. Of course, this style of visitation will reduce the number of homes that are visited.

## Guidelines for Home Visiting

The following represents some important considerations which should be addressed in any program of home visitation:

1. It is extremely important to establish rapport with the parent being visited as quickly as possible. Part of the process of establishing rapport has to do with how willing the home visitor is to get involved with parents and convey to them that she is

a helping person. If you as a home visitor can't establish good feelings with parents quickly, then you are lost.

2. It is important to have specific goals and objectives relating to the program and to what the home visitor is going to do. In this way, both parents and home visitors know what the program is about and what it is that will be accomplished.

3. Preparation for the visit is crucial. If the visitor is unwilling to prepare for the visit, then the process will not be as effective as it should be. To a large extent, success is proportional to the amount of planning that occurs. In this respect, administrators should provide staff with sufficient planning time. The amount of time usually deemed sufficient for planning is a half day to a whole day depending on the case load of the visitor.

4. The home visitor should enter every home with an open mind, ready to experience anything. This means the home visitor must accept the values, conditions, traditions, and culture of the home.

5. If you don't like to be around people, don't become a home visitor. The process is too important to jeopardize it on someone who cannot get along with others.

6. The home visitor must begin where the parent is in terms of:

   a. How the parent feels about himself as a person and a parent.

   b. The knowledge and skills of parenting the parent possesses.

   c. The ecological problems the parent must live and deal with (and which the home visitor must help the parent deal with).

7. The home visitor should know the community and local areas in which the homes are located. It may take special time and effort to learn this demographic and geographic information, but it is worthwhile to do so. By effectively knowing the community, the visitor will be able to link the family to more community services and opportunities and will be more able to involve the parent in the community.

8. The home visitor must be willing to go where the parent is. This means not only the home but also the place of employment in order to deliver even a minimum amount of services.

## A Home Visit Can Occur Anywhere

A home visit does not necessarily take place in the home! The parent may not spend enough time in the home to have a "home visit" there. For example, a home visit may occur in a bar, place of employment, hospital, or wherever it is necessary to meet the parent. You must meet the parent where the parent is, at a time and place comfortable to and appropriate for the parent, if you are sincere in your efforts to establish contact and communication with the parent.

We should remember also that a home visitation process is only one part of a comprehensive program of parent involvement. Unfortunately, there may be a tendency to place the majority of the emphasis on home visiting.

## Developmental Nature of Home Visits

Just as every effort should be made to individualize programs with children, so every effort should be made to individualize programs for families. One plan of home visitation will not be sufficient for every family. Also, a family just beginning to receive home visits will have quite different needs from families who have been receiving them for six months, a year, or longer. In addition, the home visitor's relationship to and style of operation with a new family will differ markedly from a family that has been visited for a period of time. Thus, individuals involved in the program should design a program which is unique to each family.

## Summary

Visiting with parents in the home in order to provide families and children the support and services necessary for self-fulfillment is where the action is. It represents the ultimate expression of what the helping professions are all about. The opportunities for creative contribution are virtually unlimited. It permits the home visitor to interact with a wide range of individuals from birth through adulthood in the intimate environment of the home. This should be conceived of as a rare opportunity.

Working with parents, families, and children in the homes is a sacred trust which should be prized. People who are willing to dedicate themselves to the task of uplifting, supporting, and promoting self-fulfillment in others are much needed.

Every person who thinks she wants to be a teacher should have a home visiting experience prior to becoming a teacher. It is only by working with parents and children in their homes that you truly come to appreciate why children are as they are and the power and influence parents have over their children. By experiencing this process first-hand, teachers would become more compassionate and tolerant of children. Perhaps they would also be more willing to provide individualized programs of instruction for children rather than demanding that all children accomplish the same activities in the same way.

## *Further Reading and Study*

Board of Cooperative Educational Services of Nassau County, Salisbury Center. *200 Ways to Help Children Learn: While You're At It*. Reston, Va.: Reston Publishing Co., 1976.
Parents will find this book an excellent reference book which provides information about how they can help their children learn and have fun during the busy homemaking schedule. The design of the book provides a quantity of easily read material and ideas for any activity.

Coles, Ann; Haul, Carolyn; Bushnell, Faith; and Weinberger, Betsy. *I Saw a Purple Cow and 100 Other Recipes for Learning*. Boston: Mass. Little, Brown and Company, 1972.
This easily read, fun account of learning activities and games really works. A great reference book to keep on hand for rainy days, party time, or fun time. The activities are fun for both child and parent. The activities are flexible for use at home or school. They are also very inexpensive and much of the required material can be readily attained in the home or classroom. A good book to have around the home.

D'Audney, Wesley. *Calendar of Developmental Activities for Preschoolers*. Omaha, Neb.: Meyer Children's Rehabilitation Institute, University of Nebraska Medical Center, 1975.
This book is an idea resource book written primarily for parents interested in teaching their children readiness and school preparatory skills. Parents will find this calendar format of developmental skills most useful. Easily followed by parents interested in assisting their children through those important formative years before they enter school.

Gordon, Ira J. *Baby Learning Through Play (A Parents' Guide for the First Two Years).* New York: St. Martin's Press, 1970.

An excellent guide to babies' games that provide pleasure for both parent and child. Also helps to develop security, a good self-concept, and intellectual growth in the young infant up to older toddlers. A good resource book to have on hand.

Jones, Sandy. *Good Things for Babies.* Boston: Houghton Mifflin Co., 1976.

Excellent resource book for parents who desire more information about products, equipment, and toys. Provides information about poison and safety control. A useful tool for locating clothing and learning materials, etc.

*Rock-A-Bye Baby.* Time-Life Films, 100 Eisenhower Drive, Paramus, N.J.

Shows the importance of parental affection, interaction, and stimulation in humans and animals. Effects of maternal deprivation in young primates and children are graphically illustrated. Must viewing for parents, potential parents, and everyone in the helping professions.

Scott, Ralph; Wagner, Guy; and Cesinger, Joan. *Home Start Ideabook.* Darien, Conn.: Early Years Press, 1976.

This book is useful for both the professional teacher as well as the parent. The activities are appropriate for all interested persons who work with children in their early and formative years. The activities are designed so they are easily made and inexpensive. Much can be gained from the interaction between parent and child when home-based learning takes place. Use this book to design a good program of home-based learning.

## Activities

1. Do you feel you would make a good home visitor? Explain why. Analyze your strengths and weaknesses. What qualities would you classify as your strengths? Weaknesses?

2. There seems to be a difference of opinion about what a home visitor should do, especially as it relates to the teaching of children in the home.

   a. What role do you think a home visitor should have in the home?

   b. Write a job description for this role.

3. As a class, develop a list of household items that could be used to teach basic concepts of language and promote fine motor skills.

   a. Develop a set of directions which can be used to help parents know how to use these items.

   b. Provide illustrations for ways in which the materials can be used.

   c. How would a list of items differ from home to home? From child to child?

4. Arrange to accompany a home visitor on a home visit. Relate your experiences to your classmates.

5. Critique the competencies suggested for a parent involvement specialist presented in this chapter. What competencies would you add? Delete?

6. In what ways could a home visitor destroy values found in a home? What would be some values that would most likely be destroyed? What values would you as a home visitor tend to stress more than others?

7. Consider the following topics:

   a. Discipline of children.

   b. Cleanliness.

   c. Employment/unemployment.

   d. Attitudes toward learning and schools.

How would these areas be viewed by different families? Would this have an effect on the role of the home visitor? In what ways?

# Parent Involvement in the Home: Some Considerations

**5**

---

## Teaching and Learning Goals

This chapter will provide the information, means, and opportunity to:

Analyze important factors which relate to success and/or failure in parent involvement programs.

Clarify and examine issues related to parent involvement programs.

Compare and contrast the similarities and differences between skills necessary for working with parents in the home and those necessary in a school setting.

Consider the full dimension and range of home visitation services.

---

## Introduction

In addition to being very rewarding, home visitation can also be a very complex process. This comment should not be interpreted to mean that only those who are highly educated should be allowed to participate in the process for this is not the case. The program of Levenstein discussed in chapter 3 shows that individuals without a great deal of formal education make very capable home visitors. However, there are many factors in the home visitation process which everyone involved in the program must be sensitive to. How influential these factors will be or if they will be present at all depends on the nature and extent of the program. The factors, as they are discussed in this chapter, are ones that could potentially affect any program, and for that reason alone, they should be examined and considered.

## Parental Qualities and Attributes

It is interesting to observe the relationships that exist between parents, their individual attributes, and their attitudes toward their children. While the overt qualities of hypothetical parents shown in table 12 are representative of only selected parents and are indicative of only a few of the qualities and combinations possible, they do help point out that anyone who works with parents should be aware of the impact these personal traits and qualities have upon how a parent perceives the child and responds to him. This interaction and response, of course, will affect how the child views himself and how he deals with the world.

While it is virtually impossible to change some parental qualities and/or conditions such as age of parent, number of children, and general way of looking at life, it is possible to ameliorate some of these conditions so they have a less devastating effect on the child. To approach the problem from a more positive point of view, it is possible to change conditions so the parent may have a more positive interrelationship with the child. In order to do this, it is necessary for the parent involvement specialist to create situations in which parents can ascertain, even if to a limited degree, what their attitudes are toward their children. Once this has occurred, help can be provided for the parents to live with these attitudes, be conscious of them, and work within these limitations in helping their children. It may take a rather long time for this insight to occur. Quite often this can mean that several weeks or months are spent before parents begin to see what their strengths and weaknesses are. Then, too, a parent may never see himself as he really is, perhaps because the process is too painful or because the parent involvement specialist is incapable of helping the process occur. Some of the ways in which self-discovery and self-awareness can occur are by communicating with the parent involvement specialist, interacting with other parents, viewing films, reading, and using value clarification techniques.

However, in order to make this process possible, several crucial factors must be accounted for. First, there must be a caring parent involvement specialist who is aware of the effect parental qualities and attributes have upon children and other family members. Such caring professionals are not always available. While working with a group of preservice teachers, who were training to be home visitors, it became obvious to me that unless the individuals were sensitive to these parental qualities and characteristics and were willing to account for them in their working relationships with the parents, the interaction would not be highly successful. A home visitor simply cannot be insensitive to these qualities.

In fact, it is increasingly surprising that the whole area of parental qualities is virtually overlooked by many preservice and inservice teachers and others who work with parents. Unfortunately, there seems to be more interest in the cognitive aspects of programs, for example, designing activities for parents to use with their children, than there is in the affective. Many home visitors are almost unaware of the importance of this area in their work with parents.

Second, in establishing situations in which parents can examine their attitudes toward and relationships with their children, parent involvement specialists should not destroy either parents' self-images and confidence as parents or the good relationships and interactions that are occurring between them and their children. With few exceptions, it is grossly unfair to classify parents as "bad parents" or lacking in any positive qualities whatsoever.

What all professionals who work with parents must do is assume a role as helper and supporter. This means, in part, building on the potentialities and strengths that all parents do possess. Many teachers/home visitors are pleasantly surprised by the talents parents do have! It is merely a matter of taking the time and effort to discover these attributes.

The third condition that must be fostered is a willingness to work with parents consistently and over a long period of time. Quite often people who work with parents expect dramatic changes almost from the beginning. While there will be instances in which such changes will occur, it is best to understand that behavior is changed a step at a time, over a period of time. Therefore, parent involvement specialists need to plan for what course of action will be best for a particular parent, implement that plan on a consistent basis, and pursue it over whatever period of time is necessary to achieve the successes planned for. This period of time may be a year or more.

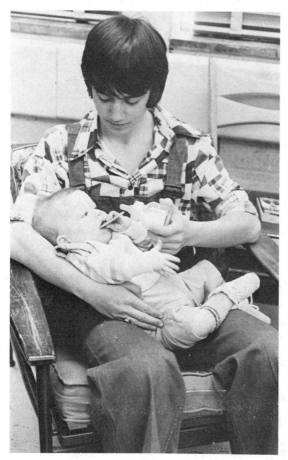

*Parent involvement means more than working with persons who already are parents. Here a high school student learns how to provide basic care for a young child.*

**TABLE 12**  A list of parental characteristics for three hypothetical parents.

| PARENT #1<br>(2 children) | PARENT #2<br>(3 children) | PARENT #3<br>(3 children) |
|---|---|---|
| *Physical Characteristics:* | | |
| Young (early twenties) Pretty (pays a great deal of attention to make-up, clothing, etc.) | Middle Aged (early forties) Conservative to sloppy dresser | Tends to be sloppy dresser Somewhat overweight Late twenties |
| *Behavior Attributes:* | | |
| Cool/cold , Unresponsive/passive Disinterested Impulsive Impatient | Acts old Quiet Feels and acts inferior to many adults Reserved Patient Wants to know all about everything | Patient Interested in knowing about child development Outgoing Verbal Considerate Reasoning with adults/children |
| *Attitudes toward Children:* | | |
| Indifferent Pays little attention to them Speaks mostly of control, e.g., "Don't do that" Keeps materials from children in order to keep a "clean" house Quick to discipline, much of this discipline is arbitrary Not much spontaneous verbal interaction Does not encourage independent behavior | Tolerant of much misbehavior Controls by reasoning and physical punishment Stresses doing things together as a family Allows children to use material even if it messses up the house Spontaneous verbal interaction Tends to overprotect | Tries to explain reasons for everything Organizes life and activities, e.g., a time for everthing, a place for everything Pays a great deal of attention to children, never too busy to do things together Spontaneous verbal interaction Tends to do things for children |

## Ecological Factors

In considering the success or failure of parent involvement programs, the ecological factors present in the lives of every family cannot be overlooked. These are factors which will determine the degree of success or failure of family efforts at self-improvement. In addition, ecological factors affect parent involvement strategies designed to uplift, upgrade, and/or revolutionize the life of a family. Some of the ecological factors involved in any family system are housing, nutrition, educational level, employment, income level, quality of neighborhood, its rural or urban nature, and support services available to the family, such as electricity, plumbing, telephone, mail service, public transportation, availability of neighbors, family and friends, educational opportunities, social service agencies, etc. All of these factors individually and collectively interact and have an impact on the family as a unit. They also affect how relationships are established and conducted among members within the family. In addition, self-perception, perception of the world, and the nature and extent of success in the world are directly proportionate to the quality and availability of these ecological factors.

The importance of this situation is stressed by Bronfenbrenner when he states:

> The essence of the strategy [parent involvement] is a primary focus neither on the child nor his parent nor even the dyad or the family as a system. Rather, the aim is to effect changes in the context in which the family lives; these changes in turn enable the mother, the parents, and the family as a whole to exercise the functions necessary for the child's development.[1]

One of the problems in considering the ecology of the family and the impact ecological factors can have on family members is that for someone who is not intimately familiar with the effects of poor nutrition, ill health, unemloyment, etc., it is difficult to appreciate or to be empathic about these conditions and their consequences. The majority of adults are used to adequate housing, reasonably good health, relatively full employment, and many of the conveniences of public utilities and services. It is often difficult to understand the impact the absence of any single one of these factors may have on a family.

## *Effect of Ecological Factors*

Any one of the ecological factors mentioned above can have an effect on how the family views itself and the world and how it interacts with the world. For example, consider the matter of housing, which is one of the most pressing problems facing many families in the Americas. Housing, that is esthetically unpleasing, dilapidated, and overcrowded; that lacks adequate heat, plumbing, and lighting; that affords little opportunity for privacy; and that does not encourage sanitary living conditions will have several impacts upon a family:

---

[1]Urie, Bronfenbrenner, A Report On Longitudinal Evaluations of Preschool Programs, Volume II, Is Early Intervention Effective?, (Washington, D.C.: U.S. Government Printing Office, Department of Health, Education and Welfare, Publication No. (OHD) 76-30025, 1974), p. 47.

1. The house may not be a home in the sense that it is a place where members of the family want to spend any length of time. Family members may, in fact, spend a great deal of their time either outside of their home or in finding ways to get out of the home. The house may literally force a separation of family members. This factor was vividly impressed upon me during a home visit in which I observed that the eldest child, a twelve-year-old boy, was absent from the home most of the time except for eating and sleeping. By talking with the boy, I was able to determine how little he enjoyed staying in the home because of the overcrowdedness, noise, and lack of "something to do"!
2. The lack of adequate housing may cause the family to spend a great deal of its time, effort, and energy in trying to find suitable housing. However, not being able to secure adequate housing because of lack of resources can promote in family members a sense of hopelessness, frustration, aloneness, and a feeling that it is not even worth the effort to try.
3. It may well be that the housing a person occupies may be reflected in his self-image. If the surroundings of a home project a feeling of depression, aloneness, and rejection; a feeling that no one cares; and a feeling of hopelessness, then this attitude will be present in the image of the particular family. Inadequate housing can lead to a feeling of self-rejection and worthlessness and to an attitude of negativism on the part of any individual family member.

## Dealing with Ecological Factors

One of the implications of these ecological factors is that, in all efforts of parent involvement in the home, these factors have to be assessed and accounted for *prior* to effectively changing other factors, or before beginning to deliver a program of educational services to the children. How can we honestly expect parents to feel good about themselves and about learning how to effectively interact with their children when their housing indicates that they are really not of much worth? How can we expect parents to be concerned with the quality of children's school work when no one cares about the quality of the neighborhood or home they are living in? Consequently, these ecological factors must become primary targets for remediation and restructuring as a necessary first step in efforts at helping families. This explains, to a large extent, why home workers, home visitors, and other social service personnel may spend weeks, months, and sometimes years dealing with ecological factors prior to delivering direct educational services to parents or children.

## Removal of Child

Because of the crucial role ecological factors play in the lives of families, some educators favor taking a child completely out of the environment in which he is being reared and placing him in an environment which is more ecologically conducive to growth and development. Such separation of the child from the home environment to a more ecologically favorable environment is a drastic and controversial procedure. However, for children in severe ecological circumstances, it may be the only available alternative, if effective change of any kind is to be made toward sound growth and development.

The necessity for this separation in certain circumstances was illustrated for me while visiting a day care center. The center staff had recently enrolled a four-year-old who was raised in a backyard pen with dogs. The child could only whine and did not talk. He spent most of his time crawling and when taken outside, ate grass. Here was a child who, because of the environment he was reared in, thought he was a dog! In cases such as this, the separation of the child from the environment is not only appropriate, but justifiable.

It is important, therefore, to become aware of and involved in the ecological conditions of all families and children you teach. Family and home visits on a regular basis are necessary for all professionals in public and private school programs, as well as those supported with federal and state monies. It is also imperative that you approach this involvement with a sincere effort to try and help families correct and overcome the environmental conditions under which they live.

## Cultural and Social Factors

Most parents feel their children are capable of doing many things. Many parents also feel their children can do things beyond their age, and that they are "smarter" than other children. This feeling, of course, is a natural reaction of parents for indeed the parents' hopes and dreams are reflected in their children. Why wouldn't a parent think their child is smart and capable of achieving a great deal? At the same time it is very ego shattering to recognize and face up to the realities of what the child is capable of doing, especially when that capability is less than what the parent wants or expects. In order to deal with this in a psychologically and socially acceptable way, parents build and create many defense mechanisms against failure or criticism. For these reasons, working with parents prior to the entry of the child into school can help parents set realistic achievement goals for themselves and their children.

Parents also feel that if their children have the right kind of help and encouragement, they can do a great many things other than what they are already doing. However, some parents tend to feel that this help should come from outside themselves and the home. Either by lack of confidence in themselves or a socially ingrained view that real learning begins in the school, parents tend to wait for the school to help.

Some parents are also concerned that their child may be "slow" or retarded. These feelings are the opposite of what we have just discussed. However, there is the nagging suspicion on the part of some parents that their children may not be as smart as they should be. This perception or feeling is often based upon limited data resulting from limited contact with other parents or children. Parents will also base their judgment of one child on the past performance of other children in the family or on limited contact with neighbors' children. Also, it may be that a parent develops an erroneous idea of what children really can achieve by watching some of the bright child "stars" on television.

Many parents are concerned about sending their children to school. While parents and most children look forward to school, it is not a trauma-free anticipation, especially on the part of the parents. Certain questions keep emerging: Will he do well? Will he get along with other children? What will his teacher be like?

Consequently, when parents see their children off that first day, be it to a Head Start Center, kindergarten, or first grade, they let them go with a mixture of joy and anxiety. By working with parents prior to their child's entry into any educational agency, many of these anxieties can be dispelled and replaced with confidence for both parents and child.

Many parents believe that boys develop slower than girls. Consequently, there is a tendency for them to expect less from sons. In addition, poor performance, in some areas, or lack of performance has a tendency to be excused by the calming saying, "He's just a boy, he'll grow out of it." This may account in part for the parental tendency to expect less of sons and to do less with sons, on a cognitive basis, in the home. Also, parents expect boys to be more physical and involved in gross motor activities such as running, jumping, and climbing. While a parent might encourage a son to play outside with other boys, there might be less concern for fine motor activities involved with cutting, pasting, and drawing.

The parent worker must also remember that parental attitudes toward the particular sex of children is often culturally determined or based on values held by a particular family or portion of society. A parent who has a strong orientation toward the "macho" image may disapprove of the son "playing" with pencils, crayons, and scissors because he views these activities as "sissyfied."

While many parents and professionals may resent the blatant sexism that exists in some homes and school situations, and while society is making many efforts toward eliminating covert and overt sexism, those who work with families cannot be blind or indifferent to the realities of what many parents view as the proper sex role identification activities for their children.

Professionals who are working with parents must also recognize that perhaps one of the reasons boys may come to school not being able to do many of the school related activities such as cutting, sitting still, and paying attention is because they were not encouraged to do these things in the family environment. It is difficult to comprehend why some teachers want to send a few children home "because they are not ready for school." If the home environment has not provided a climate for readiness prior to entry into school, the chances of it providing a climate for readiness are slim unless a concerted, planned program of readiness is undertaken in the home under the direction of a competent home visitor or teacher.

Many parents are physically isolated from the world of other parents, children, and opportunities for their children. We have a tendency to assume that most parents have access to people, places, and things. This is not the case in a great many instances. While all forms of deprivation are debilitating, I feel that one of the worst forms of deprivation comes from isolation. This isolation is particularly true in rural and sparsely populated areas. Not only does the child have no place to go, such as the story time at the nearest library, but he also has no other neighbor children to play with.

In addition, the lack of available public and private transportation is also a hindering factor. Not all families have the availability or means to use public transportation. As we mentioned before, in a one-car family, the father more than likely needs the car to go to work. Consequently, the mother and children are left home with no means to go any place, even if there were some place to go.

## Controversy with Genetic Factors

So far, the majority of the evidence provided as a rationale for parent involvement has been based upon environmental or ecological factors. We have discussed the importance of mother-child interactions and the consequences that health, nutrition, housing, and other ecological factors play in the ability of the family to cope with the process of living, education, and child rearing. The evidence seems to suggest that when ecological factors, family conditions, and parent/child interactions are negative or do not provide optimum qualities or conditions for child growth, then intervention can improve the quality of the family life. A number of the home-based and parent intervention programs conducted in the past have been designed to enhance the child's ability to deal with schooling and to increase his ability to achieve in traditional school subjects such as reading, writing, and arithmetic. In other words, many professionals assume that if environmental factors are overcome and/or corrected, families will be able to lead more productive and self-fulling lives.

However, there exists a controversy between professionals who adopt this environmental point of view and those who reject it. This second group favors heredity and genetics as a cause of lack of achievement. Those holding this genetic point of view maintain that the I.Q. of a child is attributable primarily to genetic factors; that is, the basis for achievement is the innate intelligence inherited from the parents. In attributing intelligence to genetic factors, there is a tendency to assume that heredity is a more important factor than environmental factors in the developmental growth of children. This genetic point of view has lead some people to believe that those with

*In the final analysis, a primary objective of parent involvement should be to enhance the lives of children. This emphasis should not be minimized in any parent involvement program.*

superior I.Q.'s are destined to high achievement. Similarly, lack of achievement is due to lack of intelligence. This genetic point of view also maintains that high I.Q. children are products of high I.Q. parents, and, therefore, there is a tendency to perpetuate achievement and economic standing from one generation to the next. What results is a continuation of intellectual and economic elitism based on genetic factors. While this position is held by a minority of people, the reader should at least be aware of this point of view.

## Problems Encountered in Home Visitations

### Sexual Factors

We should not hide from or pretend that factors relating to sex are not involved in the home visitation process. There are concerns that do relate to sex and sexual roles. The following are some of the problems related to sexuality that can be encountered by working with parents in the home:

1. The jealousy of one parent arising from the sex of the home visitor. If the home visitor is male, the husband in the family may be jealous because he thinks the visitor is making advances toward his wife. The reverse may be true if the home visitor is female.

2. There is a cultural factor found in rural as well as urban areas which is very subtle. It is the belief that a husband owns a woman. The male, by virtue of marriage, possession, living arrangements, etc., owns a woman much in the same sense that one owns an automobile, home, etc. This attitude may make it difficult for the parent involvement specialist to work freely with the mother.

3. Role stereotyping. Certain men feel that they should not baby-sit, wash dishes, etc., because these roles are traditionally viewed as "woman's work." Some men just will not take care of children. This stereotyping makes it difficult for some women to free themselves for other activities.

4. The home visitor, in trying to involve children in certain activities, may find resistance from one or both of the parents depending on their concepts of what *maleness* and *femaleness* means. Some parents feel that boys don't need to cut, girls don't need to learn much academically. The family has stereotyped sex roles for their children, and the home visitor may have to overcome them or work within them.

5. Many males resent the invasion of their "territory," the home, by another male or female. In such cases, efforts will have to be made to placate or assure the parent that there is no direct or implied threat to their position (and, therefore, sexuality) as a male, family provider, etc. Every effort should be made to involve the father as much as possible in the home visitation process, for his own benefit as well as his family's.

6. Occasionally, female home visitors have to resist advances, either actively (by retreat) or covertly (by getting the males involved in another topic such as auto mechanics) and divert the male's attention from the sexuality of the home visitor. In this respect, the home visitor should dress appropriately when conducting a home visit.

## Other Siblings

Quite often during a home visit, the presence of other siblings in the home will create a problem for the parent involvement specialist when trying to provide services for one child. The immediate question and concern is what to do with those other children? One solution is to enroll the other children in the program. They can benefit from the program too.

Sometimes, an effort can be made to send the other children out of the home, for example, to story time with local libraries, van libraries, grandparents, etc. However, these strategies generally require more work than they are worth and create problems in and of themselves. In addition, most often there is no place else to send the other children.

If the program is designed so that the main emphasis is on working with the child rather than the mother, then the mother can work with the other children while the home visitor works with the child for whom the service was designed. However, since some home programs are designed so that services are delivered to the child through the mother, this strategy is often a poor one to follow since it tends to isolate the mother from meaningful involvement during the home visit.

The most responsible solution would seem to be to involve all children in the programs that are delivered to the family. Consequently, objectives for the program may have to be expanded to include these other children. This strategy may also require that the parent involvement specialist will have to receive special training in order to work with several children at one time.

It is also possible to provide for other children in the home by utilizing two parent involvement specialists in the same home at the same time. This approach means that while the "regular" specialist is working with a specific child, the other one (who can be an aide) can work with the other children. If this strategy is adopted, then both parent involvement specialists should make sure that they coordinate their activities and plan together for what will be done during the home visit.

## Length of the Home Visit

Another problem often encountered is the amount of time that should be spent in a home visit. The average time spent is forty-five minutes to one hour. However, the one-hour time span may be too long or too short depending upon the type of program and the needs of the child and family. Where the parent involvement specialist has established good rapport with the parents, has a thorough knowledge of working with young children, and a background of experience in home visitations, then one hour does not seem to be sufficient. Generally, the length of a visit depends on the needs of family, level of communication between visitor and parent, activities being delivered, etc. Quite often, also, home visitors find themselves being invited to join the parent for coffee, tea, sharing of domestic information, discussions concerning child-rearing practices, etc. Where this kind of involvement is part of the program, more time will be required.

## Value Conflicts

One problem that can frequently occur is that the value system of the home visitor can come into conflict with the value system of the home. This conflict should be avoided and can be if the following points are kept in mind:

1. Don't expect every home to be like the one you came from. Every home is not as clean as yours nor are the parents as well dressed as you are.

2. Don't expect every parent to have the same amount of interest in your home program as you have. You may have to "sell" your program.

3. Don't expect the parents' view of working with the child to be the same as yours. You may say you would spend time (fifteen minutes) every day working with your child, but many parents either are not willing or are not able to spend that much time.

4. A week or more is a rather long time between visits. (Some programs visit every other week.) During this time period, parent, child, *and* home visitor can lose the continuity of the program. Here are some solutions to this problem of continuity:

    a. Twice a week visits. However, this increased visitation also escalates the cost of the program in terms of either time spent or visitors needed.

    b. Contact by telephone. This offers a convenient and low cost way to maintain contact with parents. However, many families don't have telephones.

    c. Contact in person. Some programs conduct a home visit once a week and a home contact the following week. A home contact is usually designed to see what progress the family is making, if there are any special problems, etc. A home contact usually takes about one-half hour.

## Finding Solutions

These problems should not be thought of as reasons for not visiting in the homes of families. Parent involvement in the home and community is much too important a process to permit rationalization about why it cannot or should not occur. Individuals who are dedicated to helping families will develop creative and appropriate solutions to all the considerations mentioned.

## Differences between Home and School Settings

Skills needed for working in a public school setting with children five years of age and above are quite different from the basic skills or competencies necessary for working in a home with children from birth to age five. Table 13 depicts some of the differences between the two settings. Some of the differences between working in a classroom and a home are so pronounced that they decide whether or not a classroom teacher (as trained by many institutions of higher education) can work successfully with parents in the home.

## Whose Homes Should Be Visited?

A bottom line question, perhaps, that needs to be asked early in any home visitation program is, Whose homes should be visited? In answering this question, a corollary question must also be asked, What priorities, if any, should be established to determine who should receive services? These are by no means easy questions to answer.

*Teacher preparation programs should include competencies for involvement with children and parents in the home. This preservice teacher is participating in. a parent involvement program as a means of developing such competencies.*

## Intervention Strategy

There is one group of parent involvement specialists who views home visitation programs as an intervention strategy designed to provide children of low-income families opportunities to receive, through the parent(s), help in acquiring the cognitive and social skills necessary for success in school settings. This approach sees the necessity for providing services to those who are in most need of it and makes sense when programs are faced with decisions of limited means and unlimited needs. In such cases, the tendency, and a defensible one, is to deliver services where the need is the greatest and where there is the greatest possibility for effecting change.

## Equal Opportunities for Everyone

On the other hand, there is that other group who feels that any program should be broad based enough so that all those who wish to participate may do so. However, there is very seldom enough programmatic monies to conduct a program for all who wish to participate. Given this economic and political reality, the advocates of a broad-based approach attempt to make the selection of those participating in the program random so that there is a possibility for participation by everyone.

One of the reasons for this equal opportunity approach is an attempt to remove any stigma which can be attached to participation in programs. Some people feel embarrassed that they have been singled out (selected) for services on the basis of need. (One criteria is usually income.) Programs sometimes win parental approval for participation in services by telling them that they and/or their children are eligible!

## Expectations for Parents

## Family Expectations

One problem that we must certainly face and consider in any attempt to intervene in the life of the family is that society has had and continues to have great expectations for the family. These expectations can and do place many burdens on the family. In today's society, the family is expected to present to the world in general a united front of solidarity, love, affection, unity, and economic progress toward some common

**TABLE 13** A comparison of school and home settings.

| *School Setting* | *Home Setting* |
|---|---|
| 1. The teacher teaches 20-30 children at one time in one large group. | 1. In the home, the home visitor is working with a single child or at the most with 2 or 3 children. |
| 2. The school represents an institutionalized setting which has been created specifically for educating. As such, a great number of rules, regulations, and controls have been legislated and ritualized to assure that the educational process occurs. | 2. The home is not usually conceived of as an educational institution. As such, many people don't view the home as a place where "real" education occurs. Thus, learning in the home is postponed until the child enters school. |
| 3. Emphasis is on academic or cognitive material. Learning in most schools is very subject oriented. The three R's have generally always held a position of pre-eminence in the majority of schools. This will very likely continue into the near future at least. While some schools are innovative and concerned with a full range of academic and affective programs, most schools are not. The majority of schools have been and will remain conservative institutions. They are conservative in the sense that they are always ten or more years behind in society. | 3. In the home, there needs to be an emphasis on health, social, and inter/intrapersonal needs as well as cognitive needs. The cognitive learnings may be least important or may not be dealt with until other needs of both parents and children are met. The priorities of the home are oriented toward physical care. |
| 4. The teacher is removed in distance, place, and authority from the parents. Parents seldom are invited to school, and seldom come to school. Parents are told that the teacher is the expert in the classroom. This discourages involvement. | 4. The home visitor is in intimate contact with the parent. The parent is most always present and watching what is occurring. The home visitor is not the person of most importance. In the home, the parent feels they know what is best for the child. |
| 5. The classroom is usually considered teacher territory. The school is considered educator territory. Many schools have signs which say, All visitors must report to the principal's office. This and other policies reinforce this territory concept. | 5. The home is the parents' territory. Parents say what they will permit to be done and who will or will not come into the home, etc. |
| 6. Elementary schools usually teach children from 5½ years on up to 12 years of age (kindergarten to sixth grade). | 6. Children in the home usually range in age from 1 day to 5½ - 6 years. Sometimes, depending on the maximum entrance to first grade, they may be older. |

**TABLE 13  (continued)**

*School Setting*

7. Teachers usually teach whole (large) classes. Quite often, their entire training deals primarily with how to teach, discipline, and manage whole groups of children. In addition, the same learning materials are used for all the children.

8. While lip service is paid to individual differences, there is seldom any concerted, systematic attempt to individualize instruction or provide for individual differences.

9. The classroom teacher seldom has to provide parents with child development advice and procedures. Usually the knowledge of the teacher is applied to curriculum decisions and materials.

10. There is a rather low frequency of communication with parents and other adults. The majority of the teacher's time, energy, and experience is geared toward communicating with children. Because of the limited nature of this communication, teachers find it difficult to communicate with adults. This may help explain why teachers don't attempt more parent communication than they do.

11. Teachers, as a rule, are rather ignorant and/or unconcerned about the influence of the home on the child's present achievement level and ability to learn. Teachers tend to place the blame for poor achievement on the home. While the child's inability to learn or poor attitude toward learning is blamed on the home, little attempt is made to do anything about it.

12. A teacher is in complete control of the classroom. The teacher determines the inter- and intrapersonal climate and the other ecological factors contributing to the classroom situation.

*Home Setting*

7. Skills, techniques, and materials for individualized instruction are needed. Individualized instruction must occur because usually there is only one or, at the most, three or four preschool children present in the home.

8. By working with children in the home, a person quickly realizes how different children are. This insight and realization that children are unique, undoubtedly comes, in part, from having to work with chilren on an individual basis.

9. Individuals who work in the home are asked about (are consulted) child-rearing practices. Much of this information relates to such topics as toilet training, discipline, eating habits, etc.

10. One of the skills which anyone who works in a home situation or any setting where there is a high frequency of contact with adults must develop is the ability to communicate well with adults. This skill includes communicating at their level and about the things they are interested in.

11. A person working with children in the home soon comes to appreciate the power, force, and consequence of all the ecological factors influencing the child. This realization leads to an effort to help the parent modify ecological conditions.

12. The parent sets the climate and affective conditions of the home. The home visitor must accept that climate and those conditions for good or bad. The effects the home worker will have on the climate of the homes are long range and dependent upon the ability and inclination of the parent to implement them.

**TABLE 13   (continued)**

| *School Setting* | *Home Setting* |
|---|---|
| 13. Generally speaking, public school teachers have not had experience with preschool children nor do they know, on a first-hand basis, the characteristics and development of the preschool child. | 13. A thorough knowledge of preschool children is essential. While it is not absolutely essential to have had child-rearing experience, many professionals feel that it greatly benefits the home visitor to have had this first-hand experience. |

goal. For all of its members, and in particular its children, the family is supposed to provide love, affection, nutrition, security, guidance, and, above all, education. In some homes and to some parents, these expectations become burdens to be carried by the family rather than joys to be cherished and challenges to be met.

When families are faced with burdens, frustrations occur. The frustrations come from several sources. One is the general lack of training for parenthood. As discussed previously, parenthood is the one most difficult job that any adult can face. For this very demanding job there is practically little, if any, help or training provided by society.

A second source which contributes to a family's burdens is economic. Most of the problems facing a family concern money. Many families do not have the financial means or the economic potential to deal with money problems. In addition, the three most necessary items needed for survival—housing, health care, and food—have been and probably will continue to be increasingly expensive.

Some of the things which money buys are the support systems necessary to deal with many of life's problems. Middle class families have the money and resources necessary to cope with problems of survival. For instance, two excellent resources are the telephone and the automobile which can be used to contact friends and relatives and find relief from the environment. These support systems are often lacking in many low-socioeconomic homes. Another excellent support system which is often lacking for many parents is child care service. Many parents cannot do things for themselves or cannot go anywhere because of their children. Good child care services readily available to parents would contribute immensely toward helping parents become more involved and autonomous.

The third obstacle to solutions to burdens placed upon the family is that of temperament. Temperament, defined as a way of looking at the world and dealing with problems, is a product of an individual's own background and relates primarily to how he deals creatively with the problems facing him. Some parents are so overwhelmed with the simple day-to-day processes of living that it is difficult for them to deal effectively or creatively with the problems encountered in the home.

In working with parents in the home, there seems to be a need to develop the idea that they are capable of teaching their children and that the home can be a learning resource. Parents need to be shown how to teach their children and how to use readily available household objects and materials for teaching children. There are those (and your author is one of them) who feel the emphasis should not be so much on importing into the home specially designed learning materials, but on how to use household items for learning.

## The Parent as Teacher

A question that can be legitimately raised is, Can parents teach their own children? The answer to this question is deceptively obvious; yes, they can teach their own children. This answer is obvious because all parents, whether they realize it or not, do teach their children. Because of the intimate nature that exists between parent and child, in the parent-child relationship, the parent does teach the child many different things.

However, many parents don't consider themselves to be teachers and conceive of learning as something which occurs only when the child enters school. For the most part, society in general and professional educators in particular have done a good job of reinforcing the idea that "real" education begins when school begins. In this sense, many parents feel that their role is that of caregiver and caretaker.

However, how effective a parent is as a teacher depends upon many factors:

1. The psychological make-up of parents which determines their particular temperaments. Parents may be highstrung, nervous, overanxious, etc., and this kind of behavior does not give them the patience necessary for teaching their children in any systematic way.

2. The feelings of the parent toward the child. For example, the parent may have a tendency to reject the child because he may be an unwanted or unexpected child, a child who does not meet the expectations of the parent, or a child who reminds one parent too much of the other parent. Or a parent may feel the child is an obstacle to some goal. For whatever reason, a parent may reject a child and, therefore, not have a good parent-child relationship which would promote the interaction necessary for teaching.

3. Time. Teaching children takes time. Time available to teach children is affected by many other interrelated factors, such as the number of other children in the home, housekeeping demands, demands from the other parent, health and nutritional problems, etc.

4. Knowledge background of the parent. The knowledge a parent brings to the child-teaching process is also extremely important for the success of the endeavor. Many parents feel a great deal of frustration in knowing what or how to teach their children. When faced with not knowing what to do, the normal reaction is to do nothing. It is much easier to do nothing than worry about doing something you don't know how to do. Besides if you don't know what to do and if you go ahead and do something, it may be wrong.

5. Availability of materials. Many parents are very well intentioned and might want to read to their children, but because they don't have anything to read or because they don't know whether or not what they have is good enough to read to children, they end up not reading to them.

6. Family problems. Problems facing the family, such as marital problems, employment problems, etc., determine how effective the parent is in dealing with the child. If parents are so immersed and consumed with problems, then certainly they are not going to have the time or desire to work with their children.

Teaching requires a warm, supportive, and loving relationship. This type of relationship between parent and child may not always be possible. For example, if a parent has been rejected and hurt by the other parent or lover, this feeling of hurt may carry over to the parent-child relationship. The parent may not allow himself to become emotionally involved in another loving relationship because of his fear of being rejected again. In other cases, parents, because of anxiety resulting from wanting their own children to do better than they reasonably can be expected to do, are too close to the situation to effectively teach their own children. They may be, on the other hand, good teachers of other children because they are removed from the imtimate teaching interaction with their own children. Because of these feelings and problems, some parents don't relate well to their children and, consequently, are not effective in teaching them.

## Parental Information Based on Needs

Parents have many needs that we overlook or ignore, thinking that they have the information when they really don't. Some of the types of information that parents need are:

*Child Development Information.*   Parents, the vast majority of them at least, don't know about child development. They don't know what to expect a child to be able to do and at what age—including walking, speaking, controlling elimination, etc. One parent thought her child was retarded because she wasn't talking at 12 months!

*Achievement Information.*   Not only do some parents not know what to do, but they also don't know how to do it. Another parent was trying to teach her four and one half-year-old daughter how to tell time. She thought her child was dumb because she couldn't figure out the quarter hours! In essence, many parents have difficulty establishing realistic achievement standards for their children. On the other hand, some parents set no goals at all. Also, many parents feel their children are retarded if they can't do certain things.

Not only do parents not know what to expect of their children developmentally, they don't know what to expect as far as achievement is concerned. Generally, parents fall into two categories as far as achievement orientation is concerned. One group expects nothing at all. They feel it is the school's job to teach the child, so they will not interfere with that job by teaching the child or encouraging the child to participate in anything resembling school achievement. The attitude is reinforced by two things:

1. *Tradition.* They as children were not taught a great deal by their parents; therefore, they are not going to teach their children anything.
2. *Teachers.* For whatever reason, be it ignorance or lack of understanding of the educative process, many teachers have encouraged parents *not* to teach their children. This encouragement of the parent not to teach their child usually sounds something like this: "Don't teach your child his letters because I'll teach him the right way when he comes to school." What I often interpret this to mean is, "If you teach him his letters, I won't be able to. That's what I have always taught, so don't take my job away."

A second group of parents want to make super-achievers out of their children. Usually, these parents get upset if their children do not achieve as much as the parent thinks they should.

*Support and Personal Reinforcement Information.* While this type of information is related to the achievement information given previously, it is different and important enough to discuss it separately. Many parents do not know if what they are doing is good or bad for the child. These parents need to talk with someone or read information that indicates they are doing good things. Many parents have a great deal of anxiety about their ability and performance with their children. When they do find out they have been doing good things for and with their children, (and we generally can find something good), they are tremendously relieved.

## Parents Should Retain Control of Educational Process

One of the merits of any educational program that delivers service to the home is that it has the potential for permitting parents to retain control over the education of their children. Notice I said it *has* the potential. I hope it is obvious to you that delivering a program of education into the home also has the potential for undermining, usurping, and destroying the self-image, confidence, and control of the parent. What is necessary is that any program of parent involvement must support the role of the parents not only as the primary providers and educators of their children, but also as the people who have ultimate and final authority over what happens to their children.

## Time to Accomplish Activities

In working with parents, we expect them to give of their time and energy to the activities we want them to do. Usually, these activities involve educating their children and/or improving their own condition. However, what we ask of the parents may not be meaningful to them or may not be on their personal priority list. Therefore, parents may not have the time or take the time necessary to accomplish what we want done.

Professionals whose main job it is to get people involved in educational process forget about the element of time associated with any endeavor. We think because we have the time (because it is part of our job) or are willing to devote time to a particular task that this is the way it should be with everyone. It is wrong for us to think this way for several reasons.

First, managing time is a skill which has to be developed and learned. Organizing one's time takes effort, desire, and know how. It is true that we all have time for what we really want to do, and it is true that all of us have more time than we really know what to do with. The problem is we don't organize and budget time well, and, therefore, we waste much more time than we use. One of the key jobs in working with parents may be to help them organize their time and use it more effectively.

Second, time orientation and one's concept of time are cultural conditions. How a person deals with time is largely a product of how his subculture deals with time and more particularly how he has been reared to deal with time. Therefore, finding time to do things and doing things on time are values that have to be learned. Not everyone is time oriented. Also, it is usually those people who are time oriented who are also task oriented. Being task oriented (wanting to get a job done) and being time oriented are almost complementary conditions. For someone who is not time oriented, getting something done on time has very little meaning. If it gets done, fine. If not, that is fine also. The attitude toward time and tasks that each person has will determine if parents do particular tasks when they should be done. The time orientation of each parent will have to be considered in the parent involvement process.

Third, for many parents, the responsibilities of child rearing and family care are fulltime jobs. Indeed, in many instances, they require more time than many parents seem to have. While many people think of a job as consisting of an eight-hour day, the job of parenting is twenty-four hours a day. Many parents, prior to the involvement of a parent involvement specialist, feel overworked and even hassled by the demands placed upon them. In such situations, the question can be raised, How many parents have the five minutes extra to spend with their children that we ask them to spend? What must be dealt with in such situations is the issue of what will best serve the interests of the parents and the needs of the child. One approach is to teach parents how to be teachers of their children while they are doing the everyday jobs of washing, feeding, bathing, etc. There are many opportunities during these times to teach concepts. Feeding can involve colors, tastes, and textures. Washing and bathing can include names of body parts, need for cleanliness, temperature of water, how to hold soap, etc. This kind of an approach would be much more constructive than asking parents to take extra time or a specific time to teach their children, particularly when time appears to be a problem in the home.

## Community Involvement

Many parent involvement specialists and home-based programs view the development of the parents in and through the community as an essential feature. In these types of programs, efforts are made to do the following:

1. Make the parents aware of the broad range of community services and activities that are available. Many of these are available free of charge depending upon the family's income.

2. Link the parents to community services and activities so that they become consumers of them. Services are only beneficial if they are utilized.

3. Encourage and provide opportunities for the parents to become involved *in* the community activities. There is a broad range of activities which parents can participate in besides being consumers of the social services.

4. A long-range goal for all parents is to become contributing members of the community. Many parents who formerly utilized the services of an agency have become volunteers, employees, and board members of these same agencies. Many parents, because they have been consumers of an agency's services, can bring to that agency insights and perspectives that might not be available from a nonconsumer.

This attitude of involvement should be the same as far as parents and public schools are concerned. Parents should be encouraged to be consumers of all the services schools offer and should be involved in all the learning programs and activities of the school.

## Additional Benefits to Parents from the Parent Involvement Process

There is a tendency to think that through the parent involvement process the majority of the benefits that occur for parents and children are those which are readily visible. For example, these benefits are often emphasized: the increased achievement of the child, the increased amount of time that the parent spends interacting with the child, the increased number of visits to a doctor, etc. In other words, we are quite often interested in that kind of data that can statistically show that parent involvement does indeed provide increased benefits to families. However, there are many other kinds of benefits parents say accrue to them which are not readily observable or easily documented. Obviously, many of these benefits relate to the affective domain and have to do with how people feel and their interpersonal and intrapersonal relationships. The following are some of the things which parents indicate are benefits to them as a result of parent involvement programs:

1. The opportunity to have company, to meet other people, to see other people, and to have other people to talk with. For many parents, particularly in rural settings, isolation for themselves and their children is a real problem. A home visitor helps break this isolation and helps to provide the parent with company and social interaction.

2. Parents relate that they become more confident in themselves and their own abilities to do things as a result of parent involvement. Where parents did not have the inclination, confidence, or the ability to perform certain kinds of acts previously, they find that the support of the parent involvement specialist brings about an increase in the ability to do and achieve.

3. Parents report that parent involvement specialists help them become aware of problems they might not have otherwise thought were areas of concern. For example, the importance of brushing teeth and other forms of dental hygiene are not as obvious to some parents as to others.

4. Parents say that they enjoy having someone who will relate to them and "treat them good" as opposed to someone who brings them problems all of the time. Thus, parent involvement specialists may represent the only or one of a few significant people in the life of a family member.

We should not be too quick then to focus only on the readily observable or documentable data available in a program. The whole range of benefits must be considered in the assessment of the worth of any program. If as a result of a particular program, a child does not achieve better in school, does this mean that a program is bad and should not continue to operate? Not necessarily. If the quality of the interaction that exists between family members increases and if family members relate that they feel better about life, then these kinds of gains are justifiable ones also. In addition, it may well be that the effects of a program may not be readily apparent. What we do with a child today may not affect his achievement today. As a result of an increased self- image, however, the child may achieve more a year or two from now; that is, direct results may be apparent only after a period of time.

## Bibliography

Bronfenbrenner, Urie. *A Report on Longitudinal Evaluations of Preschool Programs, Volume II, Is Early Intervention Effective?* Washington, D.C.: U.S. Government Printing Office, 1974.

## Further Reading and Study

Harben, Gloria, and Cross, Lee. *Early Childhood Curriculum Materials—An Annotated Bibliography*. Washington, D.C.: Office of Education, U.S. Department of Health, Education, and Welfare, 1975.

A useful source for locating programs, books, and skill kits for gross motor and fine motor development, perception and reasoning skills, language development, social skills, and infant training. This bibliography names the program, states the purpose, provides a description, and lists the vendor. Useful for the parents who wish to help their child in any of the described areas.

Hope, Karol, and Young, Nancy. *The Source Book for Single Mothers*. New York: New American Library, 1976.

This unique collection of articles helps the single parent learn, understand, and solve some of the many simple and complex problems they face every day as single parents. This book is a collection of articles written for the magazine *Momma* and has many contributions from the *Momma* organization.

McLaughlin, Clara J. *The Black Parents Handbook*. New York and London: Harcourt Brace Jovanovich, 1976.

A timely book for black parents, since many child care and child development books are written from the point of view of white, middle-class parents. Gives the black parent a thorough, comprehensive analysis of parenthood and its joys and problems. A must for today's concerned black family.

Marzallo, Jean, and Lloyd, Janice. *Learning Through Play*. New York: Harper Colophon Book, Harper and Row, Publishers, 1972.

Parents have a great deal of influence on their children's development (physical, intellectual, and emotional) since they are the first teacher. This book will help parents learn how to teach their children through play. It provides many useful and well-designed activities to help parents learn with their children.

## Activities

1. List the reasons why you would want to be a home visitor. Discuss these with your classmates. What are the similarities and differences among yours and theirs?

2. Observe a family, your own or that of relatives. Determine if you can, how competently they are functioning as individual persons, parents, and members of the community.

3. List five qualities, attitudes, or feelings your parents have transmitted to you. Also, list five of these qualities, attitudes, and feelings which you would want to transmit to your children. Compare your list to your classmates'. What are the similarities and differences? How do you account for these similarities and differences? Are all of these factors positive? What value(s) has been transmitted to you which you wish you could change or shed altogether? Why has this shedding been difficult to do?

4. What values do you think a family possesses which a home visitor could easily destroy? Have you had a value destroyed by someone else? How could it have been avoided?

5. What are some of the personal values (e.g., cleanliness) which you think parents easily transmit to their children? What are some values others (including loved ones) have tried to impose on you? Why were they successful or unsuccessful?

6. What national priorities would you establish for improving social services such as health, housing, etc. List priorities specific to your local community or college.

7. Compile a booklet of all the social service agencies in your area. Include the name of the agency, services rendered by the agency, to whom the services are rendered, cost of the services, if any, eligibility requirements, contact person, etc.

    a. Interview key personnel at these agencies to determine what efforts are being made by that agency to let the public know about the particular services.

8. Not everyone is in agreement that food stamps are a good idea. List the pros and cons of their use and benefits. Interview someone who is receiving food stamps to determine how they receive them, their cost, the limitations placed on their use, etc.

9. Under what conditions do you feel it is justifiable to remove a child from the environment in which he is reared? Cite specific examples.

10. Given a situation in which there were more families who could benefit from a home-based program than there were parent involvement specialists to service the families, develop a set of priorities which determines those families who would receive the services first, second, third, etc.

# Parent Involvement in Early Childhood Programs

# 6

---

## Teaching and Learning Goals

This chapter will provide the information, means, and opportunity to:

Examine specific strategies for working with parents whose children are in early childhood programs.

Analyze issues and problems inherent in programs and strategies for parent involvement in early childhood programs.

Design a program for incorporating parents into early childhood programs.

Develop specific strategies for parent involvement in early childhood programs.

---

## Lack of Parent Involvement in Early Childhood Programs

For purposes of this discussion, *early childhood program* means any educational setting for any child between birth and age eight. This definition includes public and private agencies, as well as grades N-3 in public and private schools. The term *school* means any educational setting for children between the ages of three and eighteen. This definition includes such programs as day care and Head Start centers and public and private programs in grades N-12.

It is rather interesting to note that when a child enters a school of any kind, be it a day care center, a public kindergarten, or other type of early childhood program,

127

the family and the parent lose, for the most part, influence over approximately six to eight hours of the child's day. This block of time is usually considered "prime time" in which the child is usually at her best. She is rested, fed, awake, reasonably alert, and depending on the circumstances, anxious to be involved. However, these are the hours and the conditions over which parents have little or no control! What is even worse, to a very large degree, the parent is shut off from control over the child and what and how she will learn! It is not a case of the parent's voluntarily relinquishing control, it is a case of the parent's literally being forced to abrogate possession of the child.

Legally, almost every state has a maximum age for compulsory education, and during this time, parents have to surrender their children to the educational process. Age and compulsory schooling are not the only circumstances under which children might have to be turned over to another agency. If a woman wants to work, receive job training, or pursue other activities, she may have to place her child in another home, day care center, private preschool, etc.

Thus, where efforts have been made to involve parents, this involvement, at best, has been limited and restrained by those in authority, usually teachers and administrators. Such control and/or domination, depending on your point of view, lasts for at least a decade, from six to sixteen, and occurs during the child's most formative years. It is precisely this lack of control over many of the factors affecting the child that programs of parent involvement seek to rectify.

The extent to which this problem can be rectified depends upon many factors. One of these is how much those who are responsible for the operation of early childhood programs, i.e., the teachers and administrators, *recognize* and *admit* that a problem exists. Many individuals who are responsible for schooling do not realize their influence over the process of education or their ability to control and direct the lives of children. It is my experience that only a few perceptive professionals truly understand the power of teachers and schools over children.

## Schools Unwilling to Involve Parents

The problem of parent involvement concerns responsibility. Are teachers and administrators willing to do anything about the problem, even if they recognize that a problem exists? Traditionally, schools have not been anxious to involve parents in the schooling process. They have consciously and perhaps unconsciously almost prevented parent involvement. At the conscious level, they have systematically organized and controlled parent involvement through such organizations and processes as the PTA, parents' clubs, parent night, parent visitation day, etc. These are all events which are sponsored by schools. As such, the agenda is almost always controlled, which means the topics discussed are subtly controlled by professional educators.

Defacto *Segregation.*   Through these above-named groups and educators' control of them, the schools have been able to limit the involvement of parents and control what they do. It has almost amounted to *defacto* segregation of parents from effective and meaningful involvement. By limiting the involvement, the extent and nature of the parents' influence are also controlled. Many administrators and teachers view this control as a legitimate means of school administration and public relations. Others call it manipulation.

*Isolation from Community.* At the unconscious level, schools have tended to isolate themselves from parents and, to a large extent, from the community. This isolation is evidenced by schools being built in places that are difficult for parents to reach, for example, many miles from the homes of the children. It is further evidenced by the walled, fenced, and fortress-like qualities many schools have.

*Making Parent Involvement Inconvenient.* In addition, schools have systematically discouraged parent involvement through such practices as making visiting hours suitable only to teachers, for example, before or after school. Rather than making visiting hours convenient to parents, schools operate at their own convenience.

*Noncommunication.* Schools tend to communicate with parents only when the child has done something wrong or when a problem exists. Consequently, there is a negative connotation to this type of involvement. What occurs is that many parents are *relieved* that the school does not contact them. The response to this lack of contact is, Everything must be all right. I haven't been called.

## Not Giving Parents Credit

Another interesting phenomenon about parent involvement is that schools take all the credit for any success children may demonstrate but are unwilling to accept any blame for nonsuccess. For example, if a child learns to read, write, and act in a socially acceptable way, the school and teachers point to this achievement as an example of their ability to conduct an exemplary program. However, if the child does not learn to read quickly and well, the school and teacher place the blame on the home and parent. Such statements as, How do you expect me to teach him to read when he comes from a home like that? and I can't work miracles by making something out of nothing, are frequently heard teacher's comments. In the area of social responsibility, teachers have been even less inclined to explore the possibility that schools may be responsbile for how children act when they are in school. It is interesting to note that teachers are more inclined to blame the home than accept some responsibility or initiate programs to help ameliorate children's behavior. Indeed, teachers quite often attribute the inability of the child to learn in school to the parents' lack of preparation of the child for school. Teachers expect parents to prepare their children for school. The paradox of this situation is that many parents don't know what to do, because they are ignorant of the curriculum of the school and because schools have not helped them learn what to do. The content of many high school curricula does not even include sessions on parenting.

## The School's Self-perception

*Control.* Why is it that schools and early childhood programs have been reluctant to encourage parent involvement? One of these reasons undoubtedly involves control. It is simply a matter of schools taking the position that teachers and administrators are in control of the schooling process, not the parents. This concept of schooling as control is reflected not only in the way parents are treated but in how schools perceive their function and process. Consequently, the majority of professionals view schooling primarily as a process of control. Schools establish many rules and regulations for controlling the lives of students. This is evidenced by fixed schedules, curricula, admittance criteria, procedures, etc. At the instructional level, it is reflected in the pre-occupation of teachers with managing classrooms and children's behavior. This is apparent in the classroom arrangement of many schools, for example, straight rows, a seat for every child, emphasis on classroom rules, etc.

*Organizational Structure.*   Part of this concept of control can be attributed to the school's traditional make-up and organizational structure. This organizational approach is based, in many instances, on that of large corporations where the predominate themes are efficiency and management. Many schools are operated to encourage efficiency, for example, time schedules, large classes, etc. On the managerial level, most administrators of educational programs, regardless of whether or not they administer in public schools or private, spend a great deal of their time and energy on *administering* rather than on developing the curricula and affective contents of schools. This preoccupation with administering is reflected in the great amount of time administrators spend ordering materials, approving lesson plans, scheduling meetings, attending meetings, and the like. Indeed, many preschool and public school administrators would probably make good managers of large five and dime stores, for this is the style of management which they prefer and exhibit. This explains, in part, why administrators seldom get involved in the process of curriculum development and also explains why the curriculum of a school, what the school teaches, is usually its weakest component.

*Threatened Teachers.*   Yet another reason schools have been reluctant to involve parents in their programs is that teachers have felt threatened by, and are often uncomfortable in, the presence of parents. Many teachers feel that, while the parent may know what is best for the child at home, they, the teachers, know what is best for the child at school. Teachers simply have not wanted parent involvement because they have wanted to do their own thing, which means teaching in their own way according to their own concept of what should be taught. Generally, the attitude of many teachers is expressed something like this; "Since I'm a college graduate, and a professional, I know what should be done. Why should I let a parent, whose job is not education, tell me what to do?"

## Communicating Difficult for Parents

If you are a parent and must communicate with a school, you will discover it is a difficult job. The tendency for even those who are in education and who are trained to deal with schools is to do nothing. It is much easier not to communicate with the schools and not to visit them. The point is that for everyone, the educated as well as the uneducated, the sophisticated as well as the unsophisticated, those trained in communication and those who are not trained in communication, the tendency is to not communicate with the schools. Even for someone who has letter-writing ability and the ability to converse well, who can go to a school in an automobile, who is accessible to a school, or who has all of these support systems available to her, communication is still a difficult process. It is even tougher if a parent does not have paper to write on or a pencil to write with. It is impossible to do if one does not know how to write or if one has hardly ever written a letter.

More importantly, what do you say when you have to communicate with the schools? After all, don't the schools know more than parents know? The fact remains then that even those who have the knowledge and ability to communicate with the school are still intimidated by it.

The issue can be raised here of where the fault lies. Is it the parents' fault because they are not more articulate, because they are not more aggressive, because they are not more prone toward communication? Or is it the schools' fault because they don't encourage participation and communication and because they have a history of not involving parents in communications and processes? As a parent (and as an educator who has been hesitant to communicate with the school) I feel that it is the fault of the schools. It is their responsibility to encourage parents to communicate their thoughts and feelings.

## *Reasons of Lack of Successful Parent Involvement*

I do not mean to imply that the schools and early childhood programs have not attempted to bring the outside world into the schools. Many worthy attempts have been made to bring the talents of people and the resources of the community into the school. However, the schools have not been overly successful in their attempts at parent involvement. Reasons for this general ineffectiveness are several:

1. Lack of real effort on the part of the majority of schools to implement an effective program of community involvement. Attempts have been of a peripheral nature but have not dealt with the central issues.

2. Lack of enthusiasm on the part of teachers and administrators to make parent programs operative. Part of this reluctance can be attributed to a fear by professional educators that their subject matter, teaching perogatives, and jobs will be made vulnerable by "outsiders" in the classroom.

Lack of efforts at and an emphasis on attempting to take the educational community into the home can be attributed in part to the failure of schools to adequately and effectively involve parents *and* to recognize that the educational process begins before entry into kindergarten and first grade.

## Rationale for Parent Involvement

A rationale for parent involvement in early childhood programs includes the following:

1. To give parents a feeling of importance and support in their role as parents and educators.

2. To enhance the self-image and performance achievement of the child.

3. To change parents' attitudes about the school. This is particularly important where the parent has a negative attitude toward the school. It also helps where the parent has little knowledge of the school or its program, for as parental knowledge about school programs increases, parental approval of the school's programs also usually increases.

4. To provide parents with skills which they can use at home with their children.

5. To provide parents with opportunities to increase their incomes by being in paid positions in educational programs. In this sense, many parent involvement programs are viewed as breaking cycles of poverty.

6. To comply with federal and/or state guidelines which stipulate parent involvement as a condition for receiving programmatic monies.

7. To provide teachers with the help they need in coping with overcrowded classrooms.

8. To utilize the services of parents as an economic commodity.

9. To relieve teachers of secretarial-type duties (such as taking attendances) and other jobs (such as recess duty) which are considered "nonprofessional."

## Initiative from Schools

In any successful program of parent involvement, the initiative must come from the schools. As many public schools have found, if they wait for the parents, nothing will happen. Effective involvement is not a matter of indifference and/or chance. Too often schools and teachers blame parents for not beating a path to the school room door! Teachers will have to realize that, like it or not, they are going to have to take the lead in any two-way relationship they wish to establish with parents.

## Large Group Approach Not Always Best

A typical and frequently used approach in attempting to have parent involvement is to approach parents through large groups. Usually these large groups are PTA's, one-time, special purpose meetings (for example, an explanation of a new grading system, textbook series, etc.), or children-produced concerts or plays. In many instances, these events are quite successful in getting the parents out ("But," teachers complain, "not the parents who really should be involved."). Usually, however, you have a teacher-parent ratio of ten or more to one. In a situation such as this, there is no way a teacher and parent can interact effectively about anything. While the evening may turn out to be a pleasant and enjoyable one for all involved, it hardly can be said that

*Parents should be involved in decision-making processes about programs which affect them. This group of parents is helping formulate plans for a series of parent meetings.*

really effective parent-school involvement or parent-teacher communication occurred. The point is that while large group approaches and activities can be used as part of the parent involvement process, they should not be the total program.

## Parent Involvement in Decision Making

### *Barriers*

One of the barriers to parent involvement in schools is the inability or unwillingness of school personnel to involve parents in decision-making processes for day-to-day operations and instructional processes within the classrooms. It is not unusual for this barrier to exist simply because it is natural for teachers, administrators, and school boards not to want to surrender any of the policy-making power they have. Indeed, in the organization of many school boards and school districts, an elected or appointed school board authority is in office at the will of the people in order to make policy decisions about the educational process. Thus, boards of education see themselves as invested with an authority-making mandate. Typical school-staff authority, then, as it emanates from the school board, is that of implementing policy established by the board of education. Of course, from day to day in the operation of any school, there are opportunities and possibilities for the administrators and teachers to make policy decisions. The majority of these decisions are of a minor nature. However, they have a great deal of effect upon the children, for they affect the nature of their interaction with other children, their self-perceptions, how well they achieve, etc. While teachers and administrators are powerless in terms of major policy making, they are powerful on an individual school and classroom basis. Many schools are run rather dictatorially and autocratically at the whim and the desire of a particular administrator. Some school administrators even view their function as "running a tight ship." It is precisely in this area of policy and decision making that schools could and should benefit from parent involvement. However, many administrators and teachers see such involvement as a threat to their authority.

Furthermore, many administrators feel they should not allow much parent participation in policy decisions because they view the operation of a school as similar to the operation of a corporation. What they forget is that the analogy between schools and private business is not a valid one for several reasons. One of these reasons is that most private businesses are profit-making entities. Therefore, their job is not necessarily to serve the public good, but to maximize profits. As such, they hire individuals who are skillful at production and management decisions and who will, in the long run, return to the owner or stockholder the highest profit margin that can be attainable. On the other hand, most schools are nonproprietary in nature and are not operated for profit.

Secondly, large corporations are, for the most part, not dealing with human services. The schools are responsible for providing a very human helping service which is to educate children. There is no other institution which deals in such a precious commodity and in which parents have such a high interest.

The third thing that is often overlooked in the school administration process is that, in the United States, control of public education is, for the most part, a local district or community concern. Oftentimes this local control concept is overlooked or ignored. The schools, by and large, have been founded, funded, and monitored by the local school district. As such, parents have a right to say what should occur in the schools. This concept of local control is reinforced time and time again by taxpayers, advocacy organizations, and parent groups that have sought to reassert their right for involvement and decision making where they feel it has been ignored or where they have not been involved as they should be.

## In Loco Parentis

The school function as it exists in relation to parents is a rather unique one in the sense that teachers and schools have always been considered to be extensions of the parent. Teachers and administrators have historically and legally been considered to be *in loco parentis,* meaning they take the place of or stand in place of the parent. This concept means that the schools and teachers may act basically in the same capacity and in the same manner as a parent would act toward the child. Vested with this authority, the teacher is free to teach, control, and discipline the child much the same way as a parent would. On the other hand, the *in loco parentis* concept also means that the teacher has to exercise legitimate care of and provide reasonable safeguards for the child just as a parent would.

Because of this *in loco parentis* relationship between children and teachers, all teachers have to be prudent in exercising authority. Unfortunately, some teachers have abused this concept because they feel they can do anything they want to the child, including corporal punishment, without threat or retribution from the law.

It seems a reasonable proposition that because teachers stand *in loco parentis,* they would want to interact with, communicate with, and involve the parents in the educational process in order to more adequately understand what parents want for their children and to more reasonably fulfill the role of parent. In a very real sense, the power given to teachers represents a sacred trust, implying that parents should be involved in the educational process of their children.

## Family Privacy

Another legal basis for parent involvement is the Family Educational Rights and Privacy Act of 1974. This act gives parents who have children in any educational agency the right to inspect the official records the agency maintains on the child. These records include such things as test scores, cumulative records, health data, teacher observations, etc. In addition, the law provides parents with the right to have a hearing during which they may challenge the content and accuracy of such records.

The act further stipulates that educational agencies cannot release any personally identifiable information about children unless parents have given their prior written consent to the release of such information. In this manner, the parent and child are both protected from people having access to information which is no one else's business but the family's.

The primary method for enforcement of the regulations specified in the Family Educational Rights and Privacy Act is by withholding federal funds from an agency currently receiving them or by not approving federal expenditures to an agency unless it agrees to the provisions of the act.

There has been some criticism of this act on the basis that it denies to researchers information and data needed in compiling and conducting studies relating to educational programs. It may be true that some agencies have been overzealous in the implementation of the provisions of the law and have not done the public relations work necessary to inform parents about the act and secure their permissions for the release of information. The purpose of the law is not to stop or prohibit the flow of research information. Rather, the purpose is to open records to parents, to have them examine these records, and to involve them in the decision-making process relating to the release of information regarding their children. Unfortunately, some educational agencies have not accomplished this involvement. While they may have informed parents of their rights, they have not encouraged parents to exercise these rights by becoming involved in the processes of examination, correction, and consent giving.

Researchers, on the other hand, will have to be more specific and discriminative in specifying the kind of data they require in their research studies. In addition, they too will have to be willing to take the time and effort necessary to inform educational personnel and parents of the purpose, nature, and methodologies of their studies in order that parents will be willing to release specific kinds of data. This process is something which not all researchers have been willing to do.

## Corporal Punishment

Most states permit educational agencies to administer corporal punishment to pupils under their care and guidance. However, a growing number of states are beginning to question the wisdom of administering corporal punishment or are prohibiting it altogether. The basis for corporal punishment is the *in loco parentis* concept which gives teachers the same powers over the child as the parent has. However, while teachers have been willing to exercise this power, they have not been willing, for some strange reason, to involve parents in a determination of how and *if* these powers of *in loco parentis* should be exercised.

With growing criticism of corporal punishment by parents, child advocates, and civil rights groups, more and more educational agencies are seeking parental permission and advice concerning the administration of disciplinary procedures. How extensive this involvement is depends upon the forthrightness and leadership concept of teachers and administrators. Some agencies merely inform the parents, usually by writing, that they will administer punishment. Others inform parents that if they do not desire their child to be punished, they must inform the school in writing. Unfortunately, there is the distinct possibility that some parents cannot read or write or might not know what corporal punishment means.

Other school districts and agencies involve parents in the decision-making process relating to discipline, student codes, rules and regulations, and what kind of corporal punishment, if any, will be administered. This process is a more reasonable, rational, and humane process. Why shouldn't parents be encouraged to be involved in these areas, especially when their childen's emotional and physical well-being are often at stake?

## Advisory Committee

The fact remains that there are many opportunities for parents and taxpayers at large to become involved in public school programs. Many school boards and school superintendents have citizens' advisory committees. These quite often meet on a regular basis in order to discuss parent and committee feelings and opinions about issues, curricula, goals, etc. It is through these citizen advisory committees that parents have an opportunity to provide input to their elected and/or appointed representative. These advisory committees are an important element in enabling schools to keep their finger on the pulse of the community. However, opportunities for meaningful contributions in terms of committee action is often limited because, by their very nature, the make-up, function, and influence of the citizen advisory committee include only an advisory role. In some instances, depending upon the make-up and disposition of the board, the recommendations of the advisory committee can become policy through board actions. However, the advisory committee is somewhat removed from direct political power and control over the decision-making process.

## Long-range Planning

Another opportunity for parent participation and involvement is the preparation of long-range plans that many school districts either develop of their own volition as a means of projecting their programs in the future or which have to be completed in order to receive state funding. These long-range plans involve the preparation of a document which details and projects the philosophy, goals, curricula, methodology, pupil enrollment, building needs, personnel requirement, etc., of the schools into the future for ten to fifteen or more years. Many schools feel that it is necessary and desirable to have citizen participation in the development of these long-range proposals. Some of these plans are developed by having citizens rather than professionals chair important committees relating to philosophy and curricula. In such a position, a committee member would have equal stature and voting power with a member of the school board, administration, or faculty. In this way, the citizen has an opportunity to exert rather considerable influence over the long-range plan of a school district.

However, several problems can occur with this process. First, the citizen who is in the position to exert this influence may or may not seek feedback from the community at large. It is entirely possible then that the views presented by her are merely her own. Secondly, quite often it is only the most influential, the most political, or the most strident critic of the school who gets to be appointed to this kind of committee. In essence then, the participation of the "rank and file" is not always sought nor is it always represented when committees are formed and plans are developed.

## Curriculum Development Committees

Another opportunity for parent involvement in decision making is in curriculum selection as it relates to deciding what will be taught in the schools and what materials will be used to implement what is to be taught. During the 1960s, one of the curricular innovations which occurred in public schools was the "new math." However, as public schools soon learned, one of the problems with the new math was that it was so new to parents they didn't know what it was or even how to do it when their children brought it home for help. Consequently, public schools had to undertake rather extensive public relations campaigns in order to explain to parents what new math was. One of the more popular ways of introducing parents to new math was to teach them how to do it. Consequently, classes in new math for parents were popular during the sixties. However, because they were not originally involved in any meaningful way about the decision relating to the inclusion of new math in the curriculum and because of their lack of understanding about what it was, many parent groups were organized in order to get rid of the new math program. Had parents been involved in the beginning in more meaningful ways, perhaps new math would have been more successful than it has been.

A national example of what can occur when parents are not involved or when they feel they are removed from the decision-making process as it relates to school curricula and textbooks selection occurred in Kanawha County, West Virginia, in 1974. Basically, parents were dissatisfied with the content of textbooks and supplementary books because they felt they dealt with immorality, ungodly topics, and, in general, contained material contrary to the teaching of the local churches. Parent protests and demonstrations were accompanied by such incidents as coal miner strikes, burning of textbooks, and public denunciations of the actions of the board members. The occurrences in Kanawha County captured national attention for several months. Certainly there would not have been as much public controversy over the discrepancy between parent opinion about what was appropriate subject matter for children and what the schools thought was appropriate had there been more parent involvement from the beginning.

Parent involvement should be conducted in a systematic way at all levels of the educational process in order that schools, administrators, and teachers can be in tune with and responsive to the feelings, opinions, and desires of the public. The purpose of parent involvement is not to avoid trouble, nor to defuse trouble before it begins, nor to make parents happy. Its purpose is to provide the best educational program for children that it is possible to provide.

## Involving Parents in Educational Programs

### Parent Volunteers

One of the fundamental decisions that has to be made in any parent involvement program is the function of the parent. Simply stated, What do you want parents to do? If you want parents to be tutors and teaching assistants and involved in the instructional process, then the involvement and training program will have to be structured to achieve that goal. If, on the other hand, parents are to be used primarily as aides and given noninstructional assignments, the training program should reflect this role.

Not only will the decision concerning the parent role affect the involvement and training procedures, it will also affect how parents are perceived and treated. When parents are restricted in the classroom to noninstructional roles and are given only those jobs which deal with grading papers, making bulletin boards, etc., they will be perceived as capable of only performing those functions. When this attitude is prevalent, it can be demeaning to the abilities and talents of the parents.

Of course, the parents' feelings and desires should be considered whenever possible. If in a school district there is more than one type of role for the parent volunteers to participate in, they should be given a choice of roles. It may be that some parents are uncomfortable in a particular role and would perform better, for example, in an aide's position rather than in an instructional tutorial role.

## Methods for Involving Parents

We have examined some of the problems associated with parent involvement and have discussed the need for having parents in the classroom. However, the ultimate question which most teachers ask once they are convinced of the wisdom of parent involvement is, How do I go about involving parents? The following information may be helpful in that process:

1. One of the first things that is necessary for people who would involve parents is the right attitude or state of mind. You have to *want* to have parent involvement in early childhood and school programs, not reluctantly but enthusiastically. Otherwise, parent involvement probably won't be as effective as it should be. This positive state of mind should include the following:

   a. You as a teacher must not be or feel threatened by parents. Much of this attitude of not being threatened by parents, or anyone else for that matter, relates to self-confidence. The more self-confident a teacher is about herself as a person and about her ability as a teacher, the less threatened she is. Self-confidence comes from being good at what you are doing.

   b. The administration of the school program must be ready for parents, and this includes the principal, the superintendent, and the school board. If the program of parent involvement has and receives frequent and continuous high-level support and recognition, it will be more successful than if this support is lacking. Indeed, when this type of support is not present, the success of the parent involvement program will be limited.

   c. You must understand that the success of your program will depend on how well you involve parents. A half-hearted effort will not do. Parents must have meaningful involvement in the program, not just the custodial jobs.

2. One of the more critical factors in the involvement process relates to planning for the program. Determine what you will have for parents to do *prior* to their involvement. However, be willing to change these plans once you have determined parent strengths, weaknesses, and needs. Ways in which parents can be involved in programs are outlined in table 14. This table shows the broad range of activities that are possible if only the teacher is creative enough and willing to utilize them.

3. Contact all parents who are available.

   a. You must seek creative ways to involve *all* parents. Remember, most parents, regardless of their level of education, are threatened by schools and school-like settings. You have to help them overcome these fears. While it may be unrealistic to expect all parents to participate, it is not unrealistic for you to give all parents a chance.

   b. Be willing to go to the parents through home visitation. Don't always make the parents come to you.

4. Provide for all levels of parent abilities, desires, and needs. Don't expect the same amount of participation from every parent and don't expect all parents to desire or be able to do the same thing. Regardless of how much or how little a parent can or wants to be involved, provide her with an opportunity to do so.

5. Invite a parent or a group of parents to help you organize and operate your parent involvement program. If you are pleasantly surprised in your efforts and have a larger program of parent involvement than you anticipated, don't feel that you have to personally supervise every detail. Your main functions will be to:

    a. Develop a program rationale and structure
        1. Write your philosophy
        2. Establish learning-teaching goals for the children
    b. Orientate/train
        1. Explain your philosophy
        2. Develop and conduct a training program
    c. Supervise
        1. Plan for and with the parent helpers
        2. Explain reasons and rationale
        3. Role model specific teaching methods
    d. Evaluate
        1. The level of performance by the parent
            a. How the parent felt she did
            b. How the children felt the parent did
            c. How the teacher felt the parent did
        2. Effectiveness of the parent involvement program in the classroom

These functions will require enough of your time, but they are functions which are more appropriate to the role of a professional educator, which is what you should be. A parent can help you operate your program through such things as calling parents, setting up schedules, matching children's needs with parent's abilities, etc.

6. Provide a well-planned orientation session for your parent involvement program in your classroom *prior* to the involvement itself. This orientation should include such things as the following:

    a. Philosophy of the school. (Parents may have been oriented to this if the district had a group orientation program.)

    b. Your philosophy of teaching/learning.

    c. Learning goals and objectives for the classroom and for the children.

    d. Rules and regulations relating to the school and to the classroom.

    e. Specific tasks of the volunteers, including how to perform these specific duties and special preparations parent volunteers will have to make, if any.

    f. Limits relating to responsibilities and duties.

    g. Classroom management and specific topics, such as student self-autonomy and control, which may need particular explanation.

    h. A survey of parent interests and abilities.

**TABLE 14**  A list of functions parents as volunteers can perform in the classroom.

| *Innovator* | *Teacher/ Instructor* | *Supervisor* | *Clerical Duties* | *Maintainer of Classroom Materials* |
|---|---|---|---|---|
| 1. Creating new learning materials<br>2. Creating bulletin boards, learning centers | 1. Providing instruction to large groups, small groups, and individuals (learning disabled, under/over-achievers, bilingual, handicapped)<br>2. Tutoring small group/individual | 1. Playground<br>2. Lunch duty<br>3. Field trips<br>4. Classroom<br>5. Extracur-ricular activities | 1. Grading and recording<br>2. Filling out records and forms | 1. Library books<br>2. Learning files |

When the parent volunteer enters the early childhood program for the first time, several processes which should occur are these:

1. Introduce the parent volunteer to the students and allow the parent to talk briefly with students. This will help the students and parent get over the initial nervousness, if any.

2. Have the parent observe the classroom routine the first day. This will allow the volunteer to see the students at work and better understand these things:

   a. teacher-student relationships

   b. student-student relationships

   c. student-material relationships

   d. age level/maturity

   e. different groups

3. Have the children show the parent around the classroom and early childhood program.

4. Be sure the parent is made to feel comfortable and welcome. This can be accomplished by introducing the volunteer to the school setting—the building facilities and the faculty and staff.

## *More Techniques for Involvement*

Here are more ways to promote and encourage parent involvement:

1. Use a parent as a parent coordinator. Parents are often the best involvers of parents. Parents can organize and operate your parent program.

2. Employ a parent involvement expert who is able to encourage parent involvement. In some programs this is a fulltime position.

3. Conduct meetings and functions. These meetings can be used as opportunities for telling parents how they can help. Door prizes can be awarded at these meetings to encourage attendance.

4. Form car pools so that parents can ride with each other. Transportation to programs is very critical and often determines whether or not a parent becomes involved.

5. Parents can sell the idea of involvement to other parents.

6. Make sure the meetings you have and the opportunities for involvement in the classroom are meaningful. Nothing will turn parents off quicker than if what they are asked to do is "Mickey Mouse" or if they are uninterested in what they are doing.

7. Provide volunteers with recognition. This recognition can occur through dinners and/or banquets, certificates of recognition, and pictures in newspapers.

## Important Processes

### *Fear of Losing Control*

There should be no concern by teachers that they will lose their professional standing or jeopardize their professional role in the classroom as a result of parent involvement. Through this involvement process, the teacher can actually strengthen her own role and self-image because parents come to see the teacher as a professional in the true sense of the word. As a professional, the teacher has the ultimate responsibility for planning the program, setting its direction, and designing learning activities that will implement programmatic goals and objectives. While the parent should be a partner in the instructional process, it is the teacher who has the ultimate responsibility for setting the direction. When a program is conducted in this manner, it is professional in the truest sense of the word, and no teacher is going to lose control.

### *Philosophy*

Parents need to be informed of the philosophy and instructional goals of the early childhood teacher who guides the day-to-day activities of a particular classroom and/or center. This understanding of the philosophy of the teacher by the parent is essential in order for the parent to know what is expected of her.

Unfortunately, many teachers have never developed a philosophy. Some, when asked if they have a philosophy, respond, "Of course I have a philosophy but I have never written it down." What this really means is that they probably don't have any philosophy at all. It is surprising the number of teachers in Head Start, day care, private preschools, and public schools who are teaching without philosophies of education to guide them. Explaining one's philosophy to parents necessitates writing it. In this respect, parent involvement forces the teacher to deal with her own philosophy.

The process of acquainting the parent with the teacher's philosophy may occur days prior to actual parent involvement. However, the time spent in explaining the philosophy is worth it because it helps parents see the total picture and helps them feel good about the process. This, of course, will increase the quality of involvement in the program.

## Planning

Regardless of how well the orientation program has been conducted and regardless of how well the teacher and/or parent think they know what the parent is going to do, it is still vitally necessary for teacher and parent to plan for what will be done. Not only does planning help set a direction for what will be accomplished, it also promotes the confidence the parent needs to experience success. The planning process can be an involved and lengthy one, although it need not be, and it is probably better if it is not. Basic planning should include (1) what is to be accomplished, (2) how the parent will proceed, and (3) materials needed.

In this type of planning process, the teacher can do most of the planning, show the parents the plan, and discuss how the plan will be implemented. However, a planning process in which the parent is an integral part is preferable. In such a process, the parent is involved in discussing what has been accomplished, setting instructional goals, and determining what instructional strategies are necessary and how they will be implemented.

Planning is a process which many teachers and parents want to ignore or skip. However, the success of any educational program depends on planning, be it for the children or for parent involvement. The teacher must also plan with the parent for what involvement the parent will have. It is extremely important that the parent understand what it is she is going to do and how she is going to do it. The intended learning outcomes must be communicated to the parent and then appropriate activities planned in order to achieve these intended learning outcomes.

## Evaluating

In the evaluative process, the teacher should be aware that evaluation can occur on several different levels. The first level is the need to examine how well the parent performs on the task or activity in which she is involved. This evaluation process should be conducted on three levels.

1. What did the parent think about her involvement? Parents can be encouraged to reflect on their behavior and introspect about their feelings.
2. How did the children feel about the parent? Their reactions and comments can do much to add insight into the instructional and involvement process.
3. What did the teacher think about the parent involvement?

The second level on which evaluation has to occur is to assess the broader program and ask the question, How effective is the process of parent involvement within the classroom and/or center? While at the first level how well the parent did in a particular assignment, activity, or task was discussed, at this level the extent to which the process of parent involvement is meaningful and successful in the classroom is examined. In this respect, such questions as the following can be examined: Is the parent being involved in the kind of activities she should be? Does the parent feel that she and the children are benefitting from the activities in which they are involved? This approach to evaluation examines the success and/or failure of the system for involving parents within the classroom.

Unfortunately the thought of evaluation for people participating in an evaluation process often means subjecting themselves to criticism and negative feelings. Evaluation, more often than not, causes fear in people, especially parents who are not used to the process. As a result, evaluation is often used and viewed as a negative process not really having much value for personnel involved in it. Therefore, it is imperative that everyone who works with parents approach evaluation from a positive point of view. Once personnel have experienced evaluation as a positive rather than a negative process, a new perspective toward evaluation will have been established. This new perspective involves a positive point of view, a nonthreatening atmosphere, and a helping attitude by those responsible for the evaluation process.

*Avoid Negativism.* In order for evaluation to meet the above criteria, it must not be negative. Neither should it be conducted in an atmosphere of intrigue and suspicion conceived of or designed as an exercise for catching parent volunteers doing something wrong. The teacher should not be viewed as the all-knowing expert. Unfortunately, this is often the concept projected when the topic of evaluation is discussed.

*Evaluation Is Not Punishment.* Evaluation, to be effective, cannot be viewed as a form of punishment. Personnel being evaluated should not think of the rationale for evaluation as indicating that they have done something wrong. Evaluation should not always be concerned with what is wrong; rather, evaluation should be used to help people determine what they are doing right. Until we stop considering evaluation as equivalent to punishment, we will never be able to assign to it the helping role in which it should be regarded.

Evaluation can satisfy a very human need, that is, the need of every person to know what kind of job she is doing. The child needs to know that she is loved in order for proper emotional development to occur. The parent volunteer needs to know what kind of a job she is doing in order to do a good job. A recurring complaint from many volunteers is that the classroom teacher never tells them what kind of a job they are doing. They think they are doing a good job, but they never really seem to be sure, and they really want to know.

Evaluation can also provide a basis and a means for improvement. It is not enough to say to volunteers that they are not doing something right. The classroom teacher must provide suggestions for improvement and correction. In addition, these strategies for improvement should be cooperative ones designed by both teacher and parent. Questions such as "How can we do better?" must be asked and answered. This is not to imply that, once strategies are designed, they are or will remain good strategies. Since this may not be the case, what is important initially is that decisions for improvement are cooperatively determined. If this strategy is followed, then positive future action is decided, clues for improvement are given, and the evaluator and parent are both placed under an obligation to assume a helping role for the benefit of everyone.

## Discussing

Budgeting time for discussion permits the parent and teacher to talk about their feelings concerning how the program of involvement is progressing. In this respect, it is often helpful if the parent keeps a daily log relating to her activities and experiences. In the daily log, the parent can relate to specific incidents; react to her feelings toward administration, children, events, the teacher, etc. Log keeping also encourages the reflective process whereby an individual gains insight into how she thinks she can do a better, more effective job.

It is entirely possible, however, that the parent is nonverbal and/or lacks the experience, skill, or background necessary for writing. In this instance, the discussion can be verbal. If this is the case, the parent must be made to feel comfortable. It is essential that the discussion situation is a nonthreatening one in order that parent feelings about the process can emerge.

It is also important in the discussion process that the parent perceives something will be done about her feelings and attitudes. There is nothing worse than discussing how you feel and then seeing no results from the input that you have given.

*Parents can benefit from involvement with children while working as aides in programs.*

## Training Parent Volunteers

### *The Importance of Training*

The training of volunteers for involvement in classrooms is as important as the original decision that the school and/or teacher make that they will have and use parent volunteers in the classroom. Quite often, parents are brought into the classrooms to work with little or no systematic program for their use or training. Training is important to assure that volunteers are used in the most effective ways that will be meaningful to them, the children, and the schools. However, without a planned, systematic training program, the volunteer process will not be successful at all. This means that every school district, every school, and most certainly every classroom teacher who anticipates using aides and volunteers in the classroom should conduct a training program.

### *Attitudes of Teachers*

The attitude of teachers toward the use of parents as volunteers in the classroom is also a very important factor in any successful program. Unless the teacher on the individual classroom level has positive attitudes toward the utilization of parents and sincerely wants their involvement in the classroom, the program will not be a success. Every effort should be made, therefore, to do one of two things:

1. Develop a positive attitude in the minds of teachers toward parents and the role that they can play. This positive attitude can be developed somewhat by an orientation session for teachers about the use of volunteers.

2. Permit teachers to have the option to have parents in their classrooms. This means that a teacher can choose whether or not she wants to have a volunteer. Those teachers who do not feel that they could work with and/or benefit from the volunteer would not have to participate in the program. In this way, negative attitudes toward the program can be elimiated in the beginning, and problems involved in the utilization of parents will be reduced.

### *Preparation for Training*

Before a training program can be developed and implemented, a series of complementary preparations must be made. Some of these preparations include the development of the program on paper, the listing of goals and objectives of the volunteer program, the solicitation of teacher cooperation, and the approval of the program by the board of education or the governing body of the school or early childhood program. It would also be quite helpful in this initial preparation period if parents themselves could be involved in the program. Nothing succeeds quite like the involvement of parents in the design and implementation of a program which is designed for parents.

### *Design of Specific Training Model*

Prior to any specific kind of training program, a design for that training program has to be developed. Figures 8 and 9 illustrate a design for the preliminaries involved in a

**FIGURE 8**  Training Parents as Tutors and Aides:  An overview

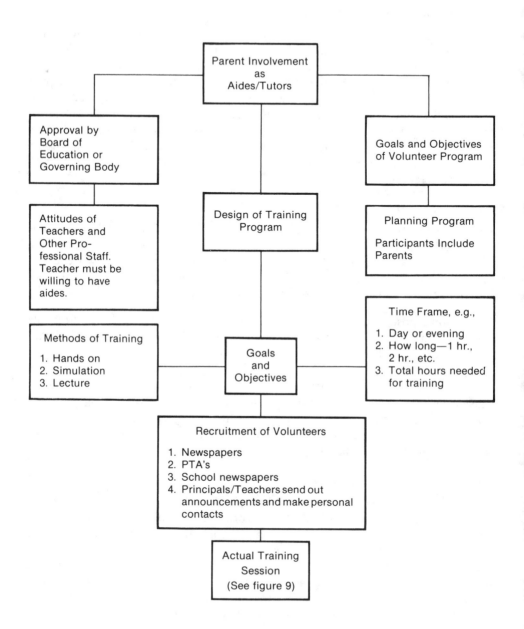

training program and an actual model for a specific training program. Some of the more important factors that have to be considered in the design are such components as the goals and objectives of the program, the methods of training that will be utilized, the materials that will be needed in the program, and the time frame within which the training program will occur. It is surprising how often these factors are overlooked in conducting training programs. One specific topic that is quite often overlooked is a specification of the goals and objectives. However, as in anything else, until and unless the goals and objectives are rather precisely defined, the training program will not be effective.

## Recruitment Process

One of the procedures that has to be conducted in any training program is the recruitment of the parents as volunteers into the program. First of all, the recruitment processes and procedures should be as comprehensive as possible. This means that every effort should be made to get the news to parents about opportunities for benefits of involvement. In order to desseminate information about involvement opportunities, such strategies as the following can be used to encourage parents: locally produced school papers, principal's news letters, teacher-made announcements sent home with children, telephone calls by other parents and by teachers, door-to-door solicitations, and announcements in newspapers and at PTA's.

In the recruitment of parents as volunteers, one of the key factors which should be emphasized is that there are many benefits that can accrue to parents in the involvement process. Instead of emphasizing these benefits, however, what often happens is that schools and teachers have a tendency to stress the benefits to the schools. Quite often these benefits are touted as freeing teachers from burdens and work such as recess duty, teaching slower students, cafeteria duty, etc. Instead, emphasis should be placed on those benefits which accrue to children and to parents.

## A Specific Training Program for Parent Volunteers

Figure 9 outlines in detail a specific training model which can be utilized in training parent volunteers to act as aides and volunteers in early childhood programs. It should be understood that, while this training model can be adapted to a wide range of situations, it would, nonetheless, have to be tailor-made to the needs and constraints of a particular program. Also, the reader should understand that what will work in one early childhood program may not necessarily work in another program.

The training session has been designed to include three two-hour sessions for a total of six hours of training. Of course, decisions relating to how long a training session will last depend upon the goals and objectives of the program and such other factors as the amount of money, if any, that is available for training. There may be some programs that feel that they can neither afford nor conduct a six-hour training session. Other programs may choose to leave the training to the classroom teacher. However, the involvement of parents in the classroom is too vital a process to jeopardize by not having a training program of some kind. In addition, while classroom teachers may be perfectly capable of conducting such training on their own, there needs to be a continuity and a commonality which can only come by an initial group training of volunteers.

The training design incorporates the important elements that need to be covered. Specifically, these are as follows:

1. There should be general overview of the program which will outline for parents the what, why, and how of the program. This general orientation can also cover a discussion of the various roles parent volunteers will assume as well as pertinent rules and regulations and characteristics of the children parents will work with. Specifically, the general orientation should be a broad overview for the parents about the general nature of the program.

2. The training program should incorporate a discussion about the specific curriculum areas the parents will be involved in. If parents will be working in the areas of language, reading, and mathematics, they should know what is involved in these areas. If the particular grade level or program area that the parent desires to volunteer in is known prior to the training, then it would be possible to subdivide

**FIGURE 9** Model for Training Parents as Aides and Tutors

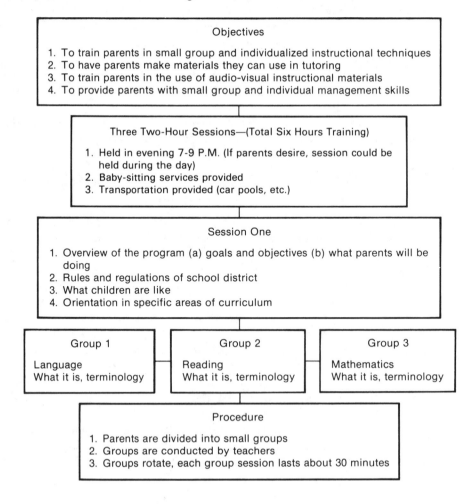

**FIGURE 9 (continued)**

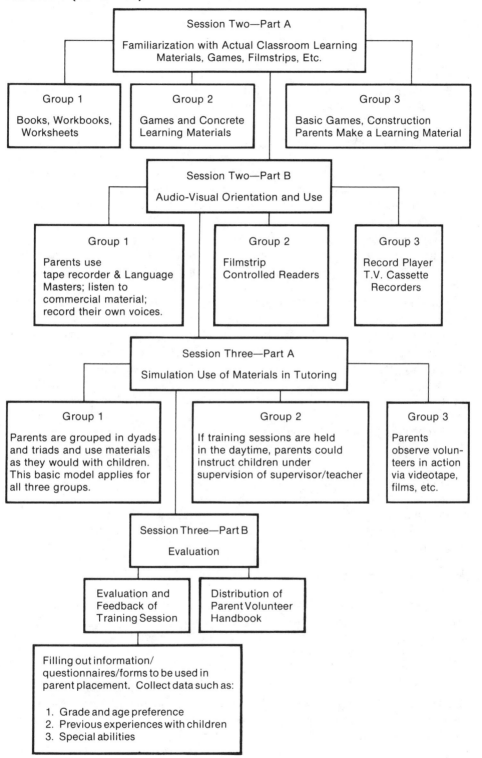

149

groups into content areas. This would allow an orientation of parents who want to deal with first graders to learn about language arts, reading, and mathematics as they are generally taught in grade one.

3. Parents should learn about materials through a "hands-on" session with actual classroom learning materials. This orientation to actual classroom materials should include both hardware and software. Parents can become familiar with materials by examining, trying out, and, in a final session, utilizing them in a simulated setting.

4. Parents should have an opportunity to learn how to use the hardware that they will be asked to use in volunteering situations. They should know how to operate tape recorders, Language Masters, filmstrip projectors, controlled readers, movie projectors, record players, calculators, etc. We cannot take for granted that parents know how to operate these devices and, therefore, should provide for this learning in our training session.

5. Parents need to use, under actual or simulated conditions, materials that they will encounter in classrooms. If the training for use of the materials cannot occur under actual conditions, this use can be simulated by having parents teach other parents. One parent can be the teacher/helper while the other parent can role play a student. One of the advantages of peer teaching is that it can occur in the training session and permits supervision by the trainers. Of course, one of the disadvantages is that actual children are not used and parents do not have the "first" encounter with children.

6. The workshop training session should end with several processes which can contribute to the success of future training programs and the continued success of the volunteer program. These two processes are evaluation and feedback. Evaluation and feedback can occur either through a written questionnaire or through solicitation of oral responses from the participants. However, every effort should be made to gather feedback about the effectiveness and the satisfaction of the training session in order that improvements can be made and the needs of the participants met.

During the final training session, it is also possible to gather from trainees material which relates to their grade level preference, subject area preference, and background of experiences. Data of this nature make it easier for those who are in charge of assigning volunteers to specific classrooms and work stations to do so with an amount of sophistication that would not be possible otherwise.

## Advantages of Parent Involvement

There obviously are many advantages of parent involvement which occur to both people and programs. Some of these advantages can be anticipated by an examination of the goals and objectives of a parent volunteer program. Specific benefits will vary from program to program.

### *Making the Teacher More Efficient and Effective*

Teachers can benefit from the help parents provide to the school and classroom through aiding, making materials, working with small groups, etc. This help, if handled by a skillful teacher, can make the teacher more efficient and effective. In addition, parent involvement can relieve the teacher of many routine tasks. Consequently, the teacher can devote more time to working with individual children, observing, planning, and working with other parents. Remember, however, the *purpose* of parent involvement should not be to relieve the teacher of routine tasks.

## Benefits to Children

Children in any educational program can and do benefit from having social interaction with a wide variety of adults who bring to the educational setting diverse and rich cultural backgrounds, skills, and points of view. Indeed, this social interaction is important and necessary for the intellectual and social development of children. Opportunities for children to interact with adults can help them "decenter" from their egocentric point of view as they begin to encounter other ideas and realize that other people have points of view differing from their own. This social interaction also contributes to the development of mental operations, such as assimilation and accommodation which form the basis of developing intelligence. A child must have an opportunity to deal with people as well as things in order to develop intellectually and socially.

## Wide Variety of Parent Talent

Adults involved in educational settings can bring an incredible number, background, and range of skills into the classroom. This contribution is not possible when parents are "shut out" of programs as they frequently are. Think of the opportunities for storytelling, sewing, baking, cooking, and many other involvements that exist by taking advantage of the talents of adults in the community. Recently, I observed a day care center program in which the children were cooking chicken stew. They prepared, cooked, and, of course, heartily ate their finished product. This very meaningful learning experience took place under the guidance and direction of a mother of three children. From her own experiences and from information and knowledge obtained by taking education courses at a local college, she knew how to conduct the cooking session. While a less-experienced teacher might not have let children use knives, cooking utensils, electric cooking pots, etc., for fear of cutting, burning, or injuring themselves, this mother/teacher knew children could use them very competently if they were supervised properly and if precautions (such as placing the pot on a low table in a corner) were taken.

## Enhanced Self-image

The self-image of the parent is enhanced through involvement in early childhood programs. When good things happen to you, you feel good about yourself. Parents who are involved in programs and who are made to feel they are worthy and contributing members of the early childhood setting, also can feel good about themselves. As they are meaningfully involved, they begin to gain confidence in their ability to be contributing members of the educational process. This feeling of self-worth will also carry over into the home and other activities in which the parent is involved.

## Enhanced Interpersonal Relations

In many instances, the quality of the relationship between the parent and the child, the parent and the home, and the parent and his/her spouse is enhanced as a result of involvement in preschool programs. The parent attends more to the child because they now have more in common, with more to talk about and more to do. The parent's increased involvement with the child widens to include the other parent so that there is more interaction among all family members. As one mother said, "For the first time in my life, I'm really listening to my daughter. When she talks to me, I look at her and listen!"

## Parents Value Education

The attitude of the parent toward education and the educational system can be changed or altered through participation in educational programs. Whereas the parent previously may have held education in low esteem or may not have fully appreciated or understood the importance of education, by participating in programs, she can come to have an increased consciousness and different perspective about what education should and can do. This increased consciousness about the role of education can be transmitted to the child. In effect, as the parent's attitude toward education is changed and enhanced, this in turn encourages and promotes a more positive attitude in the child.

## Teachers Empathetic toward Family

Teachers, by having an opportunity to interact with parents, can begin to have a more empathetic attitude toward and appreciation for the role of parent. They can begin to see children from the parents' point of view. In addition, they begin to be aware of parent philosophies, points of view, and family objectives of and for education. They can gain a first-hand appreciation for individual differences in children and begin to understand parent and home influence. By working with parents, teachers see and appreciate the power of parents to shape and mold the lives of children.

## Problems Encountered in Working with Parents

It should not be assumed that the process of working with parents is without problems or pitfalls. Some of these problems can be anticipated and their effects minimized if we are aware of them. The following problems may or may not occur. The individual who works with parents should not seek to create problems; there will be enough problems sufficient to the situation without looking for or creating them.

## Classroom Discipline

One area in which teachers who use parent volunteers frequently have difficulty is discipline. Some teachers complain that parents don't or won't exercise discipline; others say parents discipline too much. Still other teachers say they don't want parents to discipline at all. Discipline is usually a problem where the parent volunteer is not included as a partner in the teaching and learning process. To expect volunteers to be in the classroom and not participate in the discipline and instructional process is unrealistic. A volunteer should not be asked to sit idly by while a child engages in disruptive or inappropriate behavior. While the teacher is responsible for setting the tone and direction of the discipline process, the volunteer can and should be involved, under the direction and supervision of the teacher. However, the teacher still has to advise the parent of her attitude toward discipline and will also have to provide the appropriate on-the-job training. Also, parents and teachers should be aware of any state or local district regulations which prohibit anyone but the classroom teacher from exercising the discipline function.

## Highly Educated Parents

In some socioeconomic areas where there is a high concentration of mothers who are college graduates, many of whom have teaching degrees, there can be a tendency on the part of these parents to feel that they know more than the school and/or teachers about what constitutes a good educational program. (Indeed, it may well be the case that they do know more than the teacher!) Quite often, what happens in these situations is that the teachers and/or school establish, either consciously or unconsciously, barriers to communication and participation by these well-educated and well-meaning parents. This strategy of noninvolvement usually leads to tension and friction between home and school. Noninvolvement can also lead to feelings of inadequacy on the part of the teacher who never knows if she is meeting the expectations parents have for her as a teacher or for the children she teaches. I don't mean to imply here that teaching and the educative process should be solely one of pleasing parents. However, parents do pay the bills for schooling, and it is important at least that the needs of society and the expectations of parents about the objectives of schooling should merge with the objectives of the school.

## Lack of Confidence

Quite the opposite situation to that discussed above and one that is frequently cited as a source of problems in effective parent involvement is the parents who feel that they don't have the knowledge or expertise to become involved in school programs. These feeling of inadequacy often are of such intensity that they create a barrier to participation so that these parents seldom, if ever, participate.

## Conflicts between Parent and Teacher

Occasionally, there may be a conscious or unconscious conflict between parent and teacher concerning what is best for the child. This conflict may tend to exasperate both parent and teacher when the parent is present in the program. However, a skillful teacher will anticipate such problems and avoid them by talking to the parent prior to her involvement about what the parent feels is best for the child. This is a problem that can be worked out by prior consultation.

## Parents as Teachers of Their Children

Should parents volunteer in classrooms in which their own children are present? Frequently this question is raised in regard to parent involvement. Many teachers object to parents in the same classroom with their children. Some teachers feel it is satisfactory to have parents in the same classroom as long as they don't (are not allowed to) work directly with their own children. Many parents are discouraged by teachers from working in classrooms where their children are present. There is nothing wrong with having parents involved with their own children in any class room. I feel the problem is one relating to teachers, rather than parents and children. Many teachers feel uncomfortable and inhibited with a parent watching while they teach and/or discipline the parent's child. This feeling of discomfort can be avoided by a conference and orientation session with the parent prior to her involvement.

The matter of whether or not the parent should work with her own child in the classroom is also a consideration which largely depends on the attitude and abilities of the parent. Some parents may not desire to work with their own children, while others may wish to do so. To others it may make no difference. Also, while in the beginning a parent may not want to work with her child, she may not mind once she has become acclimated to the classroom and the educational process. Other parents may begin to work with their children but find as they progress that they would rather not.

Rather than make an arbitrary and hard-and-fast rule, teachers and parents should not let the presence of the parents' children in the classroom interfere with or prohibit a meaningful classroom experience for everyone.

## Increased Contact between Home and School

One way to increase parent involvement is to increase the visability of the teacher and the amount of contact that the parent and teacher have with each other. As the contact and opportunities for interchange between parent and program increase, parents are more knowledgeable of programs and are more willing to participate. With the inclusion of a home visitor in a program, contact between program and family increases. This use of a home visitor represents a rather obvious and, in a sense, traditional way for increasing parent involvement. However, there are other equally effective ways.

### A Parent Meeting

The following schedule represents a format for a parent meeting that can be conducted in any type of parent involvement program, from a home-based approach to a public school orientation/information session.

10:00A.M.—Meeting begins, opportunity is provided for parents to talk with each other.

10:15—Business meeting.

10:45—Main topic of the meeting, for example:
1. A speaker on mental health.
2. Films and discussion on child development.
3. Panel discussions (including parents) of learning activities used in the home.
4. Nutrition workshop (This could include a demonstration by a home economist on cooking, canning, etc.).

5. Training for working in the classroom.

6. Explanation of school policies, procedures, regulations, etc.

12:00—Lunch/Snack, prepared and served by parents. This could include a covered dish brought by each parent, or a committee could buy lunch meats, etc., and have a delicatessen-type lunch. Other possibilities include having the lunch catered or going to a local restaurant. Children could join the parents for lunch or they could eat by themselves depending on needs and desires.

1:30—Several activities can occur.

1. Planning for future meetings.

2. Recreation— songs, games, etc., planned and conducted by parents.

3. Time for group interaction, conversation, etc.

2:30-3:00— Meeting ends.

1. Feedback about the meeting. This should include how the parents liked the meeting; what they liked best, least, etc.

2. Transportation is provided for parents to their homes when necessary.

Several significant things should occur if the parent meeting is to be successful:

1. Parents should help in the planning. This means parents will help determine the format and the specific activities which will occur.

2. The meeting should be well publicized. If people don't know about a meeting, how can they come?

3. Child care services should be provided. If parents can't find or afford child care services, they won't attend.

4. Car pools should be formed. Otherwise, parents won't attend if they can't drive, don't have a car, can't walk, and no public transportation is available or they can't afford to use it even if it is available.

5. If possible, a regular meeting date, for example, the third Friday of every month, should be scheduled. This helps parents plan on and around the meetings.

## Van Ride Classroom Extension

A program can make the transporting of children an extension of the classroom by having teachers, aides, and parents ride on the bus or van with children. This strategy can be used to conduct learning activities and can increase the opportunities for parent contact and involvement.

In the Erie, Pennsylvania, Head Start Program, the Head Start teaching team composed of a teacher, teaching assistant, and a teaching volunteer is responsible for providing the second adult (in addition to the driver) on the van which transports children to the center. The teaching team members take turns riding the van. A class of fifteen children from the same neighborhood are in the same class in the center and are transported together on the van. The teaching team member is the first person a child sees when picked up in the morning, and the parent, by taking her child to meet the bus, also has contact with the teaching team member and the classroom.

In this type of arrangement, the home in essence turns the child over to the classroom. Then, in the afternoon, the classroom turns the child back over to the parent, caregiver, or surrogate. This process allows staff to find common experiences among the children and provide for sharing these experiences in the classroom. In addition, teaching can be based on what was observed in the home or on information gathered from parents and children. Also, at the end of the day, events that occurred in the classroom can be reinforced or extended while traveling on the van. The classroom team member who is riding the van can personally communicate to the parent about any unusual or outstanding events that happened to the child or class.

In addition, special needs of the child and program announcements can be given on a first-hand basis to the parent. Specifically, this type of classroom extension does the following:

1. Encourages contact between the parent and the teaching team members.
2. Allows teaching team members to become familiar with the child's neighborhood and parents.
3. Permits the teaching team to monitor absences of the child and encourage attendance.
4. Permits the teaching team to share with the parents the child's achievements in an informal manner.
5. Provides the parent with another adult to talk with and share ideas.

## Involvement with Parents Outside of Classrooms

One method of parent involvement which is often overlooked is for teachers, principals, and all who desire parent support to *become involved with* parents outside of the classroom. School people want parents to become involved with them at school and at the center, but it seems that the simple idea of becoming involved with parents has been overlooked, ignored, or both. Educators have thought of becoming involved with parents in their homes but look upon this as a political and educational strategy, something to be accomplished within an educational or political context. Also, many educators involve parents in school programs and decision-making processes because federal or state guidelines for the monies they receive mandate that parents have to be involved.

What can be done in a more humanistic manner is to become involved with parents *in* the community at personal and social levels. Teachers should live where their students live, go to church where the families of their students worship, shop for their food in the same supermarkets, go to the same movie houses, etc. In essence, education should become involved in the community by being part of the community. This can also include becoming involved in community clubs, organizations, and activities.

This idea will upset many teachers who view such community involvement as an invasion of privacy and an infringment on their personal rights. Teacher unions will undoubtedly take exception with the idea that teachers should have to socially interact with families. But this is precisely the point. As long as we have teachers who have to be told to pursue this humanistic and very personal interaction, the parent involvement process will never really be as effective as it could be. What is needed are teachers who don't have to be told, forced, and legislated to become involved. What is needed are teachers who want to be involved because it is good and right and beneficial to families to do so.

However, on the other hand, there does appear to be a tendency for some school districts to legislate that their teachers live in the district in which they teach. At the present time, this tendency seems to be related to community residency and based more on economic considerations rather than on social ones. Why shouldn't teachers pay taxes to and spend their money in the school district which pays their salaries?

In many schools which make an honest effort at implementing open education, teachers soon discover that in order for them to maximize all the potential from the open education process, they must become involved with students, parents, and other teachers on a social level. By getting to know people better outside the educational institution, we can begin to provide better services for all their needs, including the educational ones within the institution.

## Home Visitations by Teachers

Frequently.the question is raised, Should early childhood teachers visit the homes of the children they teach? The answer to this question depends to a great extent on your philosophy and point of view. Some teachers would answer with an emphatic "No!" Others would answer, "Yes, but I don't have the time." or Yes, but only if you pay me." Others would complain that while it would be nice, it is not an essential priority and certainly is not related to the education of children in school.

The idea that parent involvement and the conditions of the home environment have nothing to do with the school life of the child seems to be precisely the problem. Also, the home life of parents and children traditionally has not been the concern of teachers of schools of education who train teachers.

Twenty or thirty years ago, home visits, if only to determine the educational interests of the child, were more common than they are today. However, it seems as though teachers and other professional educators have become too sophisticated to deal with the essentials of education.

Home visits should be an integral part of the educative process. This means that every teacher should visit the home of every child at least once a year. This strategy, of course, depends upon a number of interrelated factors, some of which are the financial resources available to the district and the number of students who are to be visited.

Some programs have sought to deal with the concern for home visitation by using parents as home visitors or by hiring individuals who visit in the home and also teach in the classroom. The Florida Parent Education Follow Through Program conducted by the University of Florida uses parents as home visitors.[1] These parents are also aides in the classroom and help teach the children in whose homes they visit.

In certain other programs such as day care and Head Start, it is not uncommon to have such personnel as the social service worker and/or the parent coordinator visit in the homes and report their findings to the classroom teachers. Likewise, when the teacher has a problem, concern, or need for parent information, this is relayed to

---

[1]Ira J. Gordon et al., "The Florida Parent Education Follow Through Program" (Gainesville, Fla.: Institute for Development of Human Resources, University of Florida, January 1974).

the social service worker or other person who makes the visit. This procedure, while better than no procedure at all, is not as satisfactory as having the teacher of the child make the home visit.

*Visitation before the School Year.*   One strategy that has been employed rather successfully by some school districts is to hire teachers for two extra weeks at the beginning of the school year for purposes of home visitation. In this situation then, the full time of the teacher is devoted to visiting in the families of those children she will teach during the coming year. During the visit, valuable information about the child and her family can be gathered and ascertained. Some of this information can include the following:

1. Health history.
2. Interests of the child.
3. Educational expectations of the parent for the child.
4. Educational support systems available in the home, for example, books, places to study, etc.
5. Attitude of the parent toward education and school.
6. Parental support of the child in the educative process, for example, encouragement to do well.
7. Interests and abilities of the parents.
8. Environmental conditions which would support and/or hinder school achievement. (For example, I taught a seven-year-old boy who always took a morning nap. On a home visit, I discovered his bed was on the fold-out living room couch. The child couldn't go to bed until his parents were done watching the late movie on television. I became more tolerant of and provided more suitable conditions for his morning nap.)
9. Desire of the parent to become involved in and with the school.
10. Attitude of the child toward schooling.

At the same time, the initial home visit can offer the teacher an opportunity to relate valuable and supportive information about the school and her classroom to the parents. Some of this information can include these points:

1. Her desire for the child to do well in school.
2. Encouragement and support for the parents to take part in the school and classroom programs.
3. Suggestions (if asked for and if appropriate) for helping the child learn.
4. A brief description of some of the curricula in which the child will be involved, for example, writing with examples, reading with samples of the kind of books children will be reading, etc.
5. Inform parents about school events, projects, meetings, etc.

*Visitation during the School Year.*   When teachers make visits to children's homes during the school year, much of the same kind of information can be gathered as that which was discussed above. However, because the teacher now has had an opportunity to teach and interact with the child, the focus of the visit can shift to include that which the child has achieved and will achieve based on the teacher's assessment of her learning style and achievement expectations.

Information that the teacher can gather during a school-year home visit should include these things:

1. How happy and satisfied the parents are with the following:
   a. The program of the school.
   b. The program and methods of the classroom teacher.
   c. The progress of the child.

2. Specific concerns the parents have about the child's achievement.

3. Special environmental factors which are not supportive of the child's educational and social achievement. I recently observed an interesting example in a second grade classroom. The teacher had assigned the children homework in mathematics. She collected the homework from all the children except one who did not have it done. When the teacher asked the child why he didn't have his homework finished, he replied, "Because we went to visit friends last night." The teacher's response was to have the child stay in from recess and miss gym class in order to do the homework. How much better would it have been had the teacher known the life style of the family so it could be ascertained if they were supportive or not (or aware) of the child's homework. A child whose family spends its evenings outside the home may never have the opportunity, time, or encouragement to do homework! Should he be penalized in school because of this? I think not.

4. How supportive the parents are continuing to be of the child's school program.

5. The parents' continued or newly emerged interest in becoming involved in the school.

At the same time, now that the teacher is knowledgeable of the child he or she can provide the parent with a different type of information not possible to provide before:

1. Information about experiences and achievements which the child has in her day-to-day school life. The continued emphasis in this sharing of information should be on the positive. The teacher should relate to the parent what the child can do, not necessarily what she cannot do. Also, remember that the parent doesn't see the child for six or more hours of the day and, as such, might not be aware of her new achievements and abilities.

2. Learning goals that the teacher has for the child. These goals are based primarily on the past achievement of the child and the teacher's knowledge of her learning abilities.

One important thing to remember is that both the parent and the teacher have valuable information about the child. This information relates to the child's abilities, interests, likes, dislikes, needs, etc. It must be shared in a positive manner in such a way that the best interests of the child can be served. Through information sharing, a better program for the child can be developed and provided.

*Uses of Information.* Information gained during the home visit can enable the teacher to do the following:

1. Design specific ways for getting the parent involved in the classroom program; for example, an unemployed father can come to school and teach children the names for various tools he uses. A mother who is adept at needlework can help the young children sew puppets and/or the costumes for a play they are going to perform.

2. Incorporate the interests of the child into the curriculum of the classroom; for example, a doll collection could be used to learn about and teach body parts, health habits, etc.

3. Design strategies for supporting the educative process in the home such as sending home with the child certain books that would be of interest to the parent as a means of fostering parent interest in books and learnings.

## Getting to Know Parents

In working with parents and in efforts to communicate and involve parents, there is a tendency to overlook the person. By this, I mean we tend to forget that parents are human and, as such, have feelings, emotions, desires, and problems and are intelligent. Unfortunately we think of the parent as Karen's mother, but not as a person in her own right. It certainly would help in the communication process if we knew as much about the parent as possible. Such helpful information would include interests, hobbies, job occupation, and family problems, all of which can form a sincere basis for communication, interaction, understanding, and help.

## Communicating with Parents

When communicating with parents at the home, center, or school, there are several things which must be kept in mind:

1. Every effort should be made to talk on the level of the parent. This does not mean that you talk down to or are patronizing to the parent. What it does mean is that you employ every effort to use words, phrases, and explanations that the parent understands and is familiar with. The communicator should remember the following:

   a. Don't use jargon and/or words that the parent cannot understand. Teachers are notorious for using jargon. Remember, it is much easier to say to the parents that you would like to ask them some questions that will help you help the child learn than it is to say that you want to perform a comprehensive diagnostic evaluation which will result in strategies which can be implemented to achieve the highest possible utilization of the child's abilities.

   b. Don't use complicated explanations with the parent. Parents really don't want long, drawn-out, involved explanations. Communicators should make every effort to simplify all their explanations.

   c. Use a natural way of communicating with parents. There is nothing worse than someone who is trying to be "with it." This style of talking is often evidenced by people who try to use slang and/or accent of the parents when it is inappropriate to do so. The only result is a projection of phoniness which leads to suspicion and lack of confidence on the part of the parent and all who are involved.

2. Accentuate the positive. Just as you don't like to constantly hear negative things or be constantly reminded about problems, neither does the parent. You should make every effort to show and tell the parent those things which the child is doing well. Communicating in this manner does not mean that you never talk to parents about their child's problems. Quite the contrary; it is how you deal with the problems that is important. When you deal with the problems of children, you put them in the proper perspective: what the child is able to do, what the goals and purposes of the learning program are, what specific skill or concept you are trying to get the child to learn, what problems the child is having in achieving. Most important of all should be a discussion of what you plan to do to help the child achieve and what specific role the parent can have in the goals of achievement. So often when we talk with parents about problems that children have, no positive plan of action is outlined. This is unfortunate because it is so negative and does not lead to positive results. A positive plan of action is absolutely necessary.

3. Never leave the parent with a sense of hopelessness or with a sense of frustration which can result from their not knowing what you are doing or what they are to do. This idea is really part of the positive plan of action. Every communication with parents should end on a positive note so that all involved know what can be done and how to do it.

*Conferences with parents provide a basis for sharing information, cooperative planning, and goal setting.*

## Parent-Teacher Conferences

An important part of any communication process with parents is the parent-teacher conference. In many early childhood programs, it is the only way parents have for receiving information about and knowledge of their children's progress. In conducting parent-teacher conferences, several factors should be considered:

1. Make every effort to make the parent feel relaxed, comfortable, and wanted. Remember, the school is teacher territory, and many parents feel uncomfortable and/or unwanted. For this reason, many parent-teacher conferences are held on neutral territory (a community center) or in the parent's home.

2. Communicate with parents on their level. Don't use a lot of jargon.

3. Accentuate the positive. Tell parents what things their children are able to do.

4. Be ready to provide specific suggestions for specific ways in which parents can help their children. Most parents want to do what is best for their children, but they don't know what to do.

The following simulated conference is written in order to provide ideas of and a feeling for what a parent-teacher conference can be like. It should not be interpreted as a model to be slavishly followed. What it can be used for is a basis for critiquing and a background against which you can develop your own conference format.

## A Parent-Teacher Conference

Parent-teacher conferences are an important part of this school's program, and teachers are provided time to have conferences when the parents are available. Miss Irwin, a first grade teacher, has spent two weeks preparing the room and materials for a conference. She has encouraged each child to prepare an art or science project to be displayed around the room for the parents' viewing. She and the children have also made a special bulletin board welcoming the parents to their room. Miss Irwin has put together folders for each child with examples of the work each has done in class. These have been placed on their desks along with name tags which will help parents locate their child's "home" area. The room is clean and well organized. These preparations have not been done just to make the room attractive but mainly to have materials and work samples for parents to see. They form a basis for discussion and provide parents with materials to examine if they arrive early for the conference. The five learning centers will also be points of discussion.

Miss Irwin is prepared for the specific topics she will talk about to each parent. She knows her children well, both the good and negative qualities they exhibit in class. In all conferences with all parents, she plans to accentuate the positive and not dwell on problem areas. She plans to greet each parent warmly and does not intend to immediately start discussing the child. She wants to take a few minutes so she can get to know each parent; their hopes and dreams for their children; for example, what kind of activities they like to see their children participate in, how much education they will encourage their children to get, etc.; problems existing between parent and child in the home; things parents and child do together; interests, hobbies, and responsibilities of the child; how and for what reasons the parent disciplines the child; does the parent view the child as good, bad, mischievious, etc. Knowing some of this information helps Miss Irwin in discussing the child's achievements with the parent.

Miss Irwin's first conference is with Kristen's mother, Mrs. Van Buren. Kristen is a very warm child and possesses many humane qualities. She is the first child to befriend any new student in the class. Although Kristen is a very warm and friendly individual, she is not a "scholar." She works very hard and tries her best but, even so, it still far behind the achievement level of most of the other children in her class. Although Miss Irwin views each of her children as individuals and tries not to compare their work, she realizes this can be a problem area for a parent. So often parents judge their child on how they compare with their peers and not how they're achieving as an individual. She wants to make Mrs. Van Buren understand that Kristen is doing well at her own level. Kristen does do exceptional work in art, and Miss Irwin continually reinforces this area. Miss Irwin hopes that by explaining Kristen's abilities in art and her qualities as an individual to Mrs. Van Buren, she can establish a positive foundation for the conference before dealing with Kristen's academic problems.

If Miss Irwin would begin the parent-teacher conference with, "Kristen isn't reading with the rest of the group, she can't add any higher than 3 + 2, and she can barely write her full name," Mrs. Van Buren's reaction would be embarrassment, inadequacy, frustration, helplessness, anger, and hopelessness. This would be a natural reaction for any parent who is told negative things about her child.

Mrs. Van Buren arrives. Both teacher and parent introduce themselves. They begin to walk around the room looking at the children's projects and also use this time to get acquainted. Mrs. Van Buren is especially pleased with the clay models that Kristen has made. Miss Irwin takes this cue and begins her conference by telling Mrs. Van Buren Kristen's abilities in art modeling and painting. She also talks about Kristen as a person, her warm qualities as an individual. She tells Mrs. Van Buren how hard Kristen does work and how she never stops trying. Miss Irwin also describes how Kristen is always asking questions and tries to do as much as she can at her own pace. Miss Irwin is very enthusiastic about Kristen's progress and feels that Kristen will continue progressing at her own pace. She explains how Kristen has difficulty in reading and how both she and Kristen decided to go back a level in her reader. Since they did this, Kristen is doing much better in her reading skills. Both she and Kristen are pleased with the progress they are making in this area.

Although Miss Irwin tells Mrs. Van Buren about Kristen's difficulties, she speaks with much hope. She explains to Mrs. Van Buren how both she and Kristen have been working together on these areas and how progress is definitely being made. She makes Mrs. Van Buren feel relaxed and confident in Kristen's progress. She knows of her daughter's academic problem but realizes that Kristen is working hard and is doing well at her own pace. This is a much better approach than that of saying what can't be done. In addition, it can help relieve feelings of self-recrimination on the part of the parent. Mrs. Van Buren thanks Miss Irwin for her time and her help and then leaves. The next conference begins.

## Conference Follow-up

In a very real sense, the parent-teacher conference is only as good as the follow-up and follow-through that occur after the conference. Too often, a conference is a one-shot deal and is thought of as something which has to be conducted and endured, and, once accomplished, is to be forgotten. A conference must be followed up. A good way to anticipate this follow-up is to ask the parent for a definite time for the next conference as you are concluding the current one.

While another conference as a follow-up is the best method of solidifying gains and extending support, it is not the only way of following through. Other acceptable means are through telephone calls, written reports, notes sent with children, brief visits to the home, etc. While these types of contacts may appear casual, they should not be conducted in a casual manner. They should be planned for and conducted in as serious a manner as any regular parent-teacher conference.

Here are some advantages to parent-teacher conference follow-up:

1. The parents get the impression that you care and are genuinely concerned about their children.

2. Clarification of problems, issues, advice, directions given, etc., are possible.

3. It encourages parents and children to continue to do their best.

4. It offers further opportunities to extend classroom learnings to the home.

5. Programs that were initiated for helping parents and child can be extended, and new plans can be formulated.

There are also certain things which parents can and should do in order to prepare for a conference with the teacher. Many of the following are not only necessary for a parent to be well prepared, they are also rights of parents under existing federal laws.

1. Request a time and place for a conference that is convenient to you as well as the school. A conference does not always have to be held only when the school and/or teacher says it can be held.

2. Request that the conference be held in your language. For example, if your primary language is Spanish and you don't understand English well, ask that some-one be there to translate. If this is not possible, take someone with you who can help.

3. Insist that the teacher explain the progress and achievement of your child in terms you can understand. If you don't understand what the teacher is saying, don't be afraid to say so.

4. Show your concern and desire for helping your child by expressing your willing-ness to help in whatever ways you can.

5. Express a desire to have the teacher develop a plan of action for helping your child learn. In this regard, don't accept all the blame for your child's lack of achievement. Insist that the school also accept some responsibility for learning and achievement.

6. Prepare a list of things you want to talk to the teacher about. There is no reason why the conference agenda should be determined entirely by the teacher. If possible, you should tell the teacher ahead of time about some of the things you wish to discuss.

7. Extend to the teacher the common courtesies you would expect to be extended to you. Some of these are being punctual for the conference, thanking the teacher for help, and leaving promptly when the conference is through.

## What Are Parents to Do?

Rearing children is a tough, demanding, time-consuming, energy-sapping, perplexing, and, yes, joyful kind of experience. However, the complexities, the frustrations, the uncertainties of child rearing make it a lonely kind of business. Quite often when faced with problems and a situation which requires action of some kind, the parent does not know what to do. The typical situation is one in which Mom waits until Dad comes home from work to talk it over with him. After a long and exhausting day at the office, he is not always the best advisor for decision making. More importantly, as we have seen in many of today's homes, there is quite often an absence of this dad for decision making. For many people within the context of home and the family, there is no help available. Faced with this dilemma of helplessness, of frustration in the decision-making process, what is the parent to do?

### *Seeking Help*

*From Friends and Relatives.* The quite obvious, yet not so easily accomplished, answer is to seek and to find help. Help can be sought from friends, neighbors, and relatives about the uncertainties and perplexities of many child-rearing and parenting problems. While these people can oftentimes be sources of support and information, they can also be sources of misinformation and noninformation. When help is sought from these sources, caution should be exercised since they may not always have or offer the best advice available.

*From Agencies.* A second thing one can do is to seek help from agencies that already exist to provide services in parenting and child rearing. While many of these agencies are set up to deal with specific problems, such as handicapping conditions; nevertheless, they can provide information about where to go if they cannot deal with a problem. One good resource tool to use in trying to find help is the telephone directory. By calling some of the listed agencies, parents will be referred to other agencies until one is found which offers the appropriate service.

*From the Public Schools.* Parents can also go to the public schools for help. Simply because the schools identify a problem or create a problem does not mean that they should be free from or excused from having a part in determining the solution and the implementation of that solution. Unfortunately, many schools, administrators, and teachers are very content to identify problems and call them to the parents' attention, but then expect the parents to act fully on their own in seeking to solve the problem. (This is often true in the case of physically and mentally handicapping problems.) For example, if the school should have problems disciplining a child, they do one of two things. They either punish the child inappropriately, i.e., corporal punishment, or they notify the parents (usually by a written communication) that their child is not performing as she should. They then expect the parents to solve the problem. It is amazing how schools expect parents to exercise at long range control over the child while she is in school. While much of the child's attitude toward school is a product of the parents' attitude toward school, it is also true that the parents' attitude toward school is a result of experiences they have had with the current school or other schools while they were young. It is equally true that the attitude the child has concerning the school is based upon the feedback she gets from

**FIGURE 10** Public Service Agencies

The following agencies can be used to help provide information and services for children, parents, and families:

Local hospitals:
  county
  private
  osteopathic
  university
  children's
Children's Cardiac Clinic
Association for Retarded
    Children/Citizens
Public Health Clinic
Council for Exceptional Children
County Board of Assistance
Children's Services
Department of Health
Mental Health and Retardation
    Association
American Red Cross
Ambulance and Inhalator Service
Dental Emergency Service
Poison Control and Treatment Service
Easter Seal Society
March of Dimes
Cancer Foundation
Kidney Foundation
Center for the Blind
Family Medicine Center
Social Security Administration
Leukemia Society of America, Inc.
Salvation Army
Welfare Office

Community Action Center or Agency,
    providing such services as:
  Parenting Programs
  Day Care/Head Start Programs
  Health Care Services
  Protective Agency
  Foster Parent Program
  Adoption Service
  Group Home Care
Your Local School, Intermediate Unit,
    School District, College and Uni-
    versity:   Services include
  special education,
  speech and hearing screening and re-
    medial programs,
  referral service for information con-
    cerning agencies and services,
  day care,
  nursery school and kindergarten,
  psychological testing,
  programs for handicapped children
Children's Service Center:
  Foster parent and adoption agencies
Children's Shelter Center—half-way
    home
Family Crisis Intervention Programs
Christian Service for Children
Family Counseling Services
State Education Association
Family and Child Service Centers
Childbirth Education Association

the school, teachers, and administrators. Therefore, the schools cannot be held blameless for the attitudes parents, families, and children have toward them. It seems that the schools should be held accountable for helping parents arrive at just, honest, equitable, and humane approaches to problems children have while they are under the care of the school. Therefore, parents should not hesitate to seek help from the schools.

In seeking help from the schools, parents will sometimes encounter the attitude that if the child isn't learning what is being taught, either she is dumb or is not extending the effort to learn. This attitude toward students at any educational level is indefensible. The teacher should feel that if the child is not learning, then one of three conditions must be at fault: (1) the instructional process is so bad that the child can't learn; (2) what is being taught to the child is inappropriate to her level of achievement or functioning; or (3) environmental conditions are such that the child does not have the basis for learning. Parents will have to force teachers to accept responsibility and accountability for developing teaching-learning strategies which will help the child learn. This, of course, is not always easy.

*From Organizations.*    One thing parents can do is to join an organization or group in order to find the help they need. There are many benefits to be derived from having other people to talk with and interact with and from having other people available to provide strength, sustenance, and support. By joining a group, by being able to talk with other people, parents soon come to realize that other people have the same hopes and desires for a good education for their children. They also realize that other parents have many of the same problems they have. Consequently, parents begin to feel that their problems are not unique. They realize that there is not something wrong with them because their child has a problem relating to learning or the school.

A group experience can also help parents realize they are not powerless; within groups it is possible to exert pressure on teachers and schools. While one parent working alone may not have much impact on the system, change can occur through a group process. Parents, by coming together in groups, by organizing, by sharing the talents that they have, can exercise considerable control and can have an impact on the system.

I am not advocating here that parents form groups or join groups in order to tear the system apart. What needs to be done is for parents to join together so that they can "radicalize" the system. By radicalizing the system, I mean changing the system so that it serves the best needs and interests of children and parents. Schools are for children, not for teachers. Schools are places where children should learn joyfully and well. They are not places of administrative convenience or where people find employment.

*From Parent-Teacher Associations.*    Another source of help can be the local parent-teacher association (PTA). Working through this local association, parents can take advantage of the organization's rapport with the schools and of the programs that are available. Parents can also take advantage of many opportunities that this organization provides for contact with teachers and administrators. The effectiveness of the local PTA, of course, depends upon the involvement that is provided to the organization by the schools. In some cases, schools effectively control PTA's and their functions by the way in which they provide opportunities for meetings, facilities, etc. Therefore, while some PTA's may be strong, others may be weak depending upon their past relationship with the schools and the amount of involvement they have from parents and teachers. It must be recognized that teachers themselves have not always been willing to provide the time and input necessary to make a parent-teacher organization a dynamic and effective one.

*From the NCCE.*    Another organization which an individual or a parent's group can join is the National Committee for Citizens in Education. This agency, formed in 1973 as the successor to the National Committee for Support of the Public Schools, has two broad-based objectives:

> 1.  To provide our membership with intelligible, jargon-free information about current issues in public education through brochures, handbooks, and a newspaper.
> 2.  To provide member organizations and individuals with training and leadership skills and other confident-building techniques which the local group feel are important in their work with local school systems.[2]

This committee seeks to actualize and encourage citizen involvement at the local level by providing citizens with the training they need to help them deal in whatever way is necessary with the educational system. Training is given through a series of citizens' training institutes held in various places throughout the United States. In addition, a field staff organization, supported by the committee, helps members who have received training put into practice the things they have learned. The committee also operates a national hotline. This toll free number, 800-NET-WORK, can be called in order to get information and help in dealing with problems as they relate to individual children or to schools in general. NCCE also helps promote educational change by becoming involved in court proceedings.

Supported by individual memberships and memberships from organizations such as parent groups, PTA's, etc., as well as grants from foundations and corporations, the NCCE seeks to encourage citizen involvement at all levels of the educational process. It hopes to become to the area of education what Common Cause is at the political and governmental area. More information can be secured by writing the National Committee for Citizens in Education, Columbia, Maryland 21044.

*From the NARC.*    Another organization which has done a great deal to help both parents and their children is the National Association for Retarded Citizens (NARC). This national organization provides services on behalf of handicapped citizens. However, NARC was originally founded in order to provide services to children and adults where services were not provided, particularly in the areas of preschool education and sheltered workshops. While the national organization and most state programs currently act in an advocacy capacity, many local programs still provide direct services to parents and children. (By *advocacy capacity,* I mean lobbying for legislation, publishing materials on how to form parent groups, or filing briefs for legal proceedings, etc.) Individuals interested in finding out more information about NARC can write to National Association for Retarded Citizens, 2709 Avenue E. East, P.O. Box 6109, Arlington, Texas 76011.

*By Starting a Parent Group.*    When there are no local and/or national organizations for an individual to join or if the individual feels that these organizations are not meeting needs in specific situations, then another alternative open to parents is to form their own parent group. Of course, this action does take initiative, assertiveness, and some organizational ability. However, there already exist organizations in a community that can help individuals develop a parent group. For example, local

---

[2]National Committee for Citizens in Education, *Case Statement* (Columbia, Md.: NCCE, January 1977), p. 1.

branches of the American Association of University Women and others usually have subgroups which meet for purposes of dealing with specific topics. These local study groups can be used as a basis for the development of parent groups.

Usually one of the first things that is necessary in developing a parent group is to determine specifically why you want to form a group. This process is important because you must be able to tell other people about the nature and purpose of the organization. Oftentimes, people feel a need for an organization but are unclear what they want that organization to achieve.

A second step would be to contact other people who you feel have and share similar concerns and problems. Ways to accomplish this contact are ads in a newspaper, notices on bulletin boards in public places, word of mouth, door-to-door campaigns, telephone solicitation, etc.

A third procedure is to convene a meeting of a group in which a discussion of the organization's goals and objectives are outlined. While it is important that these goals and objectives be written, an organization should not become bogged down in writing, nor should it become preoccupied with the creation and development of a constitution. While constitutions for organizations are in many ways necessary, it is not always of immediate concern to develop these at the initial meeting. The initial meeting should be reserved for action and for the development of plans to do what it is the committee was organized to do. Such things as constitutions, bylaws, etc., if deemed necessary and appropriate by the group, can come later. During the first several meetings of a committee, however, efforts should be made to identify and, if necessary, elect leaders. In this way, the group can have the benefit of leadership which is necessary for any successful venture.

The next thing the parent group should do is develop plans for dealing with the problems for which it was organized. Of course, what plan the parent group develops will depend upon the specific problems it must deal with.

The effectiveness of any parent group will depend somewhat upon how willing other professionals are to work with the group. If a parent group can get lawyers, social workers, educators, civil rights advocates, etc., involved in its cause, the chance for success is enhanced. In addition, it helps if a group has a good cause and can elicit the support of the general public in that cause. Public support, opinion, and pressure are key ingredients in the success of any endeavor. Parent group leaders should make every effort to seek and secure such support.

## Developing Good Parent-School Relationships

The following outline reviews some of the ways discussed in this chapter that can be utilized to involve parents in early childhood and school programs:

1. Communications with the home
   a. Letters
      (1) Informal by teachers or other parents
      (2) Monthly newsletters
      (3) Letters to parents by children

    b. Achievement reports. These are not the same as a report card, but are minireports to parents on a daily, weekly, or monthly basis about what their child is able to do.

    c. Television. Spot announcement on TV especially where there is a Public Television Network and/or a community service channel.

    d. Telephone. Teachers can use the phone on an informal basis to inquire about the child's health or invite the parent to help. Also, some agencies utilize a twenty-four-hour answering service which provides messages about school events, lunch menus, etc.

    e. Student progress reports and follow-up reports

2. Classroom visiting programs. An organized program of encouragement for parents to come to the early childhood program and school on an informal basis and visit with the teacher and children should be established by every agency.

3. Programs of parent involvement. Parents can be utilized as volunteers and/or paid aides in the classroom.

4. Home visits

    a. By teachers to the homes of children

    b. By groups of children to children's homes

5. Classroom observation. A planned program during which parents are involved in:

    a. The observation of the classroom in general

    b. The observation of the learning activities for children

6. Parent-teacher conferences

    a. These conferences can be held before or after school, while the parent picks up or delivers the child, etc.

    b. Conferences can and should be on a regular or scheduled basis.

7. Programs to help parents help students learn at home

    a. Such programs can provide tips on how to help with homework

    b. Sessions can be conducted which help parents learn the content and knowledge they need to help their children

8. Referral services. Referrals can be used very effectively by schools to involve parents in already existing services. This process doesn't require additional outlay of time or money.

    a. Referring parents directly to an agency which will help parents get more welfare aid

    b. Providing parents with information about where they can get help, for example, Crippled Children's Society, Easter Seal Program, local department of health, etc.

9. Specific strategies for getting parents to work with children. Suggestions can be made to parents which will encourage them to help their children at home. These strategies could include:

    a. Establish specific times for study

    b. Provide parents with specific directions for helping their children

    c. Give each child something to do which the parent has to help with

10. Parent group meetings on a regular basis. These meetings can deal with a continuing series of the same topic such as What Makes a Good Parent? or How to Help Your Child Learn at Home?

11. Materials center. This center is similar to a library where parents can borrow books, toys, films, filmstrips, tape recorders, filmstrip projectors, pamphlets, etc.

12. Programs which utilize guest speakers. These special programs can be arranged on the basis of parent need and speaker availability. Many of the speakers could be people already employed in the school district such as speech therapist, school psychologist, etc. A speaker could also be someone who is available in the community such as a professor of pediatrics from a local medical school.

13. Parent Committees. Parent committees can be established to help with a wide variety of school processes. For example, parent committees can be used to:

    a. Help advise about report cards, transportation problems, testing programs, etc.

    b. Organize and conduct specific activities such as field trips, fund raising events, etc.

14. Dissemination of information relating to parents. The teacher and/or school can send home material related to child-rearing/education practices. This information can be secured from federal, state, and local sources. Also, the teacher can develop her own materials.

The above is not meant to be an exhaustive or comprehensive list. It represents a sample of some of the parent involvement strategies that can be used. The number and kind that are ultimately implemented are limited only by the imagination, creativity, and resourcefulness of parents and educators working as a team for the benefit of parent, child, and family.

## Qualities of an Effective Parent/School Involvement Program

In trying to assess or develop an effective program of home/school relationships and involvement, you will find it helpful to keep in mind some of the more important features which these programs should possess. These features are reviewed in the following:

1. The program should be conducted for the benefit of the children and families. Program personnel have to decide where the focus will be: primarily on the child, primarily on the parent, or an equal emphasis on both, etc. A program should not exist primarily for the benefit of teachers.

2. A good program should involve all parents, at whatever level they are willing and able to become involved. The young mother of twenty-three who has four children has to be involved differently from the professional woman of thirty with only one child.

3. Family attitudes, values, and culture must be taken into consideration. Simply because the values and attitudes of the parents differ from those of the school does not mean they are wrong, bad, or should not make a difference.

4. The purpose of any parent involvement program should be explained to all concerned. Such questions as the following should be asked:

    a. What is the purpose of the program?

    b. Why is the program being conducted?

    c. How is it relevant to parents and children?

5. Meetings should be held when parents can attend. Don't hold a meeting at a time when parents can't attend and then complain that nobody comes. Quite often meetings are held during working hours when parents who work can't attend.

6. Make an honest effort to inform all parents about the opportunities for their involvement.

If any agency of any kind is honest and sincere in its desire for and efforts toward parent involvement, then that involvement will occur. It is when agencies are insincere in their efforts that parent involvement does not occur. Parent involvement can better people's lives. We should do everything we can to assist in the process.

## Bibliography

Gordon, Ira J. et al. "The Florida Parent Education Follow Through Program." Gainesville, Fla.: Institute for Development of Human Resources, University of Florida. January 1974.

National Committee for Citizens in Education. *Case Statement.* Columbia, Md.: NCCE, January 1977.

## Further Reading and Study

Arnold, Arnold. *Teaching Your Child to Learn: From Birth to School Age.* Englewood Cliffs, N.J.: Prentice-Hall, Inc., 1971.

Deals with complexities of modern life and how an effective parent can use these difficulties to their advantage. Discusses developmental stages of growth and how learning experiences are more valuable when they grow out of spontaneous, natural events. Views television as a worthwhile and stimulating educational aid as a means of establishing positive parent-child interaction.

Brock, Henry C., III. *Parent Volunteer Programs in Early Childhood Education.* Hamden, Conn.: Shoe String Press, 1976.

Discusses a three-phase program format of design, implementation and evaluation for using parents in the classroom. A practical resource guide for initiating or strengthening a parent-volunteer program. Deals with proven successful methods of integrating parents into scheduled learning situations in the school. Discusses background information such as pertinent research, legal implications, orientations, training, and screening. Makes a strong case for the use of parents in benefitting and enhancing the education process.

Fisher, Seymour, and Fischer, Rhoda L. *What We Really Know about Child Rearing*. New York: Basic Books, Inc., 1976.

Assembles in a usable form a body of knowledge concerning practical guidelines to child rearing and a way to apply this knowledge to everyday situations. Discusses children's emotional and cognitive needs as well as their rapidly increasing physical growth. Examines the modern day dilemma of children left alone without care. Explores the topic of parenting from the viewpoint of an occupation requiring skill and hard work.

Lamb, Michael. *The Role of the Father in Child Development*. New York: John Wiley and Sons, 1976.

Covers a range of issues which attempt to establish and more clearly define the role of the father in child development. Each chapter deals with different topics. The auther does not play down the role of the mother but views fathers as sharing positions of parenting with females. Also reviews research pertinent to contributions made by fathers to the socialization process of children.

Lynn, David B. *The Father: His Role in Child Development*. Monterey, Calif: Brooks/Cole Publishing Co., 1974.

Takes a historical and cultural look at the father's role in child development. Examines role of male in animals, early man, and man in other countries. Compares cultural experiments such as the Israeli Kibbutz and describes father roles as found in various socioeconomic groups. Explores reality of the absent father-child interaction.

Maddox, Brenda. *The Half-Parent*. New York: M. Evans and Co., 1975.

Living with other people's children is the basis for this personal and humorous narrative. Deals with problems and tensions of a step-parent and describes from first-hand experiences the often perplexing step-parenting role. Presents the step-parent's point of view and examines the lack of information on the subject.

Pickarts, Evelyn, and Fargo, Jean. *Parent Education: Toward Parental Competence*. New York: Appleton-Century-Crofts, 1971.

This book explores the need for parent education and focuses on content and methodology for such a program. Examines the importance of programs available and assesses goals and strengths. Assumes previous knowledge of child development and presents viewpoint of parenting as a "becoming" process. Relates authors' experiences in a parent-child program.

Retting, Edward B. *ABCs for Parents*. Van Nuys, Calif.: Associates for Behavior Change, 1973.

Title refers to Antecedents-Behaviors-Consequences. Designed in a progammed instruction format dealing with a behavioral modification approach to learning. Asks the reader to use specific processes to change their own behavior and that of their children. States that parents are in a better position to deal with problems than professionals. This text strives to perfect parental techniques in modifying behavior. Stresses the development of behaviors that are measurable. Describes sample cases and gives tests to parents. Provides guidelines for developing future intervention programs.

# *Activities*

1. Write a letter to a parent inviting her to your first grade classroom for a conference. Her child, who is seven, has had difficulty adjusting during the first two weeks of the new school year.

2. Make arrangements with a local school district to be present during a parent-teacher conference. Discuss with the teacher, prior to the visit, her objectives and procedures that will be used. Following the conference, have a debriefing session with the teacher to assess the success of the conference.

3. Simulate with your classmates a parent-teacher conference. Establish objectives and procedures for the visit. Analyze this conference. A good method for analyzing this simulation is through videotaping the visit.

4. Recall from your school experiences instances of parent-teacher conferences, involvement, etc. What particular incidents have had a positive or negative effect on you?

5. Make a list of the various ways teachers communicate pupils' progress to parents.
   a. What do you think are the most effective ways? Least effective?
   b. What specific methods do you plan to use?

6. You are responsible for publicizing a parent meeting relating to ways in which the school plans to involve parents. Describe the methods and techniques you would use in publicizing the meeting.

7. What would be the essential similarities and differences among a home visitation program conducted by a preschool program, by a federal agency, and by a public school primary program.

8. Why are the courts reluctant to take a child away from the family and/or natural parents?
   a. Interview a juvenile court judge to help determine your answer.

9. You have just been appointed the program director for a parent involvement program in grade one. Write objectives for such a program. Develop specific activities for involving parents in the classroom. What specific methods would you use to train parents? What specific classroom activities would you have parents become involved with?

10. How would a parent-home involvement program conducted by a public school be similar to or different from one conducted by a social service agency?

11. Write (rewrite) your philosophy of education. Explain it to a parent. What problems did you encounter in explaining it? In what specific ways did the parent agree/disagree with your philosophy?

12. Would you, as a parent, consent to have corporal punishment administered to your child? Why? Why not?

13. Cite instances in which corporal punishment was detrimental to the physical and/or emotional well-being of a child.

# Parent Involvement with Handicapped Children

# 7

---

## Teaching and Learning Goals

This chapter will provide the information, means, and opportunity to:

Develop a rationale for involving parents in the education of handicapped children.

Examine programs for involvement of parents in the education of handicapped children.

Trace the development of parent involvement programs for the education of handicapped children.

Design a program for parent involvement with handicapped children.

Identify and evaluate issues relating to the involvement of parents with handicapped children.

---

## Interest in Parents of Handicapped Children

While there is an interest in parent education in general, there is a great deal of emphasis in particular on the education of parents of handicapped children. There are several reasons for this interest:

1. Court cases and legal decisions have extended to the handicapped the same rights and privileges that have been enjoyed by everyone. In order to assure that these rights and privileges are accorded to the handicapped child, parent involvement is a

necessity. In some instances, court decisions have encouraged and/or ordered this involvement. In the absence of the handicapped person's ability to be his own advocate, the courts, agencies, and parents are assuming that function.

2. Legislation enacted at the state and federal levels has specified that the handicapped must receive a free and appropriate education. In essence, this legislation is promoting and encouraging the development of programs for the education of the handicapped. This legislation also provides for parent involvement. Thus, educators are involving parents of handicapped children because they must.

3. There is a great deal of federal money available for the development of programs for the handicapped. It is surprising how the presence of money will encourage programs! In many ways, of course, this is good because without the funds and resources, it is difficult to initiate programs.

4. There is an increased social consciousness toward the handicapped person. This increased social consciousness recognizes that the handicapped have often been treated as second-class citizens and have been victims of oppression and degradation. As such, there is an effort to make reparations for past behavior and attitudes.

5. Many young people see the teaching of the handicapped as a very rewarding and meaningful profession. The opportunities to contribute are unlimited. They feel that they can serve society, children, and themselves best by teaching the handicapped and their parents. There is a feeling on the part of many preservice professionals that the "normal" child will probably learn on his own, but the handicapped child needs help and training. Consequently, there are many bright, young educators who are devoting their lives to helping the handicapped.

## The Right to an Education

One of the reasons for the breakthrough and subsequent interest in the education of the handicapped and their parents is due, in part, to the landmark court case, *Pennsylvania Association for Retarded Children* (PARC) v. *the Commonwealth of Pennsylvania* which occurred in 1971. (PARC is now the Pennsylvania Association for Retarded Citizens.) Historically, Pennsylvania and many other states have tended, by law, to exclude handicapped children from the public schools. Typically, a child was excluded from the public school if he had not, in the opinion of a psychologist, attained a certain mental age; if it was felt that the child was uneducable; and if the child could not benefit from public education. Because of this point of view, many children were excluded from access to and the benefits of a publically supported education.

It was felt by many parents and advocacy groups that this exclusion represented a violation of individual privileges, especially the opportunity to enroll in public education. Specifically, the PARC case, as it is commonly referred to, involved the privilege guarantees embodied in the Fourteenth Amendment of the U.S. Constitution. Article One of this amendment states, "No state shall make or enforce any law which shall abridge the privileges or immunities of citizens of the United States; nor shall any state deprive any person of life, liberty, or property, without due process of law; nor deny to any person within its jurisdiction the equal protection of the laws."[1]

---

[1]U.S. *Constitution,* Amend. 14, sect. 1.

PARC argued that this section of the amendment was violated on two counts. First, the privilege of attending school on the part of many handicapped children was violated, and, second, by the nature in which many handicapped children were excluded from school, for example, without a hearing or due process, their right to due process under the law was also violated.

The PARC case was settled through a consent agreement with the Commonwealth of Pennsylvania.[2] Specifically, it was agreed that the state would agree to the following:

1. Not postpone or in any way deny to any mentally retarded child access to a free public program of education and training.

2. Not deny tuition or tuition maintenance to any mentally retarded person except on the same terms as may be applied to other exceptional children.

3. Not deny homebound instruction to any mentally retarded child merely because no physical disability accompanies the retardation or because retardation is not a short-term disability.

4. Provide to every retarded person between the ages of six and twenty-one years access to a free public program of education and training appropriate to his learning capacities.

5. Wherever a program of preschool education exists, to provide children less than six years of age a free public program and training appropriate to his learning capacities.

6. Provide notice and the opportunity for a hearing prior to a change in the educational status of any child who is mentally retarded or thought to be mentally retarded.[2]

Specifically the PARC case provided for mentally retarded children to have an appropriate and free education. In addition, the child and parent (or guardian) had a right to a hearing before any change of original assignment could be made in the child's educational status. As a result, the Fourteenth Amendment guarantees of the privileges of citizenship and due process under the law were provided for all mentally retarded children in Pennsylvania.

While the PARC case applied specifically to the mentally retarded, these same privileges and due processes have been extended to other handicapping conditions by other court decisions and federal legislation.

## Due Process

Another significant factor about the PARC case was the due process procedure. By providing an opportunity for a hearing if the parents were not satisfied with the educational program of their child, it set the stage for the involvement of the child and parent (or guardian or surrogate) in decision making relating to the child's education placement and status. This provision has prompted parents, child advocates, and other agencies to insist that public schools provide due process to all

---

[2] *Pennsylvania Association for Retarded Children* v. *Commonwealth of Pennsylvania,* 334 *F. Supp.* 1257 (E.D. Pr. 1971).

*There is a growing awareness that a free and appropriate education is the right of all children. Hopefully this concept will become a reality rather than an unfullfilled promise.*

handicapped individuals. Consequently, the possibility that parents will become effectively and meaningfully involved in the education of their child has increased. This, in turn, of course, encourages involvement in and with the schools. The due process procedure reinforces the concept that parents can be significantly involved in decision making about those things which have a profound effect upon the immediate life of the child as well as his life-long status and achievements.

The due process provision also involves the concept of the accountability of the public schools to parents and children. No longer can the parent be bypassed or ignored. Parents' options and desires must be taken into consideration. The burden of proof relating to providing for a free and appropriate education for the child rests with the school district.

## Federal Legislation

Many of the provisions and guarantees to children and their parents provided by the PARC case applied only to the state of Pennsylvania. While the case set many precedents, which have since been enacted into law in other states, these provisions did not apply to all the states. Consequently, there were no uniform standards or procedures. This was particularly true in relation to federal programs and federal money expended in state and local programs. What was lacking was a uniformity of processes and procedures for providing for the education of handicapped persons. This uniformity was achieved in part by Public Law 94-142.

## Public Law 94-142, The Education for
## All Handicapped Children Act

This federal law was made official in November 1975 and is designed to provide handicapped children with an appropriate and free public education. Rather than being a "new" law, P.L. 94-142 represents a revision of part B of the Education of the Handicapped Act (P.L. 93-380). Section 3 of P.L. 94-142 states:

> (C) It is the purpose of this Act to assure that all handicapped children have available to them, within the time periods specified in section 612(2) (B), a free appropriate public education which emphasizes special education and related services designed to meet their unique needs, to assure that the rights of handicapped children and their parents or guardians are protected, to assist States and localities to provide for the education of all handicapped children, and to assess and assure the effectiveness of efforts to educate handicapped children.[3]

The time frame specified in section 612(2) (B) states:

> (B) a free appropriate public education will be available for all handicapped children between the ages of three and eighteen within the State not later than September 1, 1978, and for all handicapped children between the ages of three and twenty-one within the State not later than September 1, 1980, except that, with respect to handicapped children aged three to five and aged eighteen to twenty-one, inclusive, the requirements of this clause shall not be applied in any State if the application of such requirements would be inconsistent with State law or practice, or the order of any court, respecting public education within such age groups in the State.[4]

P.L. 94-142 also extends many of the privileges and processes to the federal level that were advanced in some states (particularly Pennsylvania) as a result of court decisions. It is through P.L. 94-142 that the federal government enforces the provisions of the act in those states and districts which receive federal monies.

*Key Provisions of P.L. 94-142.* Key provisions of public law 94-142 are as follows:

1. It provides for a free and appropriate education (FAPE) for all persons between the ages of three and twenty-one. The key term here is *appropriate*. This is meaningful in the sense that now the child has to be provided with an education that is suited to his age, maturity, handicapping condition, past achievements, and parental expectations. This means that it is no longer possible to assume a program is appropriate for a child or to develop a program for the child. Traditionally, what has been rather common practice is that an individual has been diagnosed as handicapped in some way and then he has been put into some prearranged and predetermined program. Whether or not that program was specifically appropriate to him was not of immediate concern or was an issue that was considered beside the

---

[3]U.S., *Statutes at Large*, vol. 89.
[4]U.S., *Statutes ...*, vol. 89.

point. Now, however, the educational program has to be appropriate to the child, which means that a plan for an appropriate education has to be developed for the child.

2. The education of the child has to occur within the least restrictive educational environment that will benefit the child. *Least restricted* means that educational environment in which the child will be able to receive a program designed to meet his specific needs. This means the regular classroom if that is the environment in which the child can learn best. This placement offers the child an opportunity to interact with children of normal intelligence and those with or without physical handicaps. The provision does not necessarily mean that the least restrictive educational environment is the regular classroom, because it may not be. However, this law provides more opportunity to be with "regular" children in a "mainstreamed" setting.

3. The law also provides that individualization of instruction and diagnosis will occur. Not only must the education for the child be appropriate, it must also be individualized to him. It must take into consideration his specific needs, handicapping conditions, wants, and desires as well as those of his parent.

4. The key to the individualization process is another feature of the law which requires that an individual educational program (IEP) must be developed for each child. This educational plan must specify what will be done for the child, how it will be done, and when it will be done. Furthermore, it must be completed in writing. In the development of this individualized educational plan, a person trained in the diagnosis of handicapping conditions such as a school psychologist must be involved as well as a classroom teacher, the parent, and, where appropriate, the child himself. There are several key implications associated with the development of this educational plan. One is that for the first time, on a formal basis, parents and children are involved in the educational determination of what will happen to the child. The second important thing is that the child must have a plan tailor-made or individualized for him. This individualization assures that accurate diagnosis and realistic goal setting as well as a responsible implementation of the program will occur. In this sense, there is an element of personalization that is brought to the process. At the same time, it increases the possibility that the teaching-learning process will be more humane.

5. The legislation specifies that the parents and child will have a role in the diagnosis, placement, and development of the individualized educational plan. The parents can state their desires for the child. In addition, information the parent has about the learning style, interests, and abilities of the child can be taken into consideration in the development of his educational plan. This is a process that was not always possible or even considered necessary prior to P.L. 94-142.

6. The law also provides for a hearing which can be initiated by the parents if they do not agree with the diagnosis of the child, his placement, and/or the educational plan that has been designed for the child. This provision gives the parent "clout" in encouraging public school personnel to provide a free and appropriate education for the child.

*Implications for Parents.*    While the implications of P.L. 94-142 are far-reaching for children and adults with handicaps, for purposes of our discussion, the important features deal with the implications for parents being involved in the educational process of the child. This law mandates that parents become involved. Therefore, if school districts want to receive money under the provisions of the law or want to continue receiving federal monies which are associated with other appropriations, then they must involve parents in the development of the educational program of their handicapped child. In this sense, the right for parents to be involved is established. No longer can school districts treat parent involvement as something that would be nice to do or something that should be done. Now involvement becomes the right of every parent of a handicapped child. If parents are not involved in this process, they can initiate legal proceedings to assure that the provisions of the act are followed.

The second implication that this act has for parent involvement is that parent ideas about and knowledge of the child can be expressed and accounted for in the planning process. This expression becomes a key factor in development of the educational plan for the child. Quite often in the teaching/learning process, parents' ideas about the education of their child, their wishes, and desires are ignored. Now in the development of the educational program for the child all of these factors can be considered.

Thirdly, parents are assured of a continued involvement in the education of their child for two reasons. First, the educational plan for the handicapped child has to be reviewed and revised at least annually. This annual revision means that, on a yearly basis at least, the parents will be involved in the educational planning for the child.

The second assurance that parents have for continued involvement is the due process features associated with the law. This due process clause stipulates that if the parents are not satisfied with the placement of the child or the educational plan, they have the right to appeal to a higher educational authority and, ultimately, to the courts.

What has occurred then as far as involvement of parents of handicapped children is that parents are now viewed as having legal rights, prerogatives, and obligations for the education of their children under the law. They are brought into the school as legal entities, with a legal right to help and aid in the education of the child. They can protect, defend, and uphold their own legal rights as well as those of their children. Parents are now viewed as consumers of the educational process.

Child advocate organizations, organizations for handicapped citizens, and civil right groups are currently directing much effort toward advising parents of their rights and responsibilities for involvement under the provisions of this act.

*Parents' Rights.* Under the provisions of P.L. 94-142, parents are thus afforded certain rights in respect to the child's education and their role in that education. Some of these rights are outlined below:

1. The parent must give his consent prior to an evaluation of the child.

2. The parent has the right to "examine all relevant records with respect to the identification, evaluation, and educational placement of the child . . . ."

3. The parent must be given written prior notice whenever a change in "the identification, evaluation or educational placement of the child" occurs.

4. This written notice must be in the parent's native tongue.

5. The parent has an "opportunity to present complaints with respect to any matter relating to the identification, evaluation, or educational placement of the child . . . ."

6. The parent has the right to a due process hearing in relation to any complaint.

7. The parent has the right to participation in the development of the individual educational program for the child.

8. The meetings to develop the IEP must be held in the parent's native tongue.

9. The meetings held to develop the IEP must be held at a time and place agreeable to the parent.

## The Federal Government and Educational Involvement

The U.S. Constitution does not provide for education. The word *education* is not mentioned. During the writing of the Constitution by our founding fathers, the procedure was to reserve certain functions for the federal government (for example, the power to make war). These functions would be the prerogative of the federal branch. Powers or functions that were not specifically reserved for the federal government were to be the responsibility of the individual states. Education, because it was not reserved or specified as a federal function, became a state function. Today, all fifty states have established regulations for and control over the education process.

How is it, then, that the federal government supports and controls an increasing number of educational processes? Basically, this influence comes from three sources.

The first of these sources is the Preamble to the U.S. Constitution. This Preamble states:

> We, the people of the United States, in order to form a more perfect Union, establish justice, insure domestic tranquility, provide for the common defense, promote the general welfare, and secure the blessings of liberty to ourselves and our posterity, do ordain and establish this Constitution for the United States of America.[5]

The federal basis for aid to education is based on the four words, *"promote the general welfare."* The federal government has passed many statutes which provide monies, services, and support to education on the general principle that, by doing so, it is promoting the general welfare.

The second source of federal support and control over education comes from specific provisions in the Constitution. As we have discussed, the legal foundation of the PARC case was based upon the Fourteenth Amendment. One of the unique features about the PARC case was that it did involve the privileges of handicapped children as they relate to federal guarantees. Prior to this case, only state statures and regulations were applied to procedures for educating the handicapped.

The third source of federal input is through federal monies provided in specific legislation. Provisions of federal legislation are enforceable at the state and local level by virtue of the fact that the states and local school districts are receiving federal monies to educate handicapped children. If state and local educational agencies want to continue to receive and use federal monies, they must comply with the federal

---

[5]U.S., *Constitution,* Preamble.

regulations and laws. Because the federal government furnishes the money, it mandates and controls how that money will be used. The alternatives that a state or local district has to not complying with federal regulations follow:

1. Defy or ignore the laws and regulations at the expense and risk of legal action.
2. Choose not to receive federal monies. The problem here, however, is that many state governments and local education agencies are so dependent on federal monies that the thought of not receiving the monies is worse than complying with a law or regulation they might not agree with or that they find objectionable.

*A mobile classroom such as the one in which these children are learning provides many opportunities which otherwise might not be possible.*

## Mainstreaming

A term that is used with increasing frequency at all levels of education from preschool through adult education is *mainstreaming*. Basically, mainstreaming means that a handicapped child will be or should be educated within the regular school classroom. Removal from the regular classroom should occur only when the regular classroom cannot provide in a meaningful way for the child.

Mainstreaming can be interpreted in one of several ways. In one way, it means that children with handicaps will be a part of the mainstream of education which traditionally has meant "normal" children and regular classrooms. In another sense, mainstreaming means that the schools are going to *return* the handicapped child to the mainstream of education from which he has been excluded for over three-quarters of a century. Whereas in the forties, fifties, and sixties, it was customary, acceptable, and thought to be educationally sound, legal, and humane to provide separate (but not always equal) education for the handicapped outside the regular classroom, it is no longer justifiable to do so if the child can benefit from an educational program in the regular classroom.

In mainstreaming, the emphasis is placed on the concept of normalcy. This concept means that the child will be treated in a normal way and educated in as normal a manner as possible. The concept of hiding children behind walls and fences is no longer defended.

## Objections to Mainstreaming

While, on the surface at least, it seems as though mainstreaming is a reasonable and humane idea, the concept and its implementation as a process are not universally embraced even by those who are responsible for implementing it. Particular resistance comes from classroom teachers who see it as an effort to add to their duties, responsibilities, and work load. Specifically, where mainstreaming involves placing the handicapped child in the regular classroom, some of the objections raised by teachers include the following:

1. The time and attention devoted to a mainstreamed student may take away or detract from time and attention usually provided to "regular" students.
2. By teaching mainstreamed students in the classroom, "regular" students are held back in their progress.
3. The mainstreamed student adds to the teacher's work load, responsibility, and time needed to prepare for instruction.
4. Regular classrooms often lack the materials and equipment necessary for effective mainstreaming.
5. Regular classroom teachers are not prepared or trained to deal with the learning needs or problems of handicapped students.

An objection that is frequently raised by the general public to any kind of special program is the cost necessary to implement and maintain it. Some people agree with the concept of providing for the needs of handicapped children and their parents but are not willing to pay for it. This attitude is unfortunate, for an educational agency usually can find money for those programs which it feels are important.

While some of these objections may have some basis in fact, they would hardly constitute reasons why mainstreaming should not occur. In addition, these objections should be viewed as challenges and opportunities rather than obstacles. A mainstreamed classroom offers opportunities for parent involvement, for parents of handicapped children can provide teachers with the insight, information, help, and time they feel they need in teaching handicapped children.

## Student Classification and Parent Involvement

In any attempt to classify the child according to his ability to achieve educationally or to determine where or in what program to place him (for example, regular classrooms, special education facility, etc), there is the interesting question of who should make the classification. Traditionally, this classification or determination of degree of educability has been made by a psychologist, either in private practice or representing the school. Occasionally, this determination has been made unilaterally. Usually, however, it is made in consultation with the classroom teacher and the school administrator. Quite often, the parent has not been involved in the process and is informed of a particular decision after the fact. While under P.L. 94-142, the parent can complain about the decision and has the right of due process in order to try and change the decision they do not agree with, this seems to be a rather negative process. The question of student placement then raises some interesting possibilities for parent involvement.

One rather obvious (but not often utilized) method of pupil placement is based on negotiations with the parent. "A completely different means of taking the classification decision out of the unilateral control of the school administration would be to require that the administration negotiate with parents. This approach downgrades the professional quality of the decision and upgrades the significance of parental consent."[6]

While the process of bargaining with parents over the educational placement of the child has some obvious inherent problems, such as what happens if the bargaining procedure breaks down, it would encourage the role of the parent as a partner in the educational process. At the same time, it would support the parent's role as the primary educator of the child. It would also draw upon the wide background of information the parent has about the interests, abilities, and experiences of the child.

Another possibility for parent involvement is through the consent process. "It is a short step from a procedure requiring bargaining with the parents to a procedure requiring parental consent for particular classification steps. Parental denial of the necessary consent would be final and the child would stay in the regular classroom as before."[7] This process would require even more parental input because of the finality of the parent decision.

## Importance of Parent Information and Knowledge

In both of the processes of parent involvement, negotiation and consent, discussed above, it becomes doubly important for the parents to be involved with their child. The inherent danger in any process which is dependent upon parents in decision making is that the parents may not have the information or knowledge necessary to make the best decision for the child. This lack of knowledge (or even ignorance) on the part of the parents is increased where there is a handicapping condition. A parent may know that her child has Down's syndrome, but she may not know what it is, what to do, etc. Therefore, it is vitally important that the parents become involved in order that they may have the information necessary to help the child.

---

[6]William G. Buss, David L. Kirp, and Peter F. Kuriloss, "Exploring Procedural Modes of Special Classification," in *Issues in the Classification of Children,* ed. Nicholas Hobbs (San Francisco: Jossey-Bass, 1975), p. 421.

[7]Ibid.

## Getting Involved

In many respects, parent involvement, regardless of the kind of children the parent is dealing with, is a matter of attitude. Just as in any endeavor, without a positive attitude, it runs the risk of failure. It helps then if parents of handicapped children try to do the following:

1. Understand your child's needs. You are the best determiner of these needs, and your information and viewpoints are needed. This is especially true when deciding what kind of services your child needs.

2. Determine what the child needs help with and seek it. Don't think that something doesn't matter or that a service isn't available.

3. Get involved in the Right to Education Program. This is especially helpful in the development of the Individual Education Program (IEP) for your child.

4. Don't feel as though there is something "wrong" with your child. Get him and yourself out and involved in the community. Try not to protect and shelter yourself or your child.

5. Don't expect someone else to do your job for you.

6. Don't get hung up on the handicap. Focus on your child as a person who has many talents and abilities. Your child is and can be a very interesting person.

7. Get the whole family involved. A father can help with sports, physical therapy, etc., and other siblings can contribute through companionship, protection, sports, etc.

Parents cannot achieve the above attitudes and processes in a vacuum. It is not good enough or right that we should say to parents, "You should do these things." Parents don't want a sermon, they want and should receive help, support, and education. Quite often, educators will say to parents, "You could understand your child if you wanted to." It is obvious that if parents knew how, they, more than likely, would understand their child. The parent educator must work out a program that will help to communicate what parents should know and should do.

## How Parents Can Get Involved

In order for parents to be more aware of their own handicapped child and to have more information in general, there are certain things that can be done.

1. Baby-sit for parents who have handicapped children. In this way, a parent can learn more about handicapped children and can provide other parents with opportunities to be involved.

2. Join and be *active* in the local chapter of your state National Association for Retarded Citizens.

3. Join various local parent groups that may be available such as infant-toddler parent groups, preschool-youth parent groups, and sheltered workshop parent groups.

4. Become involved in fund raising for various local groups such as Right to Education Committee, Advocacy Committee, and Legislative Committee.

5. Counsel with other parents in the home. This counseling process can also occur in a hospital immediately following the birth of a child who is identified as having a handicapping condition.

6. Go to open houses that are held by schools and agencies.

## Why Is It Hard to Get Parents Involved?

There may be a tendency to think that parent involvement is an easy and natural process; this is not the case. While parent involvement *per se* is frequently a process that requires a great deal of time and effort, this can be doubly true when working with parents of handicapped children, for some of the following reasons:

1. Because many programs for working with the handicapped already exist, parents are *demanding* services rather than being involved in developing the services. When services are not available, parents can be appealed to on the basis that their help is needed. However, once a service is available there is a tendency to think that the job is accomplished. However, unless everyone who is eligible is using the service, it is not being utilized to its fullest extent. Unless parents get involved in the development of the individual educational plan, it won't work. Part of the job of parent involvement revolves around convincing people there is still work to do.

2. Whereas women were demanding involvement, many are now too busy pursuing their own careers. Rather than giving of their time in volunteer ways, they are devoting their time and energy to their careers. This is a condition common to the entire parent involvement process, not necessarily just parents of handicapped.

3. Certain kinds of volunteering can and do take a great deal of time, which many parents are unable or unwilling to give. The degree and nature of the child's handicapping condition will also determine how much time the parent thinks she can spend on other activities.

4. Parents don't want to admit to themselves or the public that there is anything wrong with their child, and, therefore, they don't become involved because they see no reason to.

*Educators are Hard to Work With.* Parent involvement is also difficult for parents with handicapped children because of the nature of the educational system and the professionals who are responsible for operating it. Educators can be difficult to work with. This attitude or tendency of being difficult to work with will tend to discourage parent involvement. Some of the reasons why educators are hard to work with are listed below:

1. Sometimes educators are very resistant to change. Society may want them to move faster than they or the schools are willing to move. Educators sometimes procrastinate and say they can't change as fast as society wants them to. This situation may be more true when dealing with handicapped children.

2. In dealing with the school system, the parent is up against a whole series of "experts." There is the psychologist, administrator, counselor, teacher, etc., all of whom consider they know what is "best." There is a tendency to convey this to parents who, in turn, feel inadequate to the situation.

3. Professionals get defensive when their knowledge and expertise are challenged. After all, they are the experts, why should their views be challenged? Parents, in addition to all their other problems, may have to deal with this defensiveness on the part of educators whose opinions are questioned.

4. Educators tend to blame the home for handicapping conditions. "What are you doing at home to make him act this way?" Of course, this response occurs in all areas of the curriculum. A parent whose handicapped son got a D in math was asked by the teacher, "Is something upsetting Johnny at home?" The teacher never questioned his own teaching ability or methods.

*Many parents are willing and able to give their time and talents by providing programs for children and the schools they attend.*

## Curricular Areas for Parent Involvement

In developing specific programs for helping parents of handicapped children, there are certain areas that should receive special emphasis:

1. Child management skills. This area includes helping parents learn how to help their children cope with problems of management and behavior and involves techniques for disciplining and directing behavior toward desirable outcomes. In this respect, there is a heavy emphasis on teaching and learning behavior modification techniques, skills, and procedures. Probably in no other field has there been such a growth and refinement of behavior management procedures than in the area of teaching the handicapped.

2. Social and self-sufficiency skills. The emphasis in this area relates to helping parents gain knowledge of and develop procedures for helping children learn how to become independent in the areas of eating, toileting, dressing, and related self-care areas. Many behavior management programs have been developed to help in this area.

3. Coping, accepting and understanding strategies. Many parents of handicapped children need help accepting the child and his handicapping condition. Therefore, many programs are directed toward helping parents adjust themselves to the child. Once acceptance is achieved, understanding is promoted. This is followed by helping strategies and techniques. The emphasis is placed on getting parents involved in and through their children. Parents are encouraged to become involved in the education of the child, in parent groups, and in advocacy relationships. In addition, there is an emphasis on the development of a warm and positive relationship between parent and child. The establishment of this relationship is seen as the key and basis to all other self-help strategies.

4. Language development. There is a recognition that parents of handcapped children need assistance in helping their children grow developmentally. A specific area in which children need help is language development with emphasis placed on communication skills and processes. There is not so much a concern for the content of communication as there is for the process of communication.

A major significance of current efforts for developing programs for the handicapped is that there is an attempt to deal with each person in an individual and humane manner, in such a way that needs are met. This approach is almost the opposite of many previous practices in which the handicapped child was placed in an educational program on the basis of his disability. Such placement by disability was not only demeaning in many ways, but also it really did not provide for the total educational needs of children so they could achieve lifelong goals and ambitions.

## Parents Need Help

The parent of the handicapped child needs help, not sympathy. This help is often best expressed when it is in the form of self-help.

One of the barriers to self-help is the feeling of the parent of a handicapped child toward his child, himself, and society. An attitude of hopelessness and helplessness toward the handicapping situation is often evidenced by the parent's agonizing over the problem. Also, many parents feel guilty that they did something to directly cause the handicap (for example, a mother's poor nutrition during pregnancy). In order to help themselves, parents need support to escape from and deal realistically with these feelings of guilt.

Many parents feel ashamed of their child and themselves. One reaction to this feeling is to withdraw from society. In this way, the parents consciously or unconsciously seek to protect themselves and the child from the public gaze, attention, and conversation. Parents need help to see that there is not something "wrong" with their child. Parents can come to understand that their child is a unique and very interesting person. This idea was brought very forceably to my attention by the mother of a child with Down's syndrome. In a conversation one day, the mother related that whenever she and her son went out in public she always felt that people were watching them. One day when her son was three years old, she was shopping in a department store. One woman in particular kept looking at her son. The mother said she was very near to crying because of this observing. In order to escape, she started to leave without purchasing what she came for. As she turned, she heard the woman remark to her friend, "Did you see how attentive that young child was? He didn't miss a thing. His eyes were looking at everything! How smart he must be!" From that time on, the mother stopped thinking that people were looking at her son because something was "wrong" with him. She also started to realize for herself how smart her son is and has become involved in helping him become more so.

Another mother I talked with has a son who is considered mentally retarded. When her child, who is now eight, was younger, he experienced many difficulties in learning to speak. This mother has spent a great deal of time and effort on the language development process. One comment she made to me about her experiences sums up an attitude all parents should have toward their children regardless of whether they are handicapped or not. She said very simply and with feeling, "My son and I have had some wonderful discussions."

Parent involvement programs, rather than being haphazard, should be directed toward helping parents see how interesting and unique their children are. Wouldn't it be rewarding if all parents and children could have wonderful discussions together!

Once it is necessary for an educational program specific to and appropriate for the child to be designed, then it requires (or at least should) the involvement of a wide spectrum of professionals. This process, of course, increases opportunities for parental involvement.

In addition, it is hoped that as professionals and parents become more involved in the development of individual educational programs for handicapped children this same concept will be extended to all children. It is unfortunate that educational agencies had to be legislated into developing individualized instruction since this is the kind of program which should be provided every child whether he is handicapped or not. Hopefully, all children and their parents will be involved in a program of individualized instruction. While some people may view this as a Utopian vision and decry the money that it will cost, I would argue that we should provide our children with the very best it is possible to provide. If children are a nation's greatest wealth, they should be treated accordingly. It is really a matter of priorities. We should put first those things which are most important. This means providing each child with the best education it is possible to provide.

# Bibliography

Buss, William G.; Kirp, David L.; and Kuriloss, Peter F. "Exploring Procedural Modes of Special Classification." In *Issues in the Classification of Children,* edited by Nicholas Hobbs. San Francisco: Jossey-Bass, 1975.

*Pennsylvania Association for Retarded Children* v. *Commonwealth of Pennsylvania.* 334 *F. Supp.* 1257 (E.D. Pr. 1971).

United States. "Amendment 14, section 1." *United States Constitution.*

United States. "Preamble." *United States Constitution.*

United States Congress. *Statutes at Large.* Vol. 89.

# Further Reading and Study

Gosciewski, Francis. *Effective Child Rearing: The Behaviorally Aware Parent.* New York: Human Sciences Press, 1976.

Presents methods for management of children's behavior. Problem situations dealing with appropriate and inappropriate behavior are outlined and solutions are suggested. One chapter deals with self-modification of parental behavior as a means of becoming a more effective parent.

Kroth, Roger L. *Communicating With Parents of Exceptional Children.* Denver, Col.: Love Publishing Co., 1975.

This book contains much practical information for enhancing parent/teacher communication. The need for gathering information about parents and children as a basis for communication is stressed. It also contains a section on behavior modification as a means of helping parents deal with children's problems.

*Laton, A Handicapped Child in Need.* Scarsdale, N.Y.: Campus Film Distributors Corp., 1976.

An excellent film designed to sensitize parents and Head Start personnel to the needs of handicapped children and the role parents can play in helping their children through involvement in Head Start. Can be used with parents, general public, and preservice and inservice public school, Head Start, and day care teachers.

Lillie, David L., and Trohanis, Pascal L., eds. *Teaching Parents to Teach.* New York: Walker and Company for Technical Assistance Development System, The University of North Carolina at Chapel Hill, 1976.

A series of articles relating to helping develop, organize, and implement parent involvement programs in early childhood programs for handicapped children. Provides for both theory and practical applications.

Stott, D. H. *The Parent as Teacher: A Guide for Parents of Children With Learning Difficulties.* Belmont, Calif.: Lear Siegler, Fearon Publishers, 1974.

An easy-to-read book that presents many practical ideas for parents and how to work with parents of learning disabled children. The author feels many learning problems relate to temperamental handicaps and maladjustments such as "inconsequence" and "unforthcomingness." Teaching children how to read is particularly emphasized.

Southwest Educational Development Laboratory. *Working With Parents of Handicapped Children.* Reston, Va. The Council for Exceptional Children, n.d.

A good resource that helps teachers understand how parents of handicapped children feel. Many practical suggestions for conference preparations. Also includes ideas for helping parents help with their children's problems.

# Activities

1. Visit in the home of parents who have a handicapped child. What problems do the parents have to deal with?

    a. Are they dealing with them adequately?

    b. What suggestions would you make for helping these parents with their problems?

2. Visit public schools. What are they specifically doing to provide individualized and appropriate programs for handicapped children? What efforts are being made to involve parents?

3. By visiting agencies, interviewing parents, and reading, determine the number of specific ways in which a handicapping condition can occur.

4. Interview parents of handicapped children.

   a. What do they feel are the parents' greatest problems?

   b. What do they consider to be the greatest needs for their children?

   c. Make a list of specific ways in which they have been involved in educational agencies.

   d.   How have educational agencies avoided or resisted providing for their and/or their children's needs?

5. Quite often we think only in terms of handicapped children as having "problems." What are some assets that many handicapped people seem to possess?

# Programs for Parenting

**8**

---

## Teaching and Learning Goals

This chapter will provide the opportunity, information, and means to:

Assess the role and importance of parenting in the lives of students and parents.

Discuss issues and controversies related to the process of parenting.

Examine what the term *parenting* means.

Develop a personal philosophy of, an attitude toward, and a plan for parenting.

Examine and critique programs designed to promote the parenting process.

---

## Parenting—What Is It?

If any one word and concept has become fashionable and popular over the last several years it is the term *parenting*. Parenting is used by many educators, program developers, and parents themselves. Agencies of all kinds and at all levels, from colleges of education to high schools to mental health programs, are conducting seminars, training sessions, and formal courses in parenting. However, in spite of all the use the term receives and regardless of the number and different kinds of parenting programs developed, there is not always universal agreement about what the term means or whom the process of parenting is for. Therefore, it is necessary to become aware of some of the different meanings of the term in order to know what people mean when they use it.

On one level, parenting can refer to becoming prepared for parenthood. In this sense, a program of parenting can be concerned with sexual awareness, sexual knowledge, and the anatomical and physiological factors related to procreation and childbirth. In this approach to parenting, the emphasis is placed on the physical facts of parenting prior to the parent's giving birth to a child. This emphasis on physical care for both parent and child can also include knowledge and practice of childbirth methods. The natural approach to childbirth is very popular in comtemporary society, especially the Lamaze method and the LeBoyer method. LeBoyer feels that there is a great deal of violence connected with childbirth as it is currently practiced especially concerning the way the child is treated and handled following birth: the bright lights of the delivery room, the manner in which and the time in which the umbilical cord is cut. LeBoyer advocates a gentleness and more humane approach to the birth process. Specifically he advocates:

1. Immediately after birth placing the child on the stomach of the mother (this means that the umbilical cord is left intact).

2. The massaging of the child with soft, delicate strokes by the mother.

3. The separation of the umbilical cord only after it has "died." This dying process may take anywhere from three to five minutes or longer.

4. Dimming of lights in the delivery room in order to protect the sensitive eyesight of the child.

5. Talking in soft tones and reducing the amount of noise in the delivery room in order to protect the auditory sense of the child.

6. Placing the child in warm water for a period of time following the birth process. This placing in warm water is to simulate the child's experience while in the uterus.[1]

Parenting programs can also emphasize family living and preparation for family living. In this approach, emphasis is placed on problems, joys, and functions that are experienced and encountered by living in a family. Topics relating to money (budgeting, how to open and use a checking account), shared responsibilities, family roles, family crises (divorce, death), and other family living experiences are examined in detail. Sometimes the participants in the parenting program experience these family situations through simulation practices. In particular, high school courses have been developed in which students participate vicariously in the processes of their own families.

In other parenting programs, the emphasis is placed on the physical care of the child. Topics such as how to feed, clothe, bathe, toilet train, deal with temper tantrums, etc., are discussed.

In some of the more popular courses and seminars dealing with parenting, the emphasis is placed on parent-child relationships. Topics such as relating to, communicating with, disciplining humanely, and other strategies for living harmoniously with children within the family are discussed. The importance of the parent-child relationship is stressed through an examination of parent-child affective needs. One

---

[1]Frederick LeBoyer, *Birth Without Violence,* (New York: Knopf, 1975).

of the central purposes of this approach is to deal with parent doubts, anxieties, frustrations, and uncertainties connected with the child-rearing process. Since many parents come to such a session on parenting burdened with feelings of guilt and doubt, part of the focus is to address and deal with these feelings. Many parents are usually very much relieved when they find out that they are not the only parents with these kinds of feelings. In this sense, the group experience is very beneficial. Quite often, merely the opportunity to talk with other parents is very helpful and reassuring. Furthermore, these sessions have a tendency to reassure parents that they usually are not doing as bad a job of child rearing as they thought they were.

This particular group of parenting programs deals with helping parents understand their children as well as helping their children understand their parents. Presumably, if understanding occurs, then more harmonious relationships will follow. The emphasis is on understanding the children so that, as a result, parents can change their behavior toward the child. This approach in relationship to the child is different from that which was used in previous generations when it was the child who changed to fit into the ways, life styles, and behavior patterns of the parents. Now the emphasis appears to be on having parents change in order to account for the behavior of the children.

Part of this switch in emphasis is due to the popularity of the child study movement and new psychological interpretations of why children behave as they do. Many of the reasons for children's behavior and, in particular, their misbehavior have been attributed to the parents. In addition, Freudian personality theory attributes many adult neuroses to patterns of parent-child relationships that occurred in the early formative years. As a result of this blame, many parents have suffered from guilt and anxiety feelings. In attempts to alleviate these feelings, parents are turning to programs which offer hope of relief from these feelings. At the same time, parents hope they will learn once and for all, exactly what to do.

## Dealing with Child Rearing

There are usually two times in the child-rearing process when parents seem to want and need help in dealing with the process of child rearing. One of these times is during the early years beginning at about six months and continuing through the preschool years. The reason for this felt need for help, advice, and support during this time appears to be the result of several conditions:

1. The process of child rearing usually represents a new experience in instances where the child is the first offspring and where the parent has not had much opportunity for surrogate parenting with siblings.

2. During the preschool years, the child is not easy to communicate with. The young child cannot always verbalize her feelings and emotions, and, therefore, the feedback the parent receives concerning child-rearing methods is largely a result of her own perceptions of it. This is the time when a great deal of doubt about the appropriateness of particular methods begins to emerge.

3. This is usually the most joyful period of child rearing; the parent is enthusiastic about the process and wants to do what is "best."

The second period of time during which parents seek help with child rearing is the teen-age years. In particular, the years from about twelve to sixteen seem to be the most difficult. The teen-age years represent one of the most frustrating times for both parent and child and quite often involve situations of aggression and conflict. The number of teen-agers who run away from home is increasing at an alarming rate and represents a serious national social problem as well as poses a threat to the family as the traditional child-rearing institution. While programs of parenting designed to deal with problems between parents and children of this age are often held, they are generally not as effective as they should be for several reasons:

1. They are usually too little and too late. The damage has already been done. Patterns of behavior have already been set on the part of both parent and child. Ingrained behavior is difficult to change, and desirable behavior does not always occur as a result of several lessons or seminars.

2. Parents seek out help because of problems. Therefore, the sessions can tend to be problem oriented. It is always better to develop a system that is based on preventing problems rather than on correcting problems.

The optimum time to deal with the parent-child relationship would appear to be during the preschool years and before. Educators should capitalize on this and institute programs designed to deal with parent's practical problems of child rearing and educating. In these approaches, the emphasis should be placed on the following:

1. Affective as well as cognitive topics.

2. A developmental approach that deals with a topic from beginning to end. For example, how to deal with problems of discipline at different ages and stages of growth.

3. The practical application of specific ideas to specific cases. This does not mean that any problems are necessarily "solved," for often quick and easy solutions don't exist. However, discussion should not be theory oriented. Theory should be discussed after people are shown or have discussed how to cope with and manage situations. Most parents are solution oriented rather than theory oriented. Theory can be used if the group wants and is ready for it following practical considerations of problems.

4. Involving fathers, surrogates, and other family members in the group sessions. Parenting sessions should not be billed as only for females or mothers. The mother is not the only person who should deal with the child. Also, any strategy of child rearing should be consistently applied by all family members. It takes support from everyone in the family to be reasonably successful in the process of child rearing. Consequently, it makes sense to include as many other family members as possible in parenting programs.

5. Providing a range of alternatives for parents to consider and choose from. Every effort should be made to avoid selling, promoting, or encouraging the one and only right, honest, and true method or approach to child rearing.

*Parenting sessions should not be billed for "mothers" only. Fathers and parent surrogates need to be involved.*

## Programs for Parents

There is a growing awareness that to prepare for parenthood when one is a parent or when one shortly expects to be a parent is much too late. It appears that the time to prepare for parenthood is long before the decision is made to become a parent. Because of this need for education prior to parenthood, there is a growing number of efforts to develop programs which would provide training for individuals during adolescence and young adulthood. The aim is to make individuals knowledgeable about the processes of child rearing and child care before they are confronted with children to rear and problems they find they are incapable of handling. There are many problems, issues, processes, and concerns associated with child care and child rearing that can be anticipated, discussed, and planned for prior to the birth of children.

Many programs being developed are comprehensive or broad focus in the sense that they cover the complete aspect of child rearing. This means that they deal with physical care, interpersonal interactions, and educational strategies. Consequently, they deal with a majority of things that people need to know in order to provide good care and education to children.

## Between Parent and Child

One of the earliest programs in the recent trend to help parents deal with problems of child rearing was that advocated by Haim G. Ginott in his book, *Between Parent and Child*. Ginott advocates that one of the ways parents can improve their relationship with their children and become more effective parents is by communicating with children in constructive ways. This constructive communication involves new skills and new ways of communicating. "The new code of communication with children is based on respect and on skill. It requires (A) that messages preserve the child's as well as the parent's self-respect; (B) that statements of understanding *precede* statements of advice or instruction."[2]

In this approach, parents are told how to respond to the feelings of children rather than to merely respond to words and facts that have been stated. Ginott feels that, by responding to children as persons and by responding to their feelings, this new method of communication will lessen the conflicts that often exist between parent and child. The emphasis is placed on understanding the child and what she is saying as a means of helping both parent and child deal with problems and conflicts.

Ginott also advocates a different method of praise than is often used by many parents. He feels that "the single most important rule is that praise deal only with the child's efforts and accomplishments, not with his character and personality."[3]

Ginott also emphasizes the difference between constructive and destructive criticism. He feels that an important technique that parents must learn is how to deal with events rather than with personalities. So often  parents convey to children the feeling that they dislike the child because of an inappropriate or improper act on the part of the child. Ginott suggests that parents learn to show children that they are still loved even though the parent disapproves of the wrong act.

It is also important that parents allow children to know how they feel. Children should learn that parents have feelings, and parents should understand that they can and should express these feelings in appropriate ways to children. This expression of feelings is premised on one condition: "We can express our angry feelings *provided* we do not attack the child's personality or character."[4]

In dealing with children, it is also necessary for parents to avoid what Ginott calls self-defeating patterns. For Ginott, "the self-defeating patterns include threats, bribes, promises, sarcasm, sermons on lying and stealing, and rude teaching of politeness."[5] Ginott believes that it is through the use of these self-defeating patterns that children reflect the behavior which they see role modeled by adults. In reality, then, parents are teaching children behavior which they do not approve of by the way they act toward the child.

The best way to develop responsibility in children is by giving them opportunities to exercise responsibility. Ginott feels that what is required is a distinction between those things over which a child can exercise direct responsibility and those things in which she can have a voice. An example Ginott cites relates to purchasing of

---

[2]Haim G. Ginott, *Between Parent and Child* (New York: The Macmillan Co., 1965), p. 21.
[3]Ibid., p. 39.
[4]Ibid., p. 51
[5]Ibid., p. 53.

clothing. He feels that the young child can select what clothing will be bought from a selection made by the parent. Within the framework of the selection that the parent has made, the child has the ability to choose.

Ginott also deals with the issue of permissiveness and limits. He feels that parents should understand what permissiveness involves. For him, "The essence of permissiveness is the acceptance of children as persons who have a constitutional right to have all kinds of feelings and wishes."[6] On the other hand, "Overpermissiveness is the allowing of undesirable acts. Permissiveness brings confidence in an increasing capacity to express feelings and thoughts. Overpermissiveness brings anxiety and increasing demands for privileges that cannot be granted."[7]

In disciplining children, Ginott believes that it is the parents' responsibility to establish and set limits for children. "A limit should be so stated that it tells the child clearly (a) what constitutes unacceptable conduct; (b) what substitute will be accepted."[8]

In addition to the practical suggestions discussed above, Ginott also deals with the topics of jealousy, anxiety in children, sex education, sexual role, and social functions.

Ginott's method is to cite situations which are of concern to parents in the child-rearing process and then to provide solutions to these situations. This approach is not without its detractors. Some parenting experts feel it is best to help parents become aware of problems and provide assistance in working out and developing acceptable solutions as opposed to providing suggestions and/or telling parents what and how they should respond. However, many parents have read Ginott's books and are satisfied they have found practical solutions to some very difficult problems encountered in child rearing.

*Program Limitations.*   The reader should be aware that Ginott's techniques appear to be limited in several ways. First, they deal mainly with a communication process. In this regard, his program can be considered to be a narrow focus program. By narrow focus, I mean it deals only with how to communicate better with children and how to solve conflicts that occur between parent and child as a result of the interactive processes that occur in child rearing.

Also, the program tends to assume that the audience is one which has children. Consequently, individuals who do not yet have children may feel that the process is more appropriate to parents with children. Of course, this is not necessarily true since we all can benefit from better communication.

## Parent Effectiveness Training (PET)

One of the more popular ways to help parents deal with the problems, frustrations, and uncertainties of child rearing is the Parent Effectiveness Training program developed by Thomas Gordon. The Parent Effectiveness Training approach is based upon a system of communication between the parent and the child. In the development and implementation of this communication process, the emphasis is on the

---

[6]Ibid., p. 93.

[7]Ibid., p. 94.

[8]Ibid., p. 99.

utilization of counseling techniques, processes, and skills. The PET program is not designed to tell parents what is the best solution to a problem; rather, the emphasis is placed on treating children as people. In this process, the parent learns how to set up, establish, and maintain a two-way system of communication so that a "no-lose" approach to problem solving is established.

The key to this no-lose approach to parent-child interactions is active listening. "Active listening is a method of influencing children to find their own solutions to their own problems."[9] Gordon feels that most parent-child relationships, as they are commonly conducted, end up in a win-lose situation. In such a situation, it is the parent who always or almost always wins and the child who loses. Parents win because they use their authority, their power position as parents, their feelings, and they maintain that they have the most experience, the greatest knowledge, etc. When the parent always wins and the child always loses, the results are that the child feels resentful and the impression is conveyed to her that her feelings and ideas don't matter. This feeling of unworthiness usually results in noncommunication between parent and child. The second "win-lose" situation is one in which the child wins and the parent loses. In this situation, parents lose to the child because they are afraid of harming the child psychologically, because of their belief that the permissive approach works best, or because they are fearful of losing the child's love and affection. Gordon feels that both situations are inappropriate for rearing children because, in the past, they have not worked with any degree of success.

As an alternative to these win-lose situations, Gordon proposes a no-lose situation. This "is a method by which each unique parent and his unique child can solve each of their unique conflicts by finding their own unique solutions acceptable to both."[10] Gordon believes that it is not necessary for parents to learn many different methods of relating to children, but by learning his no-lose method, parents will be able to resolve conflicts that occur in the child-rearing process. As Gordon explains:

> My thesis is that parents need only learn a *single method for resolving conflicts,* a method useable with children of all ages. With this approach, there are no "best" solutions applicable to all or even most families. The solution best for one family— that is, one that is acceptable to that particular parent and child—might not be "best" for another family.[11]

Gordon believes that many of the problems that arise between parent and child are due to a lack of honest two-way communication. This lack of communication also generally involves a tendency on the part of children and parents not to account for each other's feelings. Gordon stresses that it is important for parents to encourage children to express how they feel, and these feelings should be taken into consideration when parents communicate with their children. It is equally important for the parent to let the child know how she, the parent, feels. For example, when the parent does not like something the child is doing, rather then ordering the child to stop, the parent could respond with an "I message" such as "I can't write this letter when your

[9]Thomas Gordon, *Parent Effectiveness Training.* New York: Peter H. Wyden, Publishers, 1970, p. 66.
[10]Ibid., p. 200.
[11]Ibid., p. 199.

*This parent learns how to conduct an activity which will be useful in the home. Parenting programs should be practical rather than abstract.*

stereo is playing so loud." Gordon feels that, by utilizing this approach, the child comes to understand how the parent feels and changes her behavior so that she acts in ways that are more in keeping with the way the parent feels. This sharing of feelings promotes an open, honest relationship between the parent and the child and provides a basis for a better interpersonnel relationship.

In using the no-lose method, six steps are involved:

1. Identifying and defining the conflict.
2. Generating possible alternative solutions.
3. Evaluating the alternative solutions.
4. Deciding on the best acceptable solution.
5. Working out ways of implementing a solution.
6. Following up to evaluate how it worked.[12]

The training for using Gordon's method occurs in a series of training sessions conducted by specially trained PET instructors. There has been a great deal of interest in Gordon's approach, and the training sessions have been very popular. Many parents have been trained in the procedures for utilizing the no-lose approach.[13]

As a program of parenting, Gordon's approach represents a method for dealing with communication and the resolution of conflicts that occur between parent and child. The program is not designed to tell parents what to do or how to do it. Rather, it is designed to show parents effective ways for dealing with their children. The

---

[12]Ibid., p. 237.
[13]Gordon has also developed a program of Teacher Effectiveness Training (TET) and is working on the development of a program dealing with Youth Effectiveness Training.

particular solution to a particular problem depends upon the parent, the child, and the values, backgrounds, and experiences which they both bring to a particular situation. In this respect, the program tends to be culture free and can be used by all economic-cultural groups.

Before attempting to use Gordon's methods, parents must understand that methods of child rearing used in the past which create conflicts and which are autocratic in nature are approaches that might not offer the best solutions to problems. Parents must want to change their methods of child rearing. Not only must the parents want to try a different method of child rearing, they must also be willing to implement the system and change some previous traditional approaches to the child. This change in child-rearing patterns and style can cause uncertainty and anxiety on the part of parents and cause them to stop using the methods of communication advocated by Gordon. Some parents may find it easier to do what they have always done rather than to change ineffective ways of relating to children.

## Systematic Training for Effective Parenting (STEP)

One of the many parenting programs designed to help parents deal with their own and their children's behavior is Systematic Training for Effective Parenting (STEP), published by American Guidance Services. The rationale for this program is based on the premise that parents are the recipients of a great deal of conflicting advice about child rearing and consequently need help. STEP is designed to help parents develop those skills and techniques which result in effective parenting. The developers of the program feel that because most present-day parents were reared in autocratic families they are ill prepared to deal with democratic processes of child rearing. STEP helps parents understand and apply the assumptions of democratic living to the parenting process.

The program has seven goals:

1. To help parents understand a practical theory of human behavior and its implications for parent-child relationships.
2. To help parents learn new procedures for establishing democratic relationships with their children.
3. To help parents improve communication between themselves and their children so all concerned feel they are being heard.
4. To help parents develop skills of listening, resolving conflicts, and exploring alternatives with their children.
5. To help parents learn how to use encouragement and logical consequences to modify their children's self-defeating motives and behaviors.
6. To help parents learn how to conduct family meetings.
7. To help parents become aware of their own self-defeating patterns and faulty convictions, which keep them from being effective parents who enjoy their children.[14]

---

[14]Don Dinkmeyer and Gary D. McKay, "Systematic Training for Effective Parenting," *Leader's Manual* (Circle Pines, Minnesota: American Guidance Service, 1976), p. 14.

These goals are achieved through nine group sessions. The topics for these nine sessions are:

| | |
|---|---|
| *Session 1* | Understanding Children's Behavior and Misbehavior |
| *Session 2* | Understanding How Children Use Emotions to Involve Parents; and the "Good" Parent |
| *Session 3* | Encouragement |
| *Session 4* | Communication: Listening |
| *Session 5* | Communication: Exploring Alternatives and Expressing Your Ideas and Feelings to Children |
| *Session 6* | Developing Responsibility |
| *Session 7* | Decision Making for Parents |
| *Session 8* | The Family Meeting |
| *Session 9* | Developing Confidence |

Materials used in the program include an introductory tape for stimulating interest in the program, invitational brochures, leader's manual, parent's handbook, five cassette tapes used to stimulate discussions, discussion guide cards, nine posters, and ten charts. The materials are contained in a carrying case also used to display some of the materials during the discussion sessions.

The leader's manual provides information relating to how to organize and conduct parent study groups. Detailed instructions for conducting each session are also included.

The STEP program relies on and uses a group approach to developing parenting skills. The developers feel the group process is important because it provides support and encouragement for parents. When someone hears someone else's problems, they realize they are not alone, that other parents have problems just as they do. In this respect, guilt feelings are also reduced. In addition. a group discussion provides the opportunity for input of a wide range of ideas and opinions, and a setting for opportunities to clarify issues and solutions to problems.

## Education for Parenthood

Because parenting is such an important topic and issue and because in the past very little has been done in terms of providing young people with information about rearing children and parenting, a national program known as Education for Parenthood has been started by the Office of Child Development in cooperation with the Office of Education. The basic purpose of Education for Parenthood is to "help improve the competency of teenagers as perspective parents." With this goal in mind, the program hopes to increase young people's understanding of the social, emotional, educational, and health needs of children. By learning about such processes through materials and in relationship with the young child, teen-agers, it is hoped, will understand the role of parents in the growth and development of the child and can appreciate the influence that families and parents exert in the lives of children. One of the reasons that the Office of Child Development is so interested in this area of providing information for young adolescents is the increase in the number of births among teen-agers, the climbing divorce rate, and the number of single-parent families.

The intent of Education for Parenthood is not to replace any parenting information that the home would provide. Rather, it wants to supplement, augment, and support traditional child-rearing and parenting information as furnished by families. In addition, the Office of Child Development conceives of its role as working through and with existing programs and agencies as a means of providing parenting information. As such, the focus of Education for Parenthood is on public schools and voluntary youth-serving organizations.

In order to implement its goals, the Education for Parenthood effort has been instrumental in supporting the development of two programs, Exploring Childhood and the National Voluntary Organization Project.

## Exploring Childhood

This program was developed by the School and Society Programs of Education Development Center, Newton, Massachusetts, under a primary grant from the Office of Child Development, with additional funding and support from the National Institute of Mental Health and the Office of Education. "Exploring Childhood is a program in which the study of child development is combined with work with young children on a regular basis. It gives students opportunities to develop competence with children, and a framework for understanding the forces that shape human development."[15]

Exploring Childhood is designed for junior high school, senior high school, preservice teachers, and organizations interested in providing child development information to parents. The program utilizes a multimedia approach revolving around three modules or units. These modules are (1) Working with Children, (2) Seeing Development, and (3) Family and Society. Multimedia materials include booklets, posters, filmstrips, records, teacher guides, and 16mm films.

Exploring Childhood seeks to provide learning and growth in the following four areas: (1) concept development, (2) skills in working with others, (3) inquiring and observation skills, and (4) personal awareness.[16]

In module one, "Working with Children," students are helped to feel competent about their working with young children. Utilizing the multimedia material, students are involved with children, teachers, families, and learning situations through case studies and use these as a basis for discussion. Emphasis is also placed on observation and observation techniques as well as the development of procedures for keeping a journal which becomes a basis for discussion and insight throughout the year.

Module two, "Seeing Development," helps the participants understand the similarities and differences among children and involves them in field site experiences as a basis for gathering data about child development. Module three, "Family and Society," explores how children learn in families and how the family and other environmental forces affect the growth and development of children. During this

---

[15] *Exploring Childhood Program Overview and Catalog of Materials* (Newton, Mass.: Education Development Center, 1976), p. 5.

[16] Ibid., p. 8.

module, films play a major role in providing a data base for students to explore how children live in families and how they are affected by what occurs in the family.

While the program is designed to be used over a school year, this time frame can be adjusted to longer or shorter intervals. In addition, while all the materials in the program can be purchased in one unit, it is also possible to purchase individual materials and films.

In order to effectively implement this program, the leader should have a thorough knowledge of the goals, objectives, and rationale for the program. It would also help if implementers received training provided by the Educational Development Center, which has a staff of people who have been involved in the program and, therefore, are experienced with its operation. In addition, there are regional field coordinators (RFC's) who help in the dissemination and explanation of material.

Exploring Childhood represents an ambitious and noteworthy attempt to present a comprehensive program of child development, knowledge, and skills. The program does not rely on specific answers to problems but, through processes and individual interactions, seeks to develop rationales and skills appropriate to individual children and participants. As such, individuals are encouraged to learn by gaining insight into themselves as people and learners while working with children. As a result of this interactive process, hopefully people will develop confidence and competence enabling them to be effective parents and/or caregivers.

## National Voluntary Organization Project

In 1972, the Office of Child Development made grants to seven national, voluntary youth-serving organizations to develop materials and conduct pilot projects in which they would explore methods and means for providing their members with knowledge about children and the parenting process. Organizations that received funding were

*This high school girl is involved in a program dealing with the rearing, education, and care of children.*

Boys Clubs of America, Boy Scouts of America, National 4-H Club Foundation of America, Girl Scouts of the USA, National Federation of Settlements and Neighborhood Centers, the Salvation Army, and Save the Children Federation (Appalachian Program). Each of these programs is encouraged to develop its own materials and explore in its own ways methods for providing information, knowledge, and skills to members about child development and family life. More information about the materials each of these programs developed can be secured by writing to each of the individual agencies.

## Parenting Programs:   Some Concerns

One pervasive issue in the whole parenting process is that there are a large number of programs and a great deal of conflicting information. Parents don't know what to do because of the many different things they are told to do. For example, parents are told not to spank their children because it will cause irreparable emotional damage. On the other hand, they are told that children need and respect firm discipline, which can include spanking. Also, one particular approach to parenting may be antithetical to a parent's basic value system.

Charlatanism is another concern. Because parenting is such a popular topic and because there is a demand for seminars, speakers, etc., everyone is suddenly an expert! Some people, with little more background than having read a book, pass themselves off to the public as a trainer of parents. Before attending a seminar or training session conducted by an "expert," parents should try to determine if the session offers a program of substance and authenticity.

Some materials currently available encourage instant expertness. The materials are packaged and presented with the idea that, with only a little background and by following the directions, one can lead parenting sessions. This can be dangerous and devastating to well-meaning parents. I do not mean to imply that someone who hasn't had training in parenting techniques would not make a good group leader. What I am suggesting is that a packaged program or a leader's guide are not assurances of a competent leader or a good program. Also, simply because someone has knowledge about parenting and group leadership is no guarantee that they can or will put that knowledge to use in effective group techniques.

There is also the issue of credibility. How honest, authentic, and accurate are some of the programs that are being touted in the market place? Do they contain substance and can people rely on them? There is the very real danger that, in their desire to purge themselves of guilt feelings, parents may believe anything.

Economics represents another issue. Parents, especially those who can afford it, are being charged a considerable price for the privilege of attending parenting seminars. In some instances, an air of hucksterism prevades attempts to solicit parent involvement.

## *The Parent as a Person*

In any effort at providing parenting information or skills of any kind, the focus should not be on information but on the application of that information. The way to become a more effective parent (or potential parent, caregiver, etc.) is not through the accumulation of knowledge but through becoming a better person. The way to be a more effective parent is by being a better person. This concept is often overlooked and/or ignored in conceptualizing the process of parenting.

Because the emphasis in parenting should be on helping people become better persons, it would seem that the process of providing awareness of parenting should begin early in life. There appears to be a rationale, then, for developing such programs for elementary school children. If what occurs to the child early in life affects her throughout life, then we should provide the best possible parent-related training in early childhood.

## Bibliography

Dinkmeyer, Don, and McKay, Gary D. "Systematic Training for Effective Parenting." *Leader's Manual.* Circle Pines, Minn.: American Guidance Service, 1976.

Education Development Center. *Exploring Childhood Program Overview and Catalog of Materials.* Newton, Massachusetts: Education Development Center, 1976.

Ginott, Haim G. *Between Parent and Child.* New York: The Macmillan Co., 1965.

Gordon, Thomas. *Parent Effectiveness Training.* New York: Peter H. Wyden, 1970.

LeBoyer, Frederick. *Birth Without Violence.* New York: Knopf, 1975.

## For Further Reading and Study

Biller, Henry, and Meredith, Dennis. *Father Power.* Garden City, N.Y.: Anchor Books, 1975.

A well-written and designed book providing today's father with insight into the challenges, joys, problems, and wonders of the world of fatherhood. Highly recommended for fathers, as well as mothers and educators who are concerned with the development of parent-child relationships.

Braga, Joseph, and Braga, Larie. *Growing With Children.* Englewood Cliffs, N.J.: Prentice-Hall, A Spectrum Book, 1974.

This book deals with the role of parents in helping children develop a positive self-concept. The authors include the writings of many noted authorities in child development as a means of promoting effective parenting. Includes many ideas to help you grow as a person.

Dodson, Fitzhugh. *How to Parent.* New York, N.Y.: Signet and New American Library, 1970.

A comprehensive and extensive look at what *to parent* means: "to use, with tender loving care, all the information science has accumulated about child psychology in order to raise happy and intelligent human beings." Dodson's book offers both parents an excellent view of what "to parent" truly is! Topics include enriching the environment, stimulating children's minds and senses, childproofing your home, choosing toys, and a developmental timetable. A must for parents.

Dodson, Fitzhugh. *How to Father.* New York, N.Y.: Signet, New American Library, 1975.

*How to Father* is oriented toward the father, the father-to-be, single, divorced, and separated fathers. It covers such important topics as how to stimulate children intellectually, successful methods of discipline, good ways to play with children, how to give children a good sex education at home, how to deal with the drug threat, and the best books for children to read.

Eimers, Robert, and Artchson, Robert. *Effective Parents, Responsible Children: A Guide to Confident Parenting.* New York, N.Y.: McGraw-Hill, 1977.

A comprehensive account of parenting that goes beyond theory and deals with actual practice. The authors have done an outstanding job in outlining a plan for using effective praise and "ignoring." Gives special attention to four groups of children: adolescents, slow learners, withdrawn and fearful children, and hyperactive children.

James, Muriel. *Transactional Analysis for Moms and Dads.* Reading, Massachusetts: Addison-Wesley, 1974.

Useful for the parent interested in recognizing unpleasant feelings and behavior in their children and themselves. Provides ways and means to turn negative attitudes into constructive, pleasant feelings and behavior. This book introduces and uses Transactional Analysis (TA) in family relationships.

Levine, James A. *Who Will Raise the Children? New Options for Fathers (and Mothers).* Philadelphia and New York: J. B. Lippincott, 1976.

Devoted to men and the care of their children, this book is designed to get fathers more involved in parenting. It explores the growing phenomenon of "Househusbands," and how this change in tradition affects children, fathers, and mothers. A timely examination of the family and the changes that are rapidly occurring in its function and structure.

Maddox, Brenda. *The Half Parent.* New York, New York: Signet, New American Library, 1975.

A unique book pertaining to the increasing phenomenon of "second parenting"; an in-depth look into the step-parent/step-child relationship. This valuable guide deals with the emotional and adjustment problems as well as the rewards of parenting someone else's child.

McDearmid, Norma J., Peterson, Maria A., and Sulherlank, James R. *Loving and Learning.* New York, N.Y.: Harcourt, Brace, Jovanovich, 1975.

An interesting work pertaining to the process of child rearing and parenting. It centers around the idea that loving and warm parent-child interaction provides much of the framework for children's physical, emotional, and intellectual growth and development. Chapters are devoted to a six-month period of a child's life, from birth to three. Provides an abundance of information, skills, games, and advice that will help any parent make a better learning environment for their child.

McFadden, Michael. *Bachelor Fatherhood.* New York: Ace, 1974.

A look at the increasing number of families being raised by the single father. In today's society, the traditional two-parent family is not what it used to be, and we as a society have to start looking at the alternatives. McFadden provides an in-depth look into one alternative, "Bachelor Fatherhood." Recommended for anyone who wishes to learn more about family relationships.

Painter, Genevieve. *Teach Your Baby.* New York: Simon and Schuster, 1971.

Dr. Painter's book is an excellent program designed to help parents create a stimulating environment for promoting physical and intellectual growth. Specific activities and suggestions are outlined for parents to use with their children, beginning at one month. The programs in this book are significant for professional educators, teachers, teachers of teachers, and parents. Will surely help parents become more effective teachers of their children.

Walters, C. Etta. *Mother-Infant Interaction*. N.Y.: Human Sciences Press, Behavioral Publications, 1976.

This book outlines many essential interactions that occur between parent and child. Specific areas of importance are emotional, social, and perceptual/cognitive areas of child development. Parents concerned with their children's overall development could use this text as a vital, useful source of information.

## *Activities*

1. What are some specific plans that individuals should make prior to parenthood? List these in order of importance.

2. Some people think that parenting programs represent invasions of privacy and sinister attempts to gain control of families. What is your opinion?

3. What will the family of the year 2000 be like? What roles will it fulfill?

4. Gather parent involvement materials, such as letters, brochures, booklets, etc. Develop a set of criteria with which to evaluate these materials. Following your evaluation, tell what were the strengths and weaknesses of the materials. How would you improve them?

5. Do you believe that everyone has a right to information about child-rearing practices? Why? Why not?

6. Do you feel the role of parent is a dignified one? How can it be made more dignified?

7. Some people feel that television provides children and adolescents distorted images of what a parent is or should be. Do you feel this is true? Cite specific examples to support your opinion.

# Issues and Trends in Parent Involvement Programs

# 9

---

## Teaching and Learning Goals

This chapter will provide the information, means, and opportunity to:

Analyze and critique issues associated with parent involvement programs.

Articulate rejoinders to issues related to parent involvement.

Determine the validity, accuracy, and meaningfulness of issues in parent involvement programs.

Consider the future of parent involvement programs in relation to societal needs.

---

## Involvement for Involvement's Sake

Some critics of parent involvement programs feel that many of the current efforts to involve parents in programs, at whatever level, represent nothing more than an attempt to do precisely that—to involve parents for the sake of involving them! These critics feel that the parent involvement response is one which is being undertaken by educators merely because it is fashionable, economically expedient, or legislatively necessary to do so without any real belief or commitment on their part to the process.

There is the very real danger that by involving parents "because we have to" the involvement will result in tokenism. If programs have this attitude, parents may be involved in areas and processes which, when accomplished, amount to very little and

211

do not provide for parent growth. If involvement is to occur, it should be meaningful; otherwise, people who are involved have been deceived and cheated.

In addition, there is the feeling that parents will be viewed, not as parents, but as simply another group who can provide help in the school or agency. If this is the case, then the question has to be asked, If we are going to treat parents as any other helpful group, then why are we concerned about their involvement? If parents are treated as any other group, there is no sense in going to all the time and effort to involve them. It is only by taking into consideration the unique needs and talents of parents and children as individuals that we can really make parent involvement a meaningful process.

*Parents are educators in more ways than we and they realize. This father helps a child at a day care center learn basic woodworking skills.*

## Parents Not Considered Educators

One reason for the reluctance of teachers to encourage parents to become involved in the educative process may be that teachers don't view parents as educators. At least some teachers don't view parents as teachers. Consequently, teachers tend to divorce parents from a role (except for that of accepting the responsibility for failure) in the formal schooling process. Once the child leaves home and enters a "school," be it a public kindergarten or a day care program, the parent is cut off from the formal act of teaching. Also, in most instances, parents are also cut off from having major input into what and how the child will learn. For teachers, *real* learning seems to be confined to school. Unfortunately, they have done a good job of convincing many parents that this fallacy is true.

### Complexity of the Educative Process

One reason many educators don't feel parents can be good educators is because the complexity of the educative process precludes parents' knowing what to do or how to do it. While it is true that a particular parent may not know what to do with his children, this is certainly not true of all parents. Also, it doesn't mean parents can't learn. There are many parents who are ready, willing, and able to be quite competent teachers of their own and/or others' children. To think or suppose otherwise is demeaning to parents.

## Blaming the Home Environment

Another factor which seems to interfere with the parent-teacher interactive process is the curious habit teachers have of blaming parents and the home environment for children's lack of success in the teaching-learning process. For example, if a child comes to school unable to hold a pencil, the teacher might say, "What do you expect me to do? If the child can't hold a pencil, how do you expect me to teach him to write?" With this approach of blaming parents and environment, teachers have, in many instances, done very little to help children. We do know that the environment plays a powerful role in the ability of the child. We also know that the parent-child relationship determines, to a great extent, the attitude of the child to learning. These factors do not mean, as some have assumed, that teaching is a hopeless task. If this were true, we might as well close down the schools and concentrate our endeavors in other areas.

## Parents Are High Risk Educators

Another reason often cited for the discouragement of parents as educators of their children is that parental failure at child rearing would seem to make them high risk educators. Basically, this argument states that, if parents can't handle child rearing, how can they handle increased teaching and interaction demands? This is particularly true for parents who have emotional problems and/or who have caused emotional problems in their children. The answer to this argument, if there is a satisfactory one, is that you should not expect the same level of interaction from all parents. We cannot expect nor should we insist that all parents provide the same kind and quality of education to their children. You must begin where the parent is, not where you think he should be. There may be many parental problems that have to be dealt with prior to the parent's undertaking direct teaching of the child.

## Knowledge Does Not Always Mean Practice

An issue that has to be recognized by all who work with and involve parents in programs is that, simply because a parent knows what to do or has been taught how to do it, does not necessarily mean that the parent will do it. Just because a home visitor has shown a parent how to read to his children, does not mean that the parent will read to the children. One parent whose home has been visited for over a year still puts the crayons, paper, scissors, etc., up on a shelf where they can't be reached by the children.

What is needed in any program is a great deal of follow-up, repeated effort, and continued counseling in order to assure that the practice and implementation of skills and concepts occur. Merely to deliver services is not enough. Any good program must go beyond this to include support and help in achieving what the parent involvement specialist feels can be accomplished.

# Who Is to Blame?

There is a very real issue of where the fault lies for the underachieving child. Several theories relate to where the blame should be placed.

## With the Environment

This theory suggests that it is environmental or ecological factors which keep the child from functioning to the full extent of his ability. The premise is that, if you give the child a better environment, different experiences, etc., you can counteract or make up for these environmental factors which are having a negative effect on the child.

## With the Parent

There is that group who feel it is the quality and nature of the parent-child relationship and the attitude of the parent toward schooling which is the cause for poor school achievement. Many parent involvement programs are based on this basis. As such, these programs are based on a deficit hypothesis, that is, because the parent-child relationship and/or environment are lacking, services should be provided to counteract this deficit.

## With the Teacher

Many people feel that teachers have been too quick to blame the child, family, and environment. Granted, the majority of teachers are not miracle workers nor are they really expected to be. However, it is not unreasonable to expect teachers to individualize their instruction based upon the needs of children. Too many teachers have a prescribed notion of what children should be able or ready to do before they begin to teach them. If a child does not or cannot achieve this preordained standard, he is unsuccessful in school. This attitude will have to change. Teachers must adjust the curriculum and their expectations to the child rather than expecting a six year old to do all the adjusting.

# Political Issues

## Loss of Jobs

Some people believe that parent involvement may put teachers out of jobs. Politically speaking, the idea of involving parents in any direct way in the educative process is very upsetting to the status quo. In this sense, parent involvement/education is very revolutionary for it threatens the office of teacher and the system of the school. Less secure teachers may view training parents as a sinister move to put them out of jobs. The argument goes something like this, "If we can train parents who are eager to volunteer their services how to teach, then what is to stop them from laying teachers off?" The argument is further extended to include the idea that every parent volunteer represents a teacher who could be hired but isn't. Thus, the teaching profession is not only fearful that parents cause a loss of jobs, but also that parents will be a factor in the further depression of the teacher job market.

## Destruction of the School System

Also, if homes become places of education, with every home becoming a miniature school, then some feel this poses a threat to the school system as a physical place where learning is officially sanctioned and conducted. Obviously, there needs to be an increased awareness on the part of the educational establishment that parents are the first and primary educators of their children and, as such, exert a tremendous influence on the development of the child. There is really no reason why schools should be fearful of losing any role or function to the home. Rather, schools should view the process as one for increased opportunities.

## Fragmentation of Efforts

A great deal of fragmentation exists in terms of who and what agency will deliver what kind of services to children and their families. There is almost a bewildering array of programs, agencies, titles, funding sources, sponsors, etc., who have developed, are developing, and are providing monies for programs. Consequently, there is a need for one agency to combine and coordinate the current efforts. In addition to a single  coordinating effort, it is also important to deliver services to all families regardless of their needs. Presently, there is a seemingly endless array of eligibility requirements based upon everything from income to health status. As such, guidelines exist for providing services to just about every problem to which a child or family could be subject. It is almost impossible to be normal!

Perhaps what is needed is to provide a full range of comprehensive services to all families who desire them as a normal part of governmental services just as all children are provided with an education. This would mean that, rather than just providing services on the basis of need, we would provide services to everyone and meet whatever needs they have.

## What Should the Goals of Parent Involvement Programs Be?

A significant question that has to be asked by any agency attempting to undertake a program of parent involvement concerns what will be the goals and objectives of that program. As the situation presently exists, there are two foci around which goals and objectives are centered.

1. The parent and the family. In these programs the emphasis is on the delivery of services to parents and families, which will increase the quality of family life. The rationale is that with improved ecological factors, families will become more self-actualizing.
2. The educational  needs of children. In programs with this emphasis, personnel are involved in delivering educational programs and activities that can promote success in school.

Program developers have to decide which set of goals and objectives they will emphasize. An easy way out of this dilemma would be to say that both kinds of services will be provided. However, this is easier to say than it is to accomplish. The ultimate question seems to rest upon what the needs of families are. If the needs of a family are not great and if the family is ready to have a program of educational services for the child, then this kind of program can be delivered. However, if a family has a great number of unmet needs and if these unmet needs would interfere with the delivery of an effective educational program to children, then the program will not have much success unless the family's needs are provided for. Some programs have met with failure because they ignored the needs of families. Upon analysis, it appears that programmatic success can be achieved rather easily when a parent is able, willing, and anxious about working with his child in the home. However, we should not measure success of programs on this basis. It should be measured by how many parents who did not have the skills, knowledge, and motivation are now meaningfully involved with their children.

## Public School Involvement

One of the very crucial issues of the whole area of parent involvement and development deals with the question, Should the public schools become involved in working with parents in the home? Not everyone agrees that they should. However, there appears to be a large-scale effort on the part of the public schools and the national teachers' organizations, such as the American Federation of Teachers and the National Education Association to gain control of already existing social service agencies and day care and Head Start programs which currently provide services to children and their families.

There are several reasons why the public schools and the teachers' organizations want to become involved in this area, which until this time they have ignored or avoided. Educators and professional organizations would like to have more influence in this area due to the declining demand for teachers. Not only has teacher demand been suppressed for the last several years, but even more alarming for prospective teachers are the teacher demand projections. The projections indicate that the oversupply of teachers will continue into the decade of the eighties. Consequently, the areas of early childhood education and parent involvement represent an untapped source of potential teaching positions. If the public schools were able to exercise their influence in this area and become recognized as the social service agency which provides current and expanded programs to families, then the total number of teachers who could be employed would be considerable. Of course, there would be a spinoff effect for teachers' unions. As the number of teachers who are employed increases, the potential number of teacher union members also increases. This means that the income from union dues that teachers would pay also increases. The economic consequences are considerable.

### Economic Backlash

The economic impact of having certified teachers assume more of a role in parent involvement in early childhood programs could be detrimental to noncertified personnel who are already employed in these programs. There would be a negative effect on these paraprofessionals, many of whom are parents, who are in training or who desire to be involved in programs. In addition, one of the reasons many parent involvement programs, day care agencies, and Head Start centers are operative is to provide parents (and often these are low-income parents) with an opportunity to earn income. Does a person with a four-year teaching degree who can compete on the open job market need such a chance? I think not. Many of the employment opportunities which are available in early childhood programs and which do not require certification should be filled by individuals without the four-year degree.

## Ineffectiveness of Social Service Agencies

Another reason why the public schools are being encouraged to become involved in the preschool and family development program areas is because of what some people consider the general ineffectiveness of the social service agencies that have been responsible for conducting these services. Quite often research is cited that shows that preschool programs, particularly Head Start, have not had long-lasting effects on children. The implication is that many preschool programs are ill designed, administered, and operated. It is further implied that a better job of educating children and achieving other supplementary goals could be accomplished by the public schools.

## Increased Demand for Services

There is a growing recognition that the number of families and children who can be served by programs is much greater than the current number of families being served. Also, the ability of already existing social service organizations to meet the needs of families is limited. The demand for services is greater than currently available resources. Therefore, many professionals and legislators feel that, since the public schools already are social service organizations existing in every town and community of the nation, it makes sense to give them the responsibility to deliver services to preschool children and their families.

In addition, the rationale for public school involvement in early childhood programs is further advanced with the argument that, when the schools are bypassed, their functions are duplicated, and this constitutes a waste of money and effort. Many educators say that it does not make sense to close schools because of declining enrollment and, at the same time, build new buildings to operate preschool programs.

## Why Public Schools Should Not Become Involved

On the other hand, there are many strong arguments as to why the public schools should not become involved in the services rendered by many social service agencies. One of the most persuasive arguments is that the public schools have not and are not doing a good job of what they are supposed to be doing. People point to the failure of the schools to carry out their traditional role of teaching the basic skills of reading, writing, and arithmetic to children. They cite the dropout rate, the illiteracy figures, and declining achievement test scores as evidence that the schools have failed in their primary purpose. Therefore, the argument continues, if the schools are already failing at a job which they traditionally have been assigned, how can the public expect them to succeed at yet an additional job which involves children? In essence, since the schools have not done a good job accomplishing their roles, they should not be given newer roles involving the same and differing clientele.

## Preschool Education Not the Function of the Schools

Critics of public school involvement in preschool and family affairs point to the historic reluctance of the schools to take responsibility for this area of education. For some reason, public schools have always been reluctant to become involved in preschool and family education. Many teachers, administrators, and taxpayers feel that preschool and family education does not represent the legitimate function of the schools. It appears that this argument will be the most persuasive one in determining whether or not schools do become involved more than they currently are.

## Lack of Trained Personnel

Another argument against public schools' involvement is that the schools do not currently have personnel who are competent by training to assume responsibilities for working with children and their families. This argument contends that colleges of education have not and are not training personnel specifically to work with preschool children and their families. On the other hand, schools of education respond that it would not take that much effort to initiate retraining programs for teachers and to undertake the design of new training programs for personnel they would train for preschool and family involvement.

The determining factor in this argument, however, depends upon the willingness of taxpayers to pay for these additional services. It is unlikely that taxpayers will want to pay for these services directly by voting for an increase in the tax levy. Also, it is unlikely that they will want to pay for these services at the expense of the property tax, simply because many property owners already feel they are overburdened in their support of the schools. However, the taxpayer may be willing to allow the federal government to allocate monies to early childhood and parent involvement programs. When the federal government pays the bill, many people feel they are not paying for the services.

## What Is Best for Children?

Part of the associated issue of unions, teachers, and schools viewing early childhood education as a solution to their unemployment problems is that the mere solving of this problem may not best address the issue of what is good and best for young children. Certainly, and without doubt, there are many jobs in early childhood which can be filled by unemployed teachers. However, everyone concerned should want to do what is best for children, not what is best for teachers. The issue is really not one of solving unemployment, although this is certainly a worthy issue. The issue is really how can we best meet the needs of the nation's children?

In addition, the issue of what is best for children is not answered best by teachers' unions and their leaders. The question has to be answered by all who are involved in the education and lives of children. One of the current lines of reasoning that one hears from teachers' unions is that what is best for teachers is also best for children and their parents. This is a reversal of priorities. Those of us who still feel that schools are for children must not allow the public to be sold on the idea that schools should be anything else or less.

## Should Society Support Programs in Parenting?

Society has done a rather poor job of providing prospective parents or new parents with information about how to rear children. As a matter of fact, many individuals claim that child rearing is one of the few jobs (one might say professions) for which no training is necessary! That is, one does not need a license to have children, permission to have children, or any special qualifications except the biological ability to procreate.

Should we allow this kind of practice to continue? While the question is certainly an interesting one, the issues involved and the accompanying answers are complicated and controversial. Since the tradition of an individual's right to bear children is considered a personal and private matter, any attempt to interfere or intervene into the family-parent-child-rearing process is looked on with disfavor and suspicion. This accounts for the resistance and the reluctance of many agencies to engage in activities and/or processes which would affect in any way parents' right to bear and rear children as they see fit. Indeed, the family is considered by society, in general, and courts of law, in particular, to be a sacrosanct institution. It is one with which many people and the judicial system seem reluctant to interfere. Also, many people feel that children are the chattel of their parents and, as such, are subject to the whim and will of their parents. For example, it is only in cases of severest child abuse that a court of law is willing to take the child from the parent and place him in a foster home. Some critics, especially those who are child advocates, say that too often this reluctance of the legal system is counterproductive to the best interests of children. On the other hand, there are those who feel that the proper place for children is with their parents except in cases of extreme child abuse.

### Science Changing Family Definition

It is imperative for society to provide more attention to the whole issue of parenting because the medical sciences are rapidly outstripping our concept and definition of the child and the family. In essence, we are faced with a cultural and scientific lag between what it is possible to do with a child and what our conceptions and feelings about childhood and the parenting processes are. Several examples of this future shock are as follows:

1. It is now possible to determine the sex of a child prior to his birth through the process of amniocentesis. Amniocentesis involves inserting a needle into the womb of a pregnant woman and drawing off some of the amniotic fluid in which the child exists and lives. This process was originally developed as a means of assessing genetic defects a child might have prior to birth. The information could then be used in making decisions concerning abortion. In some instances, this technique is being used to help individuals determine whether or not the sex of the child is appropriate to their family plans. Based upon parent desires for a particular family pattern, decisions about whether or not to terminate the pregnancy can be made. A great deal of controversy surrounds this kind of process and the resultant decisions and con-

sequences. However, the fact remains that, while we are becoming very sophisticated about scientific processes concerned with procreation and child bearing, we have greatly neglected the area of education about parenting after the child is born.

2. The process and science of eugenics is an area that is receiving increased attention. Eugenics is the science of determining what an individual will be like based upon the genetic make-up of the parents. By studying their genetic make-up couples can try to avoid having children because of physical and/or mental problems that might occur based upon genetic predictions. For example, it is possible for a couple to assess their chances of procreating a child who would be subject to hemophilia. Knowing what the chances are genetically, a couple can decide whether or not to bear children. This process can be taken one step further, and couples can decide whether or not they want to be married, based on their genetic characteristics.

## Home-based Education

### *Should Agencies Intervene in the Lives of Families?*

The issue of intervening in the lives of children in their homes prior to their entrance into private or public early childhood programs has to be addressed with greater insight, clarity, and caution than in the past. The resolution of this matter represents an urgent necessity for society.

There are some professionals who charge that involvement with parents in their home amounts to nothing more than interference in the home. It is further believed that this interference has a tendency to weaken the home and erode the relationship

*It will take a full range of programs and personnel to provide families and children with the services they need. Here a grandparent volunteers her services and helps first graders with their reading.*

that may already exist between parent and child. People who feel this way believe that what occurs between parent and child is no one's business except the parent's and the child's. This concept can be defended only as long as that relationship between the parent and the child is one that is legal and does not abuse and/or harm the child. Many critics of parent involvement in the home say that the home is one of the last institutions which, to a very large extent, is free from governmental intervention, outside interference, etc. Of course, if an individual or an agency decides to provide services to a family, it should be very cautious that its program of services constitutes a helping function rather than an interfering function.

## Destruction of Traditional Family Units

Many people also feel that, by providing a home-based program, those who deliver these services pose a very real threat to the destruction of traditional family values, folkways, mores, and methods of child rearing. This threat of destroying traditional family values is particularly acute in instances in which the individual who is delivering the services to the family is either ignorant and/or uncaring of traditional family values. The situation may be compounded when the home visitor is of an ethnic and cultural background different from that of the family to whom the services are being delivered. There is a tendency on the part of the home visitor to deliver his own particular attitudes toward earning a living, child rearing, etc. Consequently, the family may think that what they have been doing is wrong, when it is not.

One of the ways that this risk of destroying traditional values can be avoided and/or minimized is to develop a program of home visitation which utilizes people of the same cultural and ethnic background in the delivery of services. Another procedure is to allow individuals who are receiving the services to have input into how the program of services will be delivered, what its content will be, and what values and mores will be stressed and supported. The risk can also be further minimized by having an advisory committee of parents monitor and evaluate the program.

## Institutional Control

A question frequently raised in conjunction with home-based and parent involvement programs is this, Does intervention with the family and child prior to the preschool years further extend the control of society and institutions over the child and the family? Many critics of preschool programs in the home and parent involvement programs see them as another attempt of society to control the child earlier, to brainwash the parent, and to make sure that the goals and objectives of society are inculcated in the parent and child long before he comes to school. Critics see the Orwellian spector of a controlled society in which the individual is programmed from cradle to grave.

*Federal Funding.* Furthermore, as you should be aware of by now, the majority of parent involvement programs are supported with federal monies. Indeed, it is questionable how many programs would be operative without this federal support. There is, without any doubt, a very strong federal influence and presence in all of these programs. This, of course, means that the type of services delivered, the point of view from which they are delivered, and the manner in which they are delivered are federally approved.

## Knowledge about Child Rearing

A very real issue is that which concerns the amount of knowledge, information, and experience that a home visitor and anyone who works in homes with parents should have. How much knowledge about child-rearing practices and child development should a home visitor have? There are those who feel that this knowledge of children should result from a first-hand experience with children, particularly through child rearing. It is my opinion after interviewing many home visitors, talking with home visitor supervisors, and observing home visitors in home settings, that knowledge about child rearing and child devleopment is essential. Yet, on the other hand, there is no reason why this knowledge and experience has to result from rearing one's own children. While it can be said that knowledge from rearing children certainly can be beneficial, there is no guarantee that simply because one has reared children one has done a good job or learned anything in the process. Furthermore, experience can occur in extended family situations, in institutional settings such as day care or Head Start, and in other agency experiences such as Girl Scouts, Cub Scouts, etc.

## Does Age Make a Difference?

Another issue closely related to the one above is the age of the home visitor. Should the home visitor be approximately the same age as the parents he visits? Again, there seems to be no hard-and-fast answer to this question. However, there is a need for maturity on the part of the visitor. This maturity does not necessarily have to occur with age. Maturity certainly can occur with learning and experience. Problems can be encountered when the home visitor is relatively young and does not have either the knowledge or the background of experiences on which to draw in order to provide the parents with information and ideas they can use. Maturity and competence are the determining factors rather than age.

## Should Home Visitors Be Teachers?

Quite often people feel that the home visitor should be a professional teacher, that is, a graduate of a four-year institution of higher education with a degree in teaching. There is nothing wrong with a teacher's being a home visitor as long as that teacher has had special and specific training for working with parents, particularly in the home. For too long, part of the teacher's role has been conceived of as telling parents what to do. Therefore, the person who has been trained as a teacher may have a tendency to assume a role of telling parents what to do rather than the helping, supportive role they should exhibit.

It should not be assumed that anyone without training can or should be a home visitor. Home visiting does require training. We should resist every effort to implement a home visitation program without specialized training for home visitors.

## Substitutes for Preschool Education
## or Kindergarten

There seems to be a tendency to believe that, by delivering a program of services to the child in the home, this program could and/or should take the place of a regular kindergarten or preschool program. This viewpoint is unfortunate since this is not the intention of many home-based programs. It is inaccurate to say that home-based programs can take the place of good center-based, school-based preschool and/or kindergarten programs. Instead, home-based programs do several kinds of things which traditional preschools and kindergartens have not done. One of these is to involve the parent as an active participant in the education of the child. A second purpose is to provide children with services they might not have an opportunity to receive in center-based preschools and/or school-based kindergarten programs. It should not be thought that home-based programs are a substitute in any way for these other programs. They are a supplement and an alternative to other programs where they do not exist.

It should be noted that, while many public schools decry the intrusion of home-based programs in preschool activities, the public schools have caused this situation. Had public schools been willing to service the needs of all children, had public schools been willing to consider education for children below the first grade and kindergarten levels, and had public schools approached this area with a little creativity there would have been little need for federal and state agencies to begin programs in this area of education. It is because the public schools have been unwilling and/or disinclined to deal with preschool programs that other agencies have filled the need.

## An Extension of the Public Schools

A question that can be legitimately raised is should home-based or educational visitor-type programs be attached to the public schools? There appears to be a great deal of merit in the public school's delivering home-based programs. One of the problems frequently encountered in home-based programs is a lack of articulation between what that agency or program does and what the program of the public school does and seeks to do. Articulation involves letting the public schools know what services an agency has provided to children. Since this function does not always occur, children who have had a particular kind of service go to the public school where these services may no longer be delivered to them. It may well be that the public schools are not aware of what services were delivered. Consequently, they may treat a child almost as though he were starting from the beginning, and any gains are lost because of this lack of articulation. Teachers do not follow up and extend the child's accomplishments. When teachers are not aware of previous programs and are not sensitive to the needs of children, it is possible that this is as detrimental to children as no program at all. One of the ways to bridge this gap between the home and the school would be to have home-based programs and/or educational visitor programs become part of the services of the public schools. Gains can be maintained and enhanced by having teachers who are knowledgeable of previous accomplishments teach these children.

Program developers should strive for an articulation of goals and objectives between programs. Of course, some people will contend that one way to deal with the issue is to build a strong articulation program. With such a program, certain people would be responsible for establishing liaisons with the public schools in order to let them know what the agency has done and can do. However, as things now exist, the public schools are not or do not appear to be anxious to have someone else or some other agency tell them what to do or how to do it.

In addition, there is the matter of what is best for the child. Research shows that children whose parents interact with them, provide a quality home environment, and engage in the parent-child interactive processes necessary for individual competence and achievement, do well in school. If the purpose of many of the home-based programs is to help the child succeed in school, then who knows best what is necessary for success in school  than the public schools? Consequently, it would seem that the public schools, if they were willing to assume the responsibility and the role, could say best what kind of programs the child needs in order to achieve in school. A home-based program isolated from a school system seems of little value. There is a need for a reciprocal support process between the two programs. The home-based program can support the educational program, and the educational system can provide support to the home-based program.

## Priorities for Inclusion

One of the issues that has to be answered by any program is priorities. Who should receive services when these services are limited? What should be the basis for eligibility criteria established for home-based programs? Obviously, those people who need the program services most should be provided for first. However, as indicated previously, there is not complete agreement that this is the right decision. Some people feel that everyone should have an equal opportunity for eligibility and for participating in the programs.

However, any effective program has to be based on the needs of the people in the program. A reasonable way to approach the matter of priority would be to involve those people for whom the services are designed in a determination of what the priorities should be for inclusion in the program. This means that people who are being delivered services have an opportunity to say what those services should be and who should receive them.

In the face of a limited number of home visitors and educational resources and an oversupply of homes and parents who need these services, there is really no way that you can side-step the issue of priorities. There are those who would argue that, since all families have needs, all families should be visited on a first-come, first-serve basis. This strategy undoubtedly appeals to our egalitarian sense, yet it is obviously neither a practical nor a realistic basis for action. While visiting all those who desire services on a first-come, first-serve basis would relieve programs of the burden of decision making, there are undoubtedly parents and families who have needs greater than others. A hierarchy of needs should be developed so that those families with the greatest needs receive first priority for services.

At the same time, home-based programs should not be something that is only for the disadvantaged. In many programs, the forgotten family is that family which is not classified as disadvantaged but which does not have the economic resources of the more affluent families. What is needed is a vision of parent involvement which includes all parents, regardless of their social or economic status.

*The needs of children should be included in any parent involvement program. Particular emphasis should be placed on these skills which promote success in school.*

## No One Approach Is Best

Although the major thrust of this text has been home-based education or parent involvement in a center or school, educators, child care advocates, and experts may lose sight of the fact that no one strategy will be sufficient or adequate to meet the needs of children or their families. The issue here is recognizing that it will require a full range of alternative services to meet the needs of all families and their children. This full range of services should include home care, center care, family involvement programs, public preschools, private programs, etc. No one particular or narrow range of services will suffice. Only comprehensive and alternative programs can provide the quality of care which children and their families need and deserve, if we are to recognize that children are indeed any nation's greatest natural resource.

Just as no one method of delivering services is best, so too, no one method of conducting an activity is best. For example, there are many different philosophies of child rearing, toilet training, individualizing instruction, etc. Parent involvement specialists should avoid giving the impression that their way is the only right, honest, and true way. Family values and traditions must be considered. Also, families can be helped without their feeling what they have been doing for years is wrong or bad.

## Economic Issues

Sooner or later, a question which must be asked is, Are parent involvement programs worth the money? This is a question which is difficult to answer. Who really knows if they are worth the money? On what basis can it truly be said that programs are or are not worth the money? Can our question really be answered in terms of a strictly monetary position? There are those who would say any money spent on preschool children and their parents is wasted money. On the other hand, if a child learns better and lives a richer, fuller life as the result of such efforts, isn't it indeed worth the money?

When a question of this nature, relating to the economic justification of a program, is asked in the area of the helping professions, it cannot be answered in economic terms. These are considerations of the market place and of production. We must also consider human terms which are not easily measured. Of course, programs can waste money. When services are duplicated, when administrators outnumber other program personnel, money is being wasted.

## Parent Involvement in the Community

One of the great educational programs which had the potential for revolutionizing and radicalizing the instructional and learning processes was open education. Simply stated, open education was an attempt to open schools to the community and vice versa. Learning in open education was to be a community effort with children living and learning in and from the community. Education was to be truly a community of scholars. However, open education has generally failed because educators did not and will not open schools to the community. Also, they have not invited the community into the schools.

Parent involvement means more than involving parents in early childhood programs and schools. Parents must be involved in community affairs, programs, and activities. This involvement should not occur in a passive consumer way, but in an activist, leadership way. If educators are sincere about enhancing the lives of children, then we must involve parents in the community. Parents can be helped to develop the skills, attitudes, and knowledge necessary for participation in groups, committees, and programs. The first step may be helping to plan the covered dish menu for a parent meeting, but that represents a beginning. Parent involvement specialists must extend their range of thinking and activities to include parent involvement in the community. If this is not done, then parent involvement may suffer the same fate of open education; a great promise, but few lasting results.

## Trends in Parent Involvement Programs

As we look forward to the next decade and beyond, it is possible to speculate about what will be some of the developments in the area of parent involvement:

1. The education profession will undoubtedly need more teachers and professionals trained in the area of parent involvement. As such, colleges and universities will be adding courses to their curricula in order to meet the demands for these trained professionals. Colleges may well view as one of their new missions the training of professionals for the entire preschool spectrum.

2. Job opportunities will become more available in the area of parent involvement. Such jobs as home visitors, program developers, counselors, and social workers will

be available and will be filled by those who are trained to do the job. Hopefully, there will be more of an emphasis on good training for all who would work with parents.

3. More federal and state monies to conduct such programs will become available. Programs such as Home Start, Child and Family Resource Centers, and home-based programs will become increasingly popular with parents. Essentially, parents will view home-based programs as ways of helping their children earlier in life.

4. Federal and state programs will continue to mandate and legislate parent involvement in early childhood programs as a means of encouraging schools to become involved with parents. This legislation of parent involvement will continue to be justified on the basis that it is necessary for the child's educational program.

5. The gains in parent involvement which are enjoyed by parents of handicapped children will eventually be extended to all parents. All parents will become involved in writing individualized education plans for their children. This parent involvement offers many opportunities and challenges to make education a truly humane and meaningful process.

6. As parents become increasingly involved, they will demand more involvements. Parental presence in schools will be a way of life for many schools. This is a process which schools will have to prepare for.

7. The distinction among the roles of educators and other members of the helping professions will become blurred and less distinct. For example, the educator's role will include more functions which were at one time thought to be those reserved for social workers, counselors, and psychologists. Consequently, teachers will be trained for a broader and more comprehensive role than the traditional narrow focus of teaching average children in a public school.

8. Teachers will have reduced contact with children and will become directors, coordinators, supervisors, and program developers. Teachers will spend more time directing the efforts of other people present in the classroom, such as parent volunteers and paid parent aides.

9. Parent education will grow in popularity. Seminars and discussion groups will be offered with more frequency and regularity. Colleges and universities will continue to add to their curricula programs devoted to parenting and parent involvement.

10. The economic consequences associated with parent involvement are such that teachers' unions and organizations will continue to press for funding for these programs. This funding will increase the likelihood that teachers will have jobs in areas which were not available to them in the past.

## Further Reading and Study

Day, Barbara. *Open Learning in Early Childhood.* New York: The Macmillan Co., 1975. Designed for teachers and administrators developing an open education learning environment for young children. However, this book can be useful to parents interested in open education by providing answers to questions about open education. It also furnishes many useful activities and learning games for such areas as communication/language arts, fine arts, home living, creative dramatics, science, math, movement, and outdoor play. Valuable reference book for parents of children attending an open education school.

Watkin, Edward. *The Battle for Childhood.* St. Meinrad, Ind.: Abbey Press, 1973.

An excellent account of what it is to be a child. This well-written book examines the ways of childhood and what it is like to be a child through the eyes and minds of children. Taken from actual accounts of children's perceptions of childhood. Useful to all parents who wish to develop a better understanding and communicating relationship with their children.

## *Activities*

1. Do you feel you currently have the competence to be:
   a. A home visitor?
   b. A teacher of two- and three-year-old children?
   c. A trainer of parents?
   What special training do you feel you would need to make you competent?
2. In what ways are parents oppressed by the following:
   a. Society in general?
   b. Television?
   c. Television commercials?
   d. Teachers?
   e. Schools?
   f. Businesses?
   What specific strategies could be developed to counteract this oppression?
3. There is a growing awareness that young children have certain rights, just as adults have certain rights. Do you believe this is so?
   a. Develop a model Bill of Rights for preschool children. Give reasons for your inclusion of particular rights.
   b. Complete the same activity for children in grades K-3.
4. Is the complaint that educators don't really have enough time or control over children's education really true?
   a. Document instances in which you feel teachers have too much control. Too little control.
   b. How much time do you think a first grader should spend in school? A preschooler? Why?
5. What do you think is the most significant issue facing parent involvement programs?
6. Do you think that education gets its fair share of the tax dollar? Support your answer with specific examples.

# New Careers in Education

# 10

## Teaching and Learning Goals

This chapter will provide the information, means, and opportunity to:

Examine new career opportunities that currently exist for working with parents and families.

Consider alternative career decisions to traditional classroom teaching.

Examine career accounts of practicing professionals concerning how they developed new careers.

## Rethinking Career Options

Those readers who are college students or paraprofessionals training for a teaching position may think that the options available are limited to those related to teaching children in the classroom. While this narrowness of career options may have been true in the past, it is no longer the case. Probably the worst thing to do is to limit your thinking and career training to classroom teaching. During the past ten years, there has been a tremendous growth in occupational skills and program areas that offer alternatives to those careers traditionally associated with education. In seeking preparation for some of these new careers, one encounters a lag between availability of appropriate training programs and jobs that are already in demand. Just as public schools are anywhere from five to ten years behind in meeting the demands of society, so too are colleges of education lagging behind. Thus the training you need for a particular job may not be available. This situation, of course, makes the necessity for self-training and inservice training more imperative.

*Appropriate and Relevant Training.*   Part of the problem has been and still is that colleges of education, in many instances, have limited their thinking to preparing individuals only for classroom teaching. Likewise, when training has been provided for many day care and Head Start personnel, the emphasis has been designed to increase competence as a classroom teacher or as a teacher of children. Unfortuntely, this has tended to make many Head Start and day care classrooms miniature kindergartens and first grades.

In addition, this problem of appropriate and relevant training has been compounded by our concept of teaching. Usually, this concept has been limited to classroom teaching. The teaching profession has not, with any great regularity, conceived for itself roles which exist beyond the four walls of a classroom. In this sense, the teacher role has been conceptualized and limited to teaching twenty to thirty children in a classroom setting. The blame for this narrow focus of teacher role can be placed on both teachers and schools of education. It can be placed on teachers because they have been content with this narrow focus. Schools of education can be blamed because of their lack of vision and leadership.

*Teaching: A Helping Profession.*   More and more, however, teaching is being viewed as an integral part of the broader range of human services and as a helping profession. Consequently, the sharp lines of demarcation which have traditionally existed among social work, the health professions, and education are gradually blurring and/or diminishing. However, there is still resistance from members of all three of these areas to recognize that other people besides themselves can provide a meaningful program of services which can complement their own. The teaching profession will be free to deliver the fullest range of services possible to all members of society only to the extent that teachers recognize it as a helping profession. The more narrow we think of our potentialities, the narrower our services will be.

You should make every effort to explore careers associated with any of the helping professions. Usually the helping professions include education, psychology, counseling, social work, the ministry, and health fields such as nursing and pediatrics. The training for these fields does not necessarily have to include a four-year degree. Many opportunities exist for working in the health professions and community service with a technical degree or an associate degree.

Readers are not being discouraged here from entering the teaching field. On the contrary, this discussion is meant to help students be realistic about their career opportunities. One way this can be done is to broaden one's horizons in relation to what is available. Whereas we used to think of many of the above fields as being separate and distinct from each other, this is no longer so. Many areas of expertise overlap and complement each other. Also, there is a trend toward resolving social problems and designing creative programs through interdisciplinary professions. In this way, the common areas of the professions can be applied to the resolution of issues while allowing each profession to contribute its own particular expertise. As a result of this interdisciplinary effort, an individual has an opportunity to contribute within a framework of appropriate services.

*There are many opportunities for helping children.*
*All possible career opportunities for involvement*
*with children should be examined and explored.*

There is also a very practical reason to encourage the reader to consider a number of career alternatives. There are already too many people in the teaching profession who don't like teaching or children. We don't need any more. For everyone's sake, a person should be happy and competent in what he or she does.

## Life Experience Cameos

You as a participant in a helping profession need to think about the many alternate options to classroom teaching. The following narratives of other jobs already existing in early childhood programs will help you get started. These narratives were written by different individuals and reflect their feelings and opinions. While the focus of the descriptions is parent oriented, don't limit your thinking to this focus alone.

*A Program Coordinator.*[1] When I graduated from college with a degree in elementary education, I had the wonderful experience of working for two years at the

[1]Contributed by George Farrow, Coordinator, Child and Family Resource Program, St. Petersburg, Florida.

same school where I did my practice teaching. In those two years I found out that, even though I love children, I did not want to spend my entire working career teaching.

In 1967, I attended an Office of Economic Opportunity Management Training Program at the University of North Carolina. Following completion of that training, I also received early childhood training at the George Peabody College, Nashville, Tennessee. Following this training, I was ready to start my second career as a supervisor of a Head Start center in Orlando, Florida, where I remained for five years.

Presently, I am with Head Start in the capacity of a program coordinator (Child and Family Resource Program). My present duties include the following:

1. Coordinating the program activities of all components.
2. Establishing a public relations system to inform the community of CFRP philosophy.
3. Coordinating the contractual agreements between agencies providing contract services to CFRP staff and families.
4. Evaluating the performance of staff and reviewing all other evaluations within the program year.

I have found great joy in my present work and would highly recommend similar work, dealing with low-income families, to people who are dedicated to helping others live a more productive life.

*A Home Visitor.*[2] I graduated from college ten years ago, full of ideas and ready to become a super teacher! I taught first grade for a year and a half, and it was a very difficult time for me. I was very fond of the children, but classroom management and organization were my weak points, and I was really drained at the end of the day. Deciding I didn't want to give up working with children, I got my required hours in early childhood and had a happy two years in a half-day nursery school with summers spent as a recreation supervisor. The relief of being less structured was enormous, but the pay was poor, and back I went to a full day, this time with Head Start. Two years back in the classroom and I had the opportunity to become part of Head Start's Child and Family Resource Program, as a home visitor.

I have found my niche! We are in our fourth year of operation as a demonstration program. My duties are quite varied. I have a case load of thirty-five families. We work with all members of the family, but the main emphasis is on children prenatal to age three. We help families set up goals within a certain time frame. Each family's needs are gone over with the help of an assessment team, made up of members from different local agencies. I serve as a resource to the different agencies we might use to help meet these goals, always keeping in mind that the family makes its own decisions; I can only suggest. I also work regularly with mothers of babies through age three in order to encourage growth and development in all areas.

---

[2]Contributed by Jane Thompson, Home Visitor, Child and Family Resource Program, St. Petersburg, Florida.

Obviously, I have discouraging days and share my families' disappointments or lack of motivation, but this is more than made up for when I get to share in successes and happiness. It's a marvelous, challenging job.

*Program Consultant.*[3]   As a high school dropout who returned to finish my education go on to college after ten years of counterproductive living, I can say that limited vision is the greatest hindrance to finding one's place in life.

If one mentions my present field of psychology, one thinks of behavioral psychologists or clinical psychologists or school psychologists or perhaps even cognitive psychologists. One seldom realizes that there are over three hundred different types of psychologists, each an open door into a world that might fit you.

It is only with a broad exposure to the many different professions related to education and within education that individuals begin to see a possible fit for themselves. In short, don't look for a niche to fit into, look for a world to discover.

As I began teaching the emotionally disturbed, I discovered my own inadequacies. As I sought to meet these inadequacies through more education, I discovered larger, related worlds that led me into teaching in the education and psychology departments of colleges. From there, I went into therapy and my own practice as a marriage and family counselor and consultant to the Head Start program.

*Van Teacher.*   Teaching is no longer limited to a classroom with four walls, screwed down seats, and a teacher assigned to thirty children. Many teaching opportunities extend to the outside world. New and better ways of reaching children and parents are being developed in a changing society. Our motorized, mobile society has also brought changes to education.

My classroom is a mobile van equipped to teach two through four-year-old children. It has "built-in" features for a classroom environment appropriate for teaching small groups. I teach approximately sixty children during the week, with each group of six to eight meeting with me two hours weekly for instruction.

Although I was trained to work in a self-contained classroom, I have had to change because my duties as a van teacher differ from those of a regular classroom teacher. A teacher today must be flexible enough to change methods of teaching in response to changing situations.

Much of my time and effort is directed toward "inservicing" parents about how to teach their children at home. Take-home packets are made by a program producer, a consultant, and myself. Much of my time is devoted to this component of the program. I not only train parents in small mini-workshops, but I also meet with them regularly in large group situations.

Working in a mobile van with the community has many advantages; it makes the program more interesting, challenging, and relevant. One advantage is not dealing with dead ideas; another is working with life itself. The van allows one to see the outside world, to stop and watch a world happening; to feed a bird, to touch a flower, to speak to a police officer. A third advantage is that one is helping a child, at an early age, get a head start in education. A fourth advantage is working with parents to help them be better parents. What other rewards could a teacher ask for in a profession?

---

[3]Contributed by Richard Wolf, Consultant, Child and Family Resource Program, St. Petersburg, Florida.

Van teaching also allows one to become a partner with parents, since you see the parents daily.

There are also some challenges to the teacher. There are always maintenance chores when no service attendant is on duty; there are other tasks, such as "gassing up," and heating the van on cold mornings.

To teach in a classroom on wheels one must be self-reliant, skillful in techniques, and flexible enough to meet the demands of children, their parents, and the weather. Inservice skills and a host of helpers make this job fulfilling. I wouldn't want to change for a more rigid classroom experience.[4]

*This adult is taking advantage of every situation to determine his honest attitude toward working with children.*

## Preparing for New Careers in Education

### Volunteer Your Services

In order to explore new careers in education there are several very practical things which any individual can do. One thing which can be done is to volunteer your services. You should seek every opportunity available to you to volunteer your services. Many students find that summer vacations, weekends, Christmas vacation, Easter vacations, spring breaks, etc., are opportune times to volunteer services as a means of exploring not only the field that they think they have chosen but also alternate fields.

Some students have a tendency to object to the volunteer approach as far as their services are concerned. They feel that if they are going to be involved they would much rather do something for which they could be paid. Quite often, this means that a student, rather than volunteering services in her particular field or in one related to

---

[4]Contributed by Mary Kay Dishner, van teacher, Bristol, Virginia Schools.

it, may end up being a waitress, clerk in a store, etc., for which she is paid. This doesn't help the individual gain experience in her professional area or find out more about an area in order to have information on which to base decisions.

*Benefits of Volunteering Services.* Volunteering services does several very practical kinds of things:

1. It allows the individual to get a range of needed experiences. Quite often the difference between getting a job in an area and not having any job at all is the amount of experience that an individual has had. Almost all employment ads in the newspapers specify some kind of experience that the employer would like the applicant to possess as a condition of employment. The lament of all new job seekers is, How in the world can I get experience when I can't get a job? One answer, while not always quite so obvious, is that prior to seeking a job on a permanent basis one can volunteer services during the training portion of their career in order to get those necessary experiences. In addition, many professions which require specialized and/or advanced training are requiring some kind of practical experience as well as academic credentials as a prerequisite for entry into the field. As a result of these conditions, students are finding that it is a combination of academic grades *and* experience which is needed for entry into many occupations.

2. Volunteering one's services allows an individual to be in the right place at the right time. Quite often, when agencies hire people, they hire people with whom they are familiar and who have shown that they are able to do the work. Many people have found that, by volunteering their services, they have been hired for jobs that have become available in the particular agency in which they have been volunteering their services. Several real-life examples relating to volunteering of services might prove enlightening.

*Personal Examples.* A young man with a B.S. degree in early childhood education could not find a job. After a long search, Larry decided to volunteer his services in a senior citizen program as a recreation aide. He spent six months in this position as an organizer and developer of recreational activities. The job that he performed as a volunteer was not a regular part of the program. However, Larry did such a good job and had such success that, during the next contract year, a job for a recreation director was included in the program. Because of his experience as a recreation aide and the excellent job he did, Larry applied for the new position and was hired. Not only was Larry able to gain a paid position because of volunteering his services, he was also able to enter a field which he had not previously considered. Larry is now taking advanced work in recreation and gerontology as a means of further developing his competency in the area.

Another student while in college volunteered her services at a social service agency. When Jayne went to the agency, she was told that there was really nothing for her to do except open the mail and do odd jobs that the staff wanted done. Jayne decided to become involved in this way and continued to do volunteer work for several months. One day, there was a need for someone to write a publicity release for the newspaper. However, all of the staff was busy, and Jayne was asked if she would do it. She welcomed the opportunity and wrote the publicity release. She did such a fine job that she was asked to do more releases for the newspaper, radio, and

*In the final analysis, the well being of our children will depend on the quality of the programs we provide for them. Parent involvement is one way these programs can be more effective.*

television. Publicity became part of her regular duties. Jayne now has a full-time, paid position as director of publicity. She also is involved in the development of new curricular materials.

It cannot be denied that both of these individuals were able to succeed in what they were doing because they were competent individuals. At the same time, they were able to succeed in these positions because they had an opportunity to demonstrate what they could do as a result of volunteering their services.

## Plan Your Educational Program

Something else individuals can do is to use any free elective and general educational electives that often exist in college curricula to explore alternate occupations. For example, most teacher education programs have a large block of general education courses. If a student has to take some general education courses in the area of social sciences, then courses in social work could be selected. In the behavioral sciences, courses in guidance and counseling would be appropriate. Every person who is going to deal with children, would, as a matter of course, probably want to take at least one course relating to handicapped children. By using these opportunities, courses can be pursued that will allow individuals to become familiar with different areas.

## Talk with Friends

An often overlooked method of finding out about other careers and opportunities in education is to talk with friends. You may have a friend who is in another occupation or knows someone who is at a college, university, junior college, technical institute, etc., who is studying for a job in one of the helping professions. You could find out from that person what she hopes to do in the area and what the requirements are for entrance into the field.

## Visit Agencies

Not only can you talk to friends, but you can also spend time visiting agencies and talking with people employed there about what they do in particular jobs. By visiting other agencies, it is possible to actually see what people do as opposed to what people say they do. Quite often, the differences between what people say they do and what they actually do is such that you may change your mind about whether or not you would want to be employed in a particular job. Some jobs are more glamorous when described than when performed.

## Counseling Services

Counselors, at the high school and college level, provide many opportunities to find out about and explore different occupational areas. One of the things that a counselor is often able to do is to help an individual become *aware* of alternate career areas. A valuable service counselors can provide is to give aptitude and interest tests which will help an individual learn more about herself in terms of occupational interests. Sometimes this testing may cost extra money. However, if it is professionally done, it is well worth the money. It is often better to spend a little money trying to find out what you are interested in than to spend a lot of money on college credits, room and board, etc., and find out you do not like a particular area.

## Reading

Reading about different occupations and different fields is another method that is often overlooked in career selection. There are many books listing different jobs and their skill requirements. Another sometimes underutilized source of reading materials is college catalogs. These outline courses of study which colleges throughout the country are offering in different fields. Oftentimes, by looking at these catalogs people get ideas about what it is they would be interested in doing.

## Looking Forward

It seems appropriate as we conclude this text on parent involvement that you should reflect on the particular role you will have in this area. I hope that each of you considers becoming an active, competent participant at whatever level you choose, be it parent, trainer, caregiver, or supporter. Avoid at all costs becoming a robot and applying to all parents and families the same procedures and strategies. People and families are different and should receive personalized programs and involvements. In providing these alternative strategies, you will have opportunities to use your education, background, and experiences. When such a process occurs, professionalism, in the fullest sense of the word, can result. Providing the best for children, parents, and families will also require that you give of yourself. This you should be willing to do, for, through giving of self, significant changes in lives can occur.

## Further Reading and Study

Danish, Steven J., and Hauer, Allen L. *Helping Skills: A Basic Training Program.* New York: Behavior Publications, 1973.

An informative, helpful, and easy-to-use program for anyone contemplating a career and/or involvement in a helping role. A great deal of insight can be gained by reading the program even if an opportunity does not exist for participation in the training program.

## Activities

1. Talk with other professionals about their careers relating to children and parents.

   a. How did they come to have the job they do? Was there evidence on their part of planning for these careers?

   b. Do you think you would enjoy an alternative career in education? Why? Why not?

2. Make a list of all the careers it might be possible for you to have that relate to working with children and parents.

3. What changes in goals, curriculum, and courses would your college or university have to make in order to provide you with other occupational opportunities relating to parents and children?

   a. Do you think the administration could or would be willing to make these changes? Why? Why not?

# Index